# THE ROYAL ROAD TO ROMANCE

# THE ROYAL ROAD TO ROMANCE

### RICHARD HALLIBURTON

TRAVELLERS'

– TALES –

CLASSICS

TRAVELERS' TALES, INC.
San Francisco

Travelers' Tales books are distributed by Publishers Group West, 1700
Fourth Street, Berkeley, California 94710.

Art Direction: Michele Wetherbee
Cover Design: Stefan Gutermuth
Page layout: Cynthia Lamb

**Library of Congress Cataloging-in-Publication Data**

Halliburton, Richard, 1900–1939.
    The royal road to romance / Richard Halliburton.
        p. cm.— (Travelers' Tales classics)
    Originally published: 1925. With new introd.
    ISBN: 1-885211-53-8 (alk. paper)
        1. Voyages and travels. I. Series.

G463 .H25  2000
910.4—dc21                                              00—044321

Printed in the United States
10 9 8 7 6 5 4 3 2 1

*To*

*Irvine Oty Hockaday*

*John Henry Leh*

*Edward Lawrence Keyes*

*James Penfield Seiberling*

*Whose sanity, consistency and respectability as Princeton*

*roommates drove me to this book*

# TABLE OF CONTENTS

Why do we travel, when we can safely and profitably stay at home? Is it the hunger of electrons for motion? A genetic survival imperative? The psyche's taste for a bit of anarchy? Or is it something deeper, a stirring of that need for discovery of the Other—the alien on far shores whom we wish to prove is really only us or the Divinity in a different guise? Surely travel is all of these, and depending on how we respond, when we respond, and especially *if* we respond, it is intoxicating or toxic. We are born strangers in a strange land, and remain so. Travel simply reminds us of this essential truth.

At Travelers' Tales we publish books that embrace this idea, that represent the essence of place and the soul of the traveler. In 1993 we began publishing anthologies of great writing about destinations and topics of special interest to travelers—the simple guiding premise being that while guidebooks present strings of data, true stories by travelers do something different: they open windows of experience and meaning. The transmission of a powerful story, one human to another, is an alchemical activity in which we are enlarged and changed. In the course of our own travels, actual and literary, we've been inspired by many explorers and writers—some whose exploits we could never hope to duplicate, and some who seemed to be kindred spirits. Richard Halliburton is both, and as such he is the inspiration for Travelers' Tales Classics, the new series of travel treasures we launch with this republication of his first book, *The Royal Road to Romance*.

Born January 9, 1900, in Brownsville, Tennessee, Richard Halliburton grew to be a boy whose favorite subject in school was geography, whose prized possession was his geography book. When he graduated from Princeton some years later, he launched himself whole-heartedly around the world like a rocket, traveling, writing, and exploring until his untimely death in March, 1939. From the Jazz Age through the Great Depression to the eve of World War II, he thrilled an entire generation of readers, beginning in 1925 with *The Royal Road to Romance*, a book we are delighted to present, in the centennial year of his birth, to a new century of wanderers.

In *The Royal Road to Romance*, Halliburton is the traveler most of us want to be: clever, resourceful, undaunted, cheerful in the face of dreadful odds, ever-optimistic about the world and the people around him, always scheming about his next adventure. He knows well the thin divide between dreaming and daring, entropy and action, and throws himself with abandon through the curtain of illusion, always in a completely charming manner, whether he is climbing the Matterhorn, crossing a Malaysian jungle, trekking to Ladakh, sneaking into the Alhambra or the Taj Mahal, or loafing about in Srinigar or Andorra. He loves history and its heroes, and in his unrelenting pursuit of both, becomes a lost hero himself, like George Mallory on Everest in 1924 and Amelia Earhart over the Pacific in 1935, when he disappears at sea while attempting to sail from Hong Kong to San Francisco on the Chinese junk *Sea Dragon*.

Some modern readers (call them jaded or cynical) might find him ridiculous, an anachronism, altogether too innocent and shamelessly exuberant, this man who wrote books such as *The Glorious Adventure* (1927), *New Worlds to Conquer* (1929), *The Flying Carpet* (1932), *Seven League Boots* (1935), *Richard Halliburton's Book of Marvels: The Occident* (1937), and *Richard Halliburton's Book of Marvels: The Orient* (1938). After all, travel in our time has become the world's largest industry—hordes of us hunting for places that have not been trod on by the rest of us. But Halliburton would agree that the world is still worth seeing, and will be worth seeing 100 years from now, simply because no amount of creeping cultural homogeneity can quell the endless variety of humanity. Travel in the end is about people, not places; places only provide different venues, so to speak, for this life in which we are all pilgrims and must talk to one another, pilgrims who may wander far, but return home in the end bearing the gifts of travel, and who do not lose sight of the true riches of home and family.

Richard Halliburton knew this well—during the last 22 years of his nearly 40 years on earth, he wrote over a thousand letters to his mother and father. There is a Publisher's Note in a collection of those letters (*Richard Halliburton: His Story of His Life's Adventures—As Told in Letters to His Mother and Father*, published in 1942) which captures the boy, the man, and the explorer:

> For him all experience was an arch wherethrough gleamed an untraveled world whose margin faded forever when he moved. Some Samarkand always lay over the horizon. He longed always to see, and to make others see, the far-flung marvels of nature and man's spectacular achievements. He was born at the advent of the new century. His manhood spanned the brief interval between the two World Wars. He is a spokesman for the youth of a generation isolated by these wars. In his own story are preserved the beauty that

inspired his appreciation, always superlative and always genuine; the illusions he proudly cherished; the history that to him was not dead past but filled with eternal heroes. The map over which he wove the web of his travels is rapidly changing. Armed forces may destroy much that he found so various, so beautiful, so new. But romance and rapture, the capacity for wonder and admiration will remain wherever there are young unregimented hearts. To such hearts and for them Richard Halliburton will continue to speak.

May *The Royal Road to Romance* stir in you the hunger you were born with for the romance of life. May you walk out of the prison of necessity—the gulag we all shamble to when distracted by the details of living, when the inner gaze is averted from the true life of the spirit. When you wake again, as you certainly will, walk beneath that "arch wherethrough gleams an untraveled world." For no matter how one may vilify oneself for not living up to childhood dreams, the truth that will be revealed to all of us when we die is that we are born adventurers. You might as well own up to it now—there's a Richard Halliburton in you, whistling as the next adventure forms out of the mist.

And if you're not quite ready to set sail or take off tomorrow morning, you've already set foot here on *The Royal Road to Romance* with Richard Halliburton as your guide, a man who once wrote, "Well, I'm grown up now. But as yet I haven't any son or any daughter to go traveling with me. And so, in their places, may I take you?"

JAMES O'REILLY
PUBLISHER

NOTE: In keeping with the spirit of the original publication in 1925, we have retained the author's spellings and styles.

# The Royal Road
# to Romance

MAY had come at last to Princeton. There was no mistaking it. The breeze rustling through our wide-flung dormitory windows brought in the fresh odors of blossoming apple orchards and the intangible sweetness of bursting tree and flower. I had not noticed this fragrance during the day, but now that night had come, it filled the air and permeated our study. As I slouched on the window-seat looking out upon the moon-blanched campus, eleven muffled booms came from the hour bell in Nassau Hall. Eleven o'clock!—and I had not even begun to read my economics assignment for to-morrow. I glanced at the heavy text-book in my hand, and swore at the man who wrote it. Economics!—how could one be expected to moil over such dulness when the perfume and the moon and all the demoralizing lure of a May evening were seething in one's brain?

I looked behind me at my four roommates bent over their desks dutifully grubbing their lives away. John frowned into his public accounting book; he was soon to enter his father's department store. Penfield yawned over an essay on corporation finance; he planned to sell bonds. Larry was absorbed in protoplasms; his was to be a medical career. Irvine (he dreamed sometimes) was struggling unsuccessfully to keep his mind on constitutional government. What futility it all was—stuffing themselves with profitless facts and figures, when the vital and the beautiful things of life—the moonlight, the apple orchards, the out-of-door sirens—were calling and pleading for recognition.

A rebellion against the prosaic mold into which all five of us were being poured, rose up inside me. I flung my book away and rushed out of the apartment on to the throbbing shadowy campus. The lake in the valley, I knew, would be glittering, and I turned toward it, surging within at the sense of temporary escape from confinement. Cool and clean, the wind, frolicking down the aisle of trees, tousled my hair, and set my blood to dancing. Never had I known a night so overflowing with beauty and with poetry. The thought of my roommates back in that penitentiary room made me shout with impatience. Except Irvine, they were so restrained, so infallible, so super-sane, so utterly indifferent to the divine madness of the spring moonlight.

All the afternoon of that day I had spent in the woods beside Stony Brook, lost in a volume of *Dorian Gray*. And now as I tramped down-hill to the lake, I began to recite aloud to the trees and the stars, lines from it that had burned themselves into my memory: "Realize your youth while you have it"…the sound of my own voice startled me, but the woods echoed back the phrase approvingly, so I took courage. "Don't squander the gold of your days, listening to the tedious, or giving your life away to the ignorant and the common. These are the sickly aims, the false ideals, of our age."…"Sickly aims, sickly aims," the crickets chirruped after me. "Live! Live the wonderful life that is in you. Be afraid of nothing. There is such a little time that your youth will last—such a little time. The pulse of joy that beats in us at twenty"—I was already a year past twenty—"becomes sluggish. We degenerate into hideous puppets, haunted by the memory of the passions of which we were too much afraid, and the exquisite temptations that we had not the courage to yield to. Youth! Youth! There is absolutely nothing in the world but youth!"

A wave of exultation swept over me. Youth—nothing else worth having in the world...and I *had* youth, the transitory, the fugitive, *now*, completely and abundantly. Yet what was I going to do with it? Certainly not squander its gold on the commonplace quest for riches and respectability, and then secretly lament the price that had to be paid for these futile ideals. Let those who wish have their respectability—I wanted freedom, freedom to indulge in whatever caprice struck my fancy, freedom to search in the farthermost corners of the earth for the beautiful, the joyous and the romantic.

The *romantic*—that was what I wanted. I hungered for the romance of the sea, and foreign ports, and foreign smiles. I wanted to follow the prow of a ship, any ship, and sail away, perhaps to China, perhaps to Spain, perhaps to the South Sea Isles, there to do nothing all day long but lie on a surf-swept beach and fling monkeys at the coconuts.

I hungered for the romance of great mountains. From childhood I had dreamed of climbing Fujiyama and the Matterhorn, and had planned to charge Mount Olympus in order to visit the gods that dwelled there. I wanted to swim the Hellespont where Lord Byron swam, float down the Nile in a butterfly boat, make love to a pale Kashmiri maiden beside the Shalimar, dance to the castanets of Granada gipsies, commune in solitude with the moonlit Taj Mahal, hunt tigers in a Bengal jungle—try everything once. I wanted to realize my youth while I had it, and yield to temptation before increasing years and responsibilities robbed me of the courage.

June and graduation.... I was at liberty now to unleash the wild impulses within me, and follow wherever the devil led. Away went cap and gown; on went the overalls; and off to New York I danced, accompanied by roommate Irvine (whom I had persuaded with little difficulty to betray commerce for adventure), determined to put out to sea as a common ordinary seaman before the mast, to have a conscientious, deliberate *fling* at all the Romance I had dreamed about as I tramped alone beside Lake Carnegie in the May moonlight.

Our families, thinking it was travel we wanted, offered us a de luxe trip around the world as a graduation present. But we had gone abroad *that* way before, and now wanted something less prosaic. So we scorned the *Olympic* and, with only the proceeds from the sale of our dormitory room furnishings in our pockets, struck out to look for work on a freighter.

To break into the aristocracy of labor was by no means as easy as we had believed. Somewhat to our dismay we found that wafting Princeton Bachelor of Arts degrees under the noses of deck agents was not a very effective way of arousing their interest in our cause. In desperation Irvine and I attempted a new method of attack. We gave each other a "soup bowl" hair-cut, arrayed ourselves in green flannel shirts, and talking as salty as possible descended upon the captain of the *Ipswich*, a small cargo boat, with the story that this was the first time in twenty-one years we'd ever been on land. The skipper was a bit suspicious, but our hair-cuts saved the day. He "signed us on"—and may as well have since we had a peremptory letter in our pocket from the president of the shipping company instructing him to do so.

And so at last on a July morning as our little *Ipswich* sailed out of New York harbor for Hamburg I waved gratefully at Lady Liberty. But she did not notice me. She does not flirt with ordinary seamen.

# Humiliating the Matterhorn

AMBURG was by no means a prearranged destination. Our adventures would have begun at Lisbon or Manila had the Ipswich happened to dock at these places. The point of embarkation upon our road to Romance was entirely unimportant. We had hoisted our sails to catch whatever winds might blow, and the winds from the west had blown us into Germany.

After squandering seven of the fifteen dollars earned at sea (part of the expenditure being for "Otto" and "Ophelia," twin bicycles on which we planned to explore Europe), we decided we had spent enough money in Hamburg and that it would not be fair to the rest of the Continent unless we scattered it impartially.

Irvine wanted to ride straight to Paris; my mind was set on Rome. In order to avoid a conflict we agreed to gamble on our next destination. Irvine closed his eyes and revolving three times before a map of Europe, struck it blindly with his index finger. On opening his eyes he found he had half covered Rotterdam—and Rotterdam it was!

Burdened with only our two-pound knapsacks, we rode first to Berlin, and then turning west rolled along so leisurely from village to village that it took us fifteen days to reach the gate with "Deutschland" painted on one side and "Nederland" on the other. Satisfied we were not escaping convicts, the officials allowed us to pass, and to pedal through Amsterdam, The Hague and so on into Rotterdam.

And now whither? Once more we disinterred our map and cast about for a new destination. Half furtively, half intuitively, my own eyes slipped south to Switzerland, and to the mountain on the Italian border marked in tiny letters: "Matterhorn." Here my heart lay, had lain ever since a picture of the regal peak had been hung in my school-boy study at Lawrenceville to dominate and stimulate every one who entered the room. Even now I had only to close my eyes and its glittering, beckoning pinnacle floated before me like the vision of swords and angels before Joan of Arc. Its majesty, its imperious sweep into the blue heavens, its romance and tragedies, fired my imagination anew until any possible substitute expedition became drab and insipid. A consuming desire rose within me to plant my foot upon this most notoriously murderous mountain in Europe. What if it had killed more people than any other? All the more reason to climb. Youth! Youth! Here was a magnificent chance to realize it. Here was a new and rare sensation worth almost any price—something beautiful, joyous and romantic all in one. We must attack the dragon now while we were responsive enough to sense its challenge. True we had no equipment and could not afford such luxuries, but neither had Moses equipment when he climbed Mount Sinai, and neither had Noah when he descended Ararat from the Ark. However if the adventure was to be considered seriously Irvine must be won over, and imbued with my own Matterhorn madness.

Before I could decide on the most strategic method of attack he spoke to me:

"Dick, I'd like to make a suggestion. I suppose it's out of the question though—too expensive—too dangerous—and all that, but it's something I've wanted to do ever since you hung that picture in our room. It's to—well—climb the Matterhorn."

To the astonishment of every one in the hotel lobby, not excepting Irvine, I gave him a furious hug accompanied by three wild cheers.

It was by now the twentieth of September, and we knew that the Matterhorn climbing season would be very shortly closed, if indeed it had not been already. There was no time to lose. "Otto" and "Ophelia" were sold, and on the proceeds we got to Cologne, turning without delay up the Rhine. Our race against inclement weather in the Alps left us little time to enjoy the river journey, but even then, in an effort to get into training for the Matterhorn assault we tarried a few days along the way to climb the towers of Cologne and Strassburg cathedrals, the soaring fortress of Ehrenbreitstein overlooking Coblenz, the famous Lorelei cliffs, the steep paths that led to half a dozen crag-topping Rhineland castles and, as a final exercise, a number of pine-clad mountains in the Alsatian Vosges through which range we tramped during a hundred-mile ramble from Strassburg to the Swiss border.

And so, when we finally arrived at Zermatt, the village at the base of our mountain, we were prepared for the great conquest, at least to the extent of blistered heels and excruciatingly painful muscles. But neither Irvine nor I was in the least disheartened. Guides were found and negotiations begun.

"Of course you have climbed other mountains," said

Adolph, one of the prospective pilots, who spoke excellent English.

We did not dare tell him that a flight of steps was our only recommendation to the Alpine Club, for it was two weeks past the end of the season, and we were afraid he would not take us.

"Oh, many," we admitted modestly, and enumerated vanquished pinnacles all the way from the Palisades to Popocatepetl.

While they had never heard of the Palisades, this sounded very difficult, and being duly impressed they agreed to make the ascent as soon as the fog and snow-storms on the heights above permitted. They despaired of us, however, when they learned that our equipment consisted of one toothbrush (each) and a safety-razor.

"But you must have cleated mountain shoes, and socks, and leggins, and mittens, and a wool helmet, and an ice-ax, etc., etc., etc. You are not climbing the Mount of Olives, you know. It will be bitter cold, and, since you have come out of season, a struggle all the way."

Irvine and I looked at each other in utter dejection. If we had to buy all these articles we would have nothing left with which to pay the guides. When we explained our predicament they responded with immediate sympathy, and outfitted us de luxe from their own equipment.

All this time because of continued fog, we had not enjoyed even the faintest glimpse of our spectacular mountain, but during the fourth night a storm broke upon the valley, and torrential rain cleared the atmosphere. On waking next morning we rushed to our window, and there aflame in the early sunshine, scorning the earth and holding itself haughtily aloof from other Alps, soared in dazzling whiteness—the Matterhorn.

At noon, with the air like wine, and the sky cloudless,

Adolph and André took courage and, laden with ropes, food and equipment, led Irvine and me up the valley from Zermatt into the paws of the crouching tiger, which the Matterhorn greatly resembles when seen from a certain position.

Right away our guides began to tell us of the mountain's evil reputation and to relate harrowing stories of its numerous victims. With more conscientiousness than tact they took us to the roadside cemetery and pointed out a number of graves of interest to prospective climbers. Standing before them we read in thoughtful silence:

"C. H. and R. H.—Perished on the Matterhorn, 1865."

"W. K. W.—Fell to his death from the Matterhorn, 1870."

"B. R. B.—With two guides on June 10th, 1891, slipped from the shoulder of the Matterhorn and fell 3,000 feet."

The near-by museum was equally encouraging. It contained the ice-axes and clothes of the immortal young English climbers, Hudson, Hadow and Lord Douglas, who along with a Mr. Whymper and three guides came to Zermatt in 1865 looking for new crags to conquer. The Swiss had always considered the Matterhorn absolutely unscalable and informed the sportsmen of the fact.

In our own climb we marveled a dozen times that they, as the first party, ever gained the summit. But the Matterhorn revenged herself for the humiliation of being at last conquered by man. On the descent, just below the "shoulder," where there is a steep snow-bank up which one is now helped by a secured chain, Mr. Hadow, a Cambridge undergraduate and the youngest member of the party, slipped on the ice, and as all seven were roped together, dragged one member after another into the abyss, until only Whymper and two of the guides were left. They threw their weight in desperation against the drag of their falling companions; and the rush was checked with the men dangling four thousand feet above the glacier. For a moment the rope remained taut, then, unable to bear the strain, it broke, and let four of the seven daring vanquishers of this haughty mountain fall to a tragic death.

It was with our thoughts on the graves and the story of the Whymper party that Irvine and I began the ascent.

After following the zigzag path for several hours we halted at the top of a promontory, and looked back down the canyon that leads to the Rhone and civilization. We could not stop long, for we had twenty-five hundred feet more of steep and, on that day, ice-covered trail to ascend before we reached the Hut, our destination for the first afternoon. Another two hours of steady climbing brought us breathless to this shelter, which overlooked the sea of glaciers stretching like fingers in five directions from the summit of Monte Rosa, glistening in the sunset, to the winding narrowing wrist, two thousand feet below, from which an icy torrent roared on down the valley. The gigantic semicircle of snow-sparkling crags loomed about us, with the mile-high precipice of the overhanging Matterhorn glowering and towering above, tossing its head defiantly into the face of the waning sun, where it became a brand of fire reflecting glowing rays of light that formed a fitting diadem for the autocrat of the Alps. The storm of the night before had covered the entire amphitheater with a glittering canopy which, intensified by a cloudless sky, made one's eyes ache from its unbroken whiteness.

A stove and bunks awaited us inside the shelter. About three hours after midnight we were up again, in order to complete as much of the climb as possible before the sun rose to melt the ice and make it treacherous. Roped, each man to a guide, we braved the freezing air and bumped our heads against the planets. The Milky Way, sweeping overhead, challenged in brilliance the last effort of the early October moon, which shone into the clear blue night, contorting the surrounding crags and illuminating the sphinx-like Matterhorn as it soared in majesty among the stars.

Feeling very much like a pet poodle being led by a chain, I barked in response to Adolph's call, and Irvine in response to André's. The first hour, our ropes dangled uselessly between us, as we were both fresh, and, by using our arms to lift ourselves from rock to rock, managed with average agility to follow at the heels of our guides. The narrow ridge pointing "this way" in the photograph was the general course of the climb all the way up. At a distance the edge looks sharp; nor does proximity disillusion one, for even on the lower slopes one must crawl up and down saw-teeth not more than twenty inches in width, with not less than three thousand feet to fall in case one did. For a stretch of one thousand feet or more we had to leave the ridge and climb up the sheer rock-face. Here ascent was especially hard. The snow and ice had filled every hollow, making it necessary for Adolph to pick them free with his ax before we could find a footing. The almost perpendicular cliffs, from six to fifteen feet in height, began to grow higher and come oftener as we labored upward, so that we had to use elbows and knees and teeth and toes as well as hands and feet to gain every yard.

The guides would see that we were safely ensconced in some crevice, whereupon they would scale the rock wall to a point twenty or thirty feet above. Then, giving us the signal to start climbing, they would begin to draw on the ropes attached to our shoulders, and with the aid of this tugging from above we were able to raise ourselves from crack to crack with a very satisfactory sense of security.

In surmounting a particularly difficult cliff, a large stone which I had seized as a support became loosened from its bed as I pulled on it. With nothing else to hold to I immediately lost my footing, and in an avalanche of snow and rocks began to glissade down the nicheless, ice-covered right wall of the Matterhorn.

"Adolph! Adolph!" I cried in desperation.

Immediately the rope tightened and I was stopped with a jerk, before I had fallen eight feet, to swing in the breeze like a sack of cement, until, mainly by the effort of the guide, I was dragged over the difficulty. From then on to the "hang-over" the rope never slacked its tautness.

Our pilots soon saw we were not the chamois-goats we had pretended to be in Zermatt, as we dropped on a ledge, blind from altitude, trembling with weariness and wondering which glacier below we were going to fall on.

And our difficulties had only begun. The passage of the ice-bound shoulder, conspicuous in a photograph, instituted a new reign of terror. The wind blew with increasing violence as we crossed the thirteen thousand-foot line and struck with enough force to blow us off the edge had we not clung like glue to the rock-face.

Beginning at the shoulder, ropes attached at the upper end to embedded iron spikes dangled downward, and only by pulling one's self hand over hand up these ice-covered cables was the ascent possible. However, even with these indispensable aids, the last six hundred feet was not a pleasure in which I would care to indulge each morning before breakfast. The rarified air made exertion exceedingly exhausting; the wind, whipping swirls of snow into our faces, stung like needles. Our arms ached from rope climbing and our hearts, unused to such a prolonged strain, palpitated in our chests.

The notorious "hang-over," half-way between the shoulder and the summit, where the top of the cliff protrudes over the bottom, found me almost spent, and only pride and the biting wind drove me on. I made one great effort to draw myself up the twenty-five feet of free-hanging cable, but half-way was my maximum. The wind caught me as I clutched the rope, blew me like a pendulum away from the cliff wall and over the sheer five thousand foot precipice. My eyes went blind; my arms ceased to exist; my head swam in half-consciousness. Once more Adolph had to come to the rescue. Having surmounted the "hang-over" with a score of parties as inexperienced as ourselves, he anticipated my predicament and heaving away at the attached line dragged me more dead than alive to his own level. Once Irvine was safe over the ledge we stretched our breathless lengths in the snow until we were refreshed. Then only did we notice that it was broad daylight, and realize that in the intensity of our assault we had forgotten to observe what must have been one of the world's most sublime pictures—sunrise from the Matterhorn.

The last hundred feet were like a stepladder, rough-surfaced and deep in snow into which we sank above our ankles at each step. Struggling doggedly on, looking nowhere but straight ahead, I noticed Adolph suddenly extend his hand to me.

"We're here," he said. "I congratulate you."

Indeed, we were on top—fourteen thousand, seven hundred and eighty feet, with all of Switzerland stretched out before us. In the cloudless air we could see nearly every mountain in the Alps. Mount Blanc loomed large and white to the west, and the Jungfrau, perpetually snow-blanketed, could be seen to the north. Italy with her lakes and haze faded into the south, and the Monte Rosa group, rising even above our soaring ridge, dominated the east. Crouching on the supreme ledge of snow we ate our breakfast, with the wind trying to tear us to pieces for presuming to enter her private domain. Savage as they were, we forgot the aroused elements in our exultation over the humiliation of the Matterhorn. In that fierce moment of intense living we felt our blood surge within us. The terrors and struggles of the climb were forgotten. The abyss beneath us, the bewildering panorama about us, cast a spell that awed me to silence. I began to believe it awed Irvine too, for I saw him clasp his hands and look out over the six thousand foot chasm with an expression that assured me he was in tune with the Infinite.

"Oh, Dick," he whispered in such unusually solemn tones that I awaited some great inspired utterance about the sublimity of nature and the glory of God.

Breathlessly, tremblingly, I listened.

"*At last,*" he continued in a far-away voice, "after talking about it and dreaming about it all these years, at last, I can *actually* SPIT A MILE!"

Only the guides restrained me from pushing him off.

No sooner had I recovered from this blow than he began to lament the fact that he had forgot to bring along his ten-pound iron dumb-bell exerciser that he had lugged all the way from Berlin and so would miss his regular morning calisthenics. I suggested curtly that he go back and fetch it.

He was equally disgusted with me when I, clinging to the wooden cross that marks the Swiss-Italian border and scrouging into the snow to keep from being blown away, got out my inseparable note-book, and with frozen fingers laboriously inscribed a thought or two on the wind-whipped page.

"If you fell from here to Zermatt," he snapped impatiently, "you'd write scenic impressions in that confounded note-book on the way down."

As I looked over the edge and saw how far such a fall would be I concluded one might write quite a lengthy document before contact with the earth jolted the pencil out of one's hand.

"That would be one way of getting my literary efforts read, Irvine, judging from the collection of fallen objects in the museum. If you want your old clothes or note-books immortalized and preserved under glass to awe future generations, just jump off the Matterhorn."

The summit of this incorrigible mountain is commonly thought to be known only to a very favored few. This is a mistaken idea, for each season a number of parties beard the old lion and return to earth content and proud, with a vow, however, of "never again." There is not a mountain left in all Switzerland that has not been scaled, so that the joy of being the first to stand upon some formidable peak which only the eagles knew before, has passed forever. But there is almost as much joy in being the tenth or the hundredth. Familiarity can never breed contempt for such vast and beautiful peaks and valleys as these. The rivers bound over the rocks with just the same abandon now as a thousand years ago. The wine-like air from the snow and pines is not less exhilarating. The charm of the Alps will never die; for where else may one find nature as spectacular, yet as serene, as in these, her favorite mountains?

It is charm below the snow-line; it is fierce joy above, fierce joy to stand at dawn on the supremacy of some soaring crag and see the amber clearness of the jagged eastern horizon grow in intensity, to scale such peaks as the Matterhorn, surrounded by a sea of mountains, with nothing to indicate that you are in the heart of civilized Europe rather than some Greenland waste. One finds a stimulation here unknown elsewhere—a feeling of having attained unto another, higher life, unto another world, a world made not of land and sea, but of crystal air, and sky, and snow, and space. It all sent a surge through our hearts. It had been a new sensation of awful power, a new element conquered, a supreme response to the hunger for exhilaration, for motion and danger and intensity of sensation. We had achieved one of the great ambitions of our young lives. We would never be haunted now by the memory of this exquisite temptation to which we had not had the courage to yield. In future years our limbs would fail, our hearts and lungs decay. But it would not matter. There would be no vain regrets. We had realized our youth while we had it. We had climbed the Matterhorn!

Ten o'clock was approaching before we could drag ourselves away from this Alpine throne and begin the precipitous homeward journey. We wondered on coming to several of the steepest and most nicheless cliffs how we would ever get down them, and once down, it was beyond our comprehension how we ever got up. The guides followed now, lowering us from rock to rock by a slow and steady extension of rope. I shall refrain from giving the details of our descent. The complete disappearance of the seats of our corduroy pants tells eloquently enough how we really came home to Zermatt.

# Largo

WHILE the Rhone Valley is not the most beautiful in Switzerland, it's too beautiful to dash through on a train. Irvine and I had not seen so much of the country that we could afford to sacrifice even this valley to rapid transportation. I began to ask myself as we bumped along in a third-class coach from Zermatt toward Lausanne why we were in such a hurry anyway. We didn't know or care where we were going; we had no schedule whatsoever. A rebellion against this waste of Alps suddenly seized me. I reached for my knapsack and informed my companion I was going to abandon that stupid third-class coach and walk a while. Then I jumped off the train, not knowing or caring how far I was from where, and leaving poor Irvine gasping at my demented behavior. Nor did my farewell suggestion that he wait for me in Paris explain this sudden departure. I was a bit surprised myself as I stood on the embankment and watched the last car disappear into the west.

The next thing for me to do was to learn where I was. A

passing pedestrian informed me that Lake Geneva was only three kilometers distant. That was joyful news, for Lake Geneva meant Montreux, and Montreux meant Chillon, and Chillon had always been to me a Castle of Romance.

Hurrying my pace, I soon caught sight of Lac Leman, blue and unruffled in the calm of an autumn afternoon. Another moment and "Chillon's snow-white battlement" rose before me. Rising out of the shining mirror in towers and turrets, surrounded by the clearest of lakes, backed by a mass of verdure, shadowed by the snow-clad Alps, this historic pile is one of the most imposing old castles in all Europe.

Eagerly I stopped to pay homage to the immortal landmark, rambled alone through its halls and dungeons, found Lord Byron's name carved on one of the seven famous columns in the prison of Bonivard that lies beneath the watersurface. Lines from *The Prisoner of Chillon* that I had learned as a boy, came to me:

> "Below the surface of the lake
> The dark vault lies wherein we lay:
> We heard it ripple night and day;
>     Sounding o'er our heads it knocked;
> And I have felt the winter's spray
> Wash through the bars when winds were high
> And wanton in the happy sky."

It was nearly sunset, and the beams came slantingly through the narrow windows high above the dungeon floor, to concentrate light on a few spots and leave the rest in darkness. I would have remained longer but the guards ordered me out, as the building was being closed for the night. Reluctantly I departed, and scrambled along the shore among the rocks and trees that border the lake from Chillon toward Montreux. Though it was after six o'clock the afternoon was so warm, Lac

Leman so peaceful, I could not resist the appeal of the water. I found a half-hidden cove, removed my dusty clothes and plunged into the glittering path of the red sunset. Striking out into the lake I again sought the castle, and swam beneath the walls of Chillon, past the bars through which the winter's spray found its way to Bonivard. The sun, huge and crimson, flashed straight against the mellowed battlements as I turned back, breathless but rejuvenated, to the cove. Upon the beach, hidden by overhanging trees, I lay till I was dry, looking toward the sun-silhouetted Alps across the lake in Savoy, and extracting a small copy of *The Prisoner* bought in the castle, I began to read:

> "Eternal spirit of the chainless mind!
> Brightest in dungeons, Liberty! thou art,
> For there thy habitation is the heart—
> The heart which love of thee alone can bind...."

The fiery ball hung suspended in the horizon clouds. Another page was turned—another canto read:

> "Lake Leman lies by Chillon's walls;
> A thousand feet in depth below
> Its massy waters meet and flow;
> Thus much the fathom-line was sent
> From Chillon's snow-white battlement..."

Once more I looked to the west. Half-hid behind the mountain wall the red disk trembled.

Canto six—canto seven—only the top-most rim remained...canto eight—one last streak of light—canto nine....

## ༞ IV. ༞

# Mademoiselle Piety

*I*RVINE and I had seen Mademoiselle Piety the first day after our reunion in Paris, in the dining-room of our little family hotel, where, pretty and appealing, she had sat opposite us at the long center table. We hadn't dared speak to her because, in the first place, she seemed painfully shy, and in the second place, we were surrounded by a number of scandalmongers who would have started meowing in chorus at such an impropriety. Not knowing the girl's name Irvine always spoke of her as "Miss Piety," concluding from her rigidly circumspect deportment that she must be taking Bible courses in some convent.

Perhaps it was her very aloofness that charmed us; perhaps it was because she was the only girl in the pension. But something about Miss Piety was so intriguing we began to concoct evil plots against her continued and unreasonable asceticism.

We had it all arranged to kidnap the damsel and drag her out to tea by force—and no doubt would have, had not a much less violent introduction offered itself in the shape of three Folies-Bergères tickets sent us by a young American and his bride who had picked me up in their honeymoon motor-car on the Lake Geneva road between Montreux and Lausanne, and given me a free ride all the way to Paris. I was asked to bring Irvine, of course, to the theater party, and one girl—any girl we liked. Naturally we hastened to accept, and immediately determined to use the third ticket as a means of bringing about a rapprochement with the demure little Madonna at our table. We had a *good* reason now to speak to her. And yet when the critical moment arrived that night at dinner, Irvine and I began to lose the nerve we had been developing all afternoon. It seemed so tactless proposing Folies-Bergères to this chaste grave violet, especially before being introduced. But she was the only girl we knew about, so it was Piety or nobody. Being the more familiar with French, I was delegated to make the attack, and, gulping down my glass of wine, I leaned across the table, trying to look as trustworthy as possible.

But I never got any further than the "Pardon, Made-moiselle—" Piety began to blush crimson at my very first word, and seeing her discomfiture I hesitated—and of course was lost. Before I could rally my forces, she had fled from the field.

We consoled ourselves, on departing girl-less for the theater, with the fact that she never in the world would have gone to such a place anyway, or if so would have made us bring her home after the second act.

As a matter of fact, the second act might seriously have been questioned as a proper spectacle for convent students. It was a voluptuous Turkish harem scene with harem maidens dressed in proverbial Folies-Bergères costumes, lounging on the divans or splashing merrily in the pool. During the height of their revels, the queen, arrayed in a few beads, burst in among them and threw herself into a wild, leaping, Oriental dance.

Irvine suddenly clutched my arm. "Look!" he gasped.

"Look at what?"

"—the dancer!"

"Do you know her?"

"Know her!" he exclaimed. "It's Mademoiselle *Piety!*"

And it was. Our shrinking saint at the pension was queen of the Folies harem. Almost overcome by astonishment, yet intrigued by this dual personality, we found her name on the program and wrote a note, requesting that she meet us after the performance if she really was our table mate, and if she was not, to meet us anyway.

Her reply came back:

*"Messieurs les Américains—Oui, je suis la méme 'demoiselle. Quand je me tiens tranquille à notre table vous me dédaignez; Quand je suis la reine d'Orient vous vous empressez. Méchants! Je ne devrais pas vous reconnaître, mais je me hasarde— à la porte de côté du théatre."*

(Messieurs Americans—Yes, I am the same young woman. When I am demure at our table, you scorn me; when I am the Oriental queen, you rush to meet me. Wretches! I ought not to recognize you, but I'll risk it—at the stage door.)

And sure enough, shortly after eleven, she appeared in the doorway, highly amused over our consternation at seeing the fragile Bible student turned Scheherazade and rioting on the Folies stage.

The problem before us now, since it was approaching midnight, was how to celebrate our alliance. I suggested a buggy ride up the Champs Elysées to the Étoile, but Irvine thought we should climb the Eiffel Tower and view the twinkling lights of Paris. Mademoiselle Piety gleefully voted with Irvine. Vividly recalling the Matterhorn outrage, I made him promise before I consented, that if we got to the top he would not make any disgusting salivary remarks.

The subway took us to the Champs de Mars station, from which point the Tower is only a short distance away. On investigation we found that our noble idea was doomed to failure, for every door was locked fast and the summit platforms were all darkness. We were bitterly disappointed. What now?

"I have it!" Piety suddenly exclaimed in excited French. "The Trocadéro towers! They must be all of three hundred feet high. We can see enough from one of these."

The Trocadéro Palais, an enormous ornamental building left standing after the exposition of 1878, loomed up just across the Seine. In a moment we had walked over the Pont d' Iéna, up the broad sweeping steps, found the concierge's house, and emboldened by numbers, knocked at his door.

"*Qu' est-ce que c' est que ça?*" growled the warden.

We knew if we mentioned the tower key at *this* hour he would never get out of bed, so we just knocked again.

In a savage humor he opened the door. Piety, whom we had chosen to be spokesman, since she had the power to charm any man into capitulation, made the request.

But our plan did not meet at all with his approval.

"*Mon Dieu!*" he moaned. "Climb the tower *now? Imbéciles! Allez-vous en!*"

Just the same, being irresistible, she got the key—and his guidance through the building as far as the tower steps as well.

Our climb to the top, round and round the long-since-abandoned elevator-shaft, was one of the strangest adventures that was to befall me on the road to romance. We could see, literally, nothing. The blackness was absolute and unrelieved.

A few windows that might have admitted a ray of starlight were covered with the grime of years. The tower had not been cleaned since the exposition, a long generation before. The steps were padded with dust. Dense masses of cobwebs festooned themselves across our path. Legions of bats, so unexpectedly disturbed, squeaked and whirred about our heads. The stagnant air was stifling. We had to feel our way upward, step by step, flight by flight. Irvine blasted our passage through the cobwebs, leading Piety by one hand, who with the other led me. Irvine and I felt very much at home, having rehearsed this adventure in more than one rickety old tower in Germany and Holland, so that the only real amateur cobweb climber among us was Piety, but she threw herself into the sport with enthusiasm and seemed to be having a glorious time. Her peals of laughter as Irvine stumbled and tumbled back upon us echoed up and down the dismal shaft and dissipated any regret we might have felt over the expedition.

By prying and jerking we opened the door leading on to the summit balcony, and stepped out into the fresh air.

Paris! Paris! Never was it so beautiful as on that autumn night. The deep blackness made the myriads of twinkling lights dance and gleam and beckon. They lined the winding Seine as it cleaved in twain the conflagration; they were marshalled in the Champs de Mars; they melted into one great blaze over the Grand Boulevards; they rushed before taxicabs across the Jena bridge and down the quays. The horizon became a fading glow. Up through the midst of this phosphorescent sea the Tour Eiffel rose in silhouette against the fire, commanding all Paris to sleep in peace while it stood guard. The Panthéon, the Dôme des Invalides, the Arc de Triomph, the Campanile du Sacré Coeur—all were hidden. Only the soaring lance of steel before us kept the vigil.

For a moment Irvine and Piety and I stood quiet, moved

profoundly by this loveliness. Then, in English, half to herself, the Oriental dancer broke the silence:

"Ze God will do."

Perhaps "Piety" was not such a misnomer after all.

## ∽ V. ∾

# Castles in France

IN Paris the greatest castastrophe of my story came to
pass. Irvine, the wit, the optimist, unexpectedly and
unwillingly was forced to hurry off to Italy, leaving me
to carry on disconsolately alone. Piety and I escorted him to
the station, bade him through tears as cheerful a farewell as
possible, and glumly watched the train take him away. We
three had committed so many delightful crimes together since
our ascent of the Trocadéro that our trio had become solidly
united, and its disruption gave Piety as much cause for lamen-
tation as myself.

Left alone, I resolved to seek consolation in the French
châteaux. But first I must write a Rhineland and a Matterhorn
story for the market, and in some more immediate way revive
my sadly drooping capital. A week of seclusion in the American Library accomplished the writing. Then, in two weeks,
having rented a "studio" and a phonograph, I revived the capital by teaching dancing lessons, with two of the pension
scandalmongers as my star pupils. Without their patronage I

should never have bicycled away from Paris, one morning early in November, with nearly as many francs in my pocket as on the day I landed in Hamburg.

Passing through Versailles and Chartres, I reached the Loire at Orleans, and clung to its banks as it rippled westward through Touraine.

For ten days I loitered in this land of poets and châteaux, tarrying with each castle as long or briefly as my fancy chose. An hour at Chambord, an afternoon at Loches, a day at Blois, two at Amboise. Chenonceaux, the loveliest and most graceful of all, captivated me completely. "Only give me Chenonceaux, and take all the rest," Catherine de Medici once exclaimed. The bloodthirsty politics of this notorious lady are open to censure, but her taste in châteaux was superb.

For me no tour of Touraine would have been complete without a visit to Chinon, since here Richard Coeur de Lion, the foremost of my boyhood heroes, breathed his last. On learning at this place that Richard's body had been carried to Fontevrault, a famous abbey some dozen miles away, and buried there, I immediately lost interest in Chinon, and scorning the approach of a stormy night sped away toward the abbey to be a pilgrim to my hero's tomb. Before I had gone a mile black clouds began to gather overhead. The wind came in wild gusts. A shepherd drove his sheep furiously to cover. An old hag in an apple-cart shrieked speed at her toy donkey and beat him into frantic haste. Man and beast scurried hither and thither to escape the impending torrents. With a crash of lightning the rain dashed to earth amid obliterating darkness. But wrapped in my coat I whirled on through the storm, stopped beneath the shelter of Château Montroreau's towering walls, past which the road led, and leaning against the great stones extracted my map and flash-light to find Fontevrault. Two miles back from the river it lay, two miles into the very teeth of the November gale. For any shrine less than Richard's I would not have stirred a foot, yet in this case, raging elements seemed to be a proper setting for the approach to such a dauntless spirit. The abbey was reached; an ecclesiastic responded to my furious knocking. Perhaps at last, even at this late and tempestuous hour, I was to stand beside the mortal remains of my boyhood idol.

"It is impossible for me to grant you permission to enter," the official informed me in positive tones. "We admit only visitors who have passes from the *préfet*. This is a prison as well as an abbey, and at present the chapel where the English kings are buried quarters convicts."

Convicts! Oh, Richard, what desecration!

Distressed more by this sacrilege than by the rebuff, I rode dejectedly back to the river and beside it into Saumur. The storm had suddenly ceased; the clouds had drifted away; a new moon and old stars came out to reflect their image in the swollen Loire.

In Paris my bicycle expedition plans had been very vague. Once the châteaux were behind I had no idea what the next step would be. Having by now run into the ocean at St. Nazaire it was necessary to make up my mind on this subject—a very simple thing for me to do with Spain so alluring and so near. True I had little more than fifty dollars left, but what of that? Where was poverty a more popular institution than in Spain! Out came my disintegrating map of Europe. Upon the Iberian peninsula my eyes came to rest. Barcelona! Alhambra! Toledo! Gibraltar! That's where I'd go—and to make it doubly beautiful and joyous and romantic I'd climb the Pyrenees on the way. But I must make haste. Already snow was piling deep in the mountain passes.

So I put my bicycle aboard a Bordeaux night express baggage-coach, and getting through the gate with a part-way third-class ticket, rode undisturbed first-class to the fourth city of France.

Any interest in this beautiful metropolis was cut short by a cold wave, which, descending over all the country, rudely jerked my attention back to the Pyrenees. The November crossing of these mountains, as yet unpenetrated by rail, would be a difficult and dangerous undertaking, and I fully understood that the later the expedition was postponed the less agreeable it would be. I had investigated the various passes into Spain, and had chosen the route from Ax because this gave me the opportunity to visit Carcassonne and Andorra, one a citadel, one a country, of such extraordinarily romantic interest that I considered them royal and indispensable stations along the road through southern France.

With Carcassonne as my first goal I overhauled my bicycle and sped out of the port city with a frosty wind behind me. The first day, driven furiously forward by wind and impatience, I covered one hundred and twenty-eight miles along the banks of the Garonne to Montauban, which is more miles than I ever care to bicycle again in one day. The next afternoon Toulouse was reached, and that night, in a flood of moonlight—Carcassonne.

*"Il ne faut pas mourir sans avoir vu Carcassonne,"* has been written of this astonishing city, no less than of Naples—and with almost as much justification. Late on that glittering November evening, armed with a flash-light, I left the modern *ville basse* on foot, crossed the seven-hundred-year-old bridge over the river that separates the fortress from the modern town, looked up at the sharp escarpment, and behold, before my eyes, nine centuries disappeared. I became an anachronism, a twentieth-century American living in sixth-century France. In one sweep the Middle Ages were revealed. A magical moonlit city of walls and towers and battlements, defiant and

impregnable, rose before me. Perhaps it was hallucination. Perhaps I had been picturing crusades and twelfth-century battles till I was "seeing things." Perhaps if I watched, the besiegers would storm up the hill with flashing armor and be met by a rain of arrows from the walls. No, it was not this; it was reality—it was Carcassonne, a fortress begun by the Visigoths and completed by St. Louis, so skilfully and formidably built it had defied the sieges of man and nature, emerging unscathed. As I was astonished by the battlements I saw before me, so by the very same battlements was Clovis in 508, were the Moors in 715, was the famous Crusader commander, Simon de Montfort in 1209, so by the same battlements were most of the great figures of the Middle Ages.

Not a person was to be seen; not a light showed, nor a dog barked as I climbed the path and walked beneath the massively fortified gate, through the double line of enormous walls, into a strange world. Incredibly ancient houses, dark and ghostly, reeled grotesquely along the crazy streets. My footsteps echoed. There was no other sound. Where were the swordsmen and cross-bowmen that should have been guarding the gate? Where were the knights in armor that should be posted about the château walls, and the ladies and banners and retinues that should be animating this corpse of a fortress? Inclines led me to the rim of the crenelated walls, and on up into a tower, where my flash-light revealed the loopholes and machicolations through which arrows and stones were showered upon the attackers. Round the walls I went, marveling at the ingenuity and shrewdness of the engineers who erected them. So impregnable was this *Cité* after the final touches given it by St. Louis, that it was *never* taken by storm.

Persistently I tried to find my way into the massive château, with ten circular defense towers, but approach was blocked. The striking Gothic chapel, so graceful and delicate amid all these grim fortifications, was likewise barred. With fifty-two towers, a mile and a half of walls, and with dungeons, tunnels, ramparts, barbicans, to examine, I did not miss the château. In this treasury of romance the night passed quickly. While I stood in a tower and looked from the battlements over the housetops, dawn broke. The dead city slowly was aroused. A man appeared in the streets, and then another and another. I knew the hours of enchantment were gone. The ghosts of Crusaders and Saracens and Visigoths, which must have been abroad that night, had marched down the shafts of the ancient wells into the subterranean caverns, to watch over the fabulous treasures which any true native of the citadel will tell you lie buried there.

With the night departed Yesterday. The real, the unromantic present lived again. I switched off my flash-light. Its gleam had faded.

## ↶ VI. ↷

# Hannibal Invades Andorra

"MAY I see the president?" I asked the kindly faced old man in pantaloons and shawl, who had come to the door of the executive mansion in response to my knocking.

"I am the president, Monsieur," he replied. "Won't you come in?"

It took me several moments to regain my composure. Presidents of republics, not arrayed in high hats and frock coats were beyond my comprehension—and here the president of Andorra stood before me in *pantaloons*! Before I could think of the French phrases to say: "Yes, thanks, I would come in," followed by appropriate apologies for this unconventional call, he added new fuel to my confusion by seizing my arm, leading me up a flight of steps into the "White House" kitchen (likewise the reception room, since it contained the only fireplace in the building), seating me in a big chair which he himself drew up before the crackling logs, requesting me to remove my wet boots in favor of a pair of his own slippers, and suggesting that I prop my feet up on the stone mantlepiece as he was doing and try one of his clay pipes.

"And now, Monsieur," he said, when I had meekly accepted all this amazing hospitality, "of what service can I be to you?"

For the first time in ten minutes I found my tongue.

"No—no special service, Monsieur. I simply wanted to have the privilege of meeting you—and—and here I am."

"How far have you come for this privilege?"

"From New York," I replied blandly.

"New York! And just to see *me*?"

"Well not altogether. I've been in Carcassonne, and am on my way to Spain, and couldn't resist paying Andorra a visit en route—it's such a funny, romantic, little country. Of course the trip over the Pyrenees, in all this snow and everything, was a fright, but I didn't mind. I liked it."

And I *had* liked it. The entire journey from Carcassonne had been as full of adventure as a chapter from Dumas. And then, too, the very idea of visiting *Andorra*, the oldest, the smallest, the highest, the quaintest, the most isolated republic on earth, had delighted me so that even the serious obstacles in my path were met and overcome with a sort of reckless enthusiasm.

For years I had not been sure whether the vaguely familiar word Andorra meant a fish or a fruit, until one day I ran across it by accident on the map, and found it was nothing edible, but an independent republic of six thousand people and one hundred seventy-five square miles, with a chief executive, a capitol building, a White House, and a congress, all lost for ten hundred years in the tops of the Pyrenees. I found that this doll democracy was perhaps the one spot left in Europe uncontaminated by the vacation flood of sightseers, for the reason that, with the exception of the capital city which communicates with the outside world by means of a sixty-mile dirt road, the entire country is inaccessible except to a sure-footed man or mule.

Long before sailing from New York I had resolved that some day, somehow, I was going to visit this little hermit republic. And at last, on reaching Carcassonne, the opportunity was at hand. Leaving the medieval citadel behind, I headed straight into the Pyrenees, (having first shipped my bicycle on to Marseilles, where I planned to go after leaving Spain), and had the thrill of realizing that here, as in the case of the Matterhorn, another dream was about to come true.

On arrival at Ax, the nearest point to Andorra reached by rail, I found I had disastrously lost my race with winter begun in Touraine. Snow and ice were two inches deep at this two thousand five hundred foot town. What would they be in the eight thousand five hundred foot pass! The hotel proprietor seemed aghast at my contemplated expedition. "It is never done at this season," he assured me. "You are a month too late. You will find the mule trail impassable with snow." He then proceeded to narrate, with all the icy details, tragic stories of men who as far back as 1800 had ignored all warning, been lost in the snow and not heard from *yet*!

His pessimistic prophecies began to discourage me. Discretion rebelled against the folly of my plans, but as usual met a crushing defeat at the hands of curiosity. Anyway what was a little snow? Hadn't I climbed the Matterhorn? "Go ahead. Risk it," said the small voice. "If Hannibal crossed the Pyrenees *with* an army, you should be able to do it without." I decided to make the venture—it was too delightfully insane to miss.

Well, if I must go, the automobile that carried the mail sixteen miles to l'Hospitalet—near the border, and the point from which the Andorra foot trail departs—could take me to that point, thus saving thirty kilometers of heavy tramping.

Naturally I took advantage of the postal carrier and climbed into the motor to be whisked up another two thousand feet. At l'Hospitalet I began to fumble in my pocket after a tip for the chauffeur when he calmly announced that the charges would be *eighty francs,* (then about seven dollars).

"I came up in a mail-wagon, not a taxicab, Mr. Jesse James, and shall pay accordingly."

"The mail-wagon is always a taxicab when it carries a passenger, Mr. Gold-Dripping American, and you will pay me eighty francs because you surely have not forgotten that I have your letters."

It was true. I had given him some important correspondence to mail when he returned to Ax, since in the rush to get away I had been unable to post it myself.

"Let's do business," he continued mockingly. "Eighty francs and I mail your letters, else—I'll hold them till you can afford that amount."

"An eye for an eye," said the ancient Hebrews. Inspired by this scripture text, I jerked the spark-plug out of his antiquated machine's battery-box, and put it in my pocket. As that was the only spark-plug in l'Hospitalet, he thought over his threat and decided that perhaps he was only joking. In the end we exchanged ransoms, supplemented on my side by a fair reward for services rendered.

Having been duly won over in Ax to recognizing the value of a donkey as a companion in the Pyrenees, I now began to look about for one. A dealer was soon found who rented mounts in season to travelers making the trip across Andorra to Seo d'Urgel, the first town in Spain, where his partner received and rerented them back to l'Hospitalet when the chance came. At first the dealer was loath to risk his mule on the difficult and dangerous November trails to one unfamiliar with the nature of the country as well as the nature of the animal. However, my statement that I had been both a horse-doctor and an Alpine guide in my youth put him at ease, and greatly accelerated my acquisition of the beast, which, bedizened with a bridle artistically studded with brass tacks, and a canvas saddle, was rented to me for a week in exchange for sixty-five francs and a sacred promise to keep it well supplied with oil, gas and water.

"What's his name?" I asked as I departed with my new traveling companion.

"Josephine, Monsieur."

"Josephine! See here, *mon vieux*, I can not have a traveling companion with a name like that! What would my family say? Think of the gossip! I shall call him 'Hannibal';" and "Hannibal" it was.

The donkey and I spent the night at l'Hospitalet, screwing up our courage for the dash next day to Soldeau, the first Andorran outpost, ten hours distant and four thousand feet higher up.

Again the villagers, gathered about the fire, tried to discourage me, but it was too late to withdraw now.

Next morning, Hannibal, having been rescued from the snow drifts that had piled against his stable door, began to lead me up the ice-hidden trail. We left l'Hospitalet at seven, under a leaden and ominous sky. Eight hours later we reached the peak of the pass in such a blizzard of rioting snow and freezing winds as to obliterate everything twenty feet away. In the storm I soon lost all sense of time and direction, and followed the little donkey's guidance with blind faith.

But just as centuries ago the original Hannibal stood on the crest of the Pyrenees and shook his fist at the Roman camps in Gaul, his unworthy namesake of a mule, following in reverse order the Carthaginian's example, brayed triumphantly when at last the summit was attained and the valleys of Andorra were seen trickling into the distance.

Once over the top the storm moderated with astonishing suddenness. With fair weather, came houses and a visible trail leading into Soldeau. Here I found a nice animal shed for Hannibal, but if he got no better accommodations there than I did at the inn next door it must have gone hard with him.

Next morning we were off at sun up, and had been descending the steep and jagged path for eight hours or more, when a turn in the trail suddenly disclosed a great rift in the mountain and a broad tree-dotted flat, where the stream ceased to roar and began to babble as it wound quietly to the opposite end. There, on the hillside, was Andorra City, climbing slightly above the verdant floor of this sunlit garden, the most pathetic, the most miserable capital city of any nation in the world. Yet appearances are deceitful, for when, nearly a week later, I bade the place farewell, it was with a heavy heart. This dirty little village houses such simple and such charming people that one is loath to leave them and return again to the world with its complexities, its unhappiness and its burdensome wisdom.

Hannibal led me on a conducted tour of the city which took nearly ten minutes. From the Grande Place we visited the two hotels. My first object was to see which had the less disagreeable odor; but as there was little choice, I registered at the one with the fewer dogs.

I soon saw that whatever Andorra was, it was not French. Owing to the difficulty of communication with the north it has been the influence of Spain that has molded the character of the country. The language is Spanish dialect, the costumes, money, customs, faces and physiques, are Spanish, though strange to say their preference for France as a nation, and loyalty to their sister republic rather than Spain, is unqualified. During the World War, this midget nation, which of all countries in the world had no irons in the fire, realized that her ancient republican ideals were in danger, and out of her six thousand people, rushed nine men to the French colors. Three returned with decorations, three came home blind or maimed, and three, to the everlasting honor of the littlest Ally, fell fighting in defense of the principles held sacred by the republic, the oldest existing republic in the world.

To these three heroes a monument is to be erected in the Place de la Concorde, and on it is to be emblazoned in French:

TO THE ETERNAL GLORY OF THE THREE ANDORRANS
WHO DIED TO MAKE THE WORLD SAFE
FOR DEMOCRACY

After dinner on my first evening I inquired from what French-speaking source I might gather more information about Andorra.

"Well, the president might accommodate you, Señor."

"Does the president receive callers at the executive mansion in the evening?"

"*Si*, Señor, unless he's spending it at the café."

And so it was that I came to call on his Excellency, and be hospitably escorted into the White House kitchen and seated in slippered ease with my distinguished host before the hearth.

From the simple appearance of his house it was obvious that the chief dignitary was truly one of the people. The big fire on the floor was not a whit different from the fires in all other houses, nor were the cooking implements less crude than those at Soldeau. A mother cat and her five kittens lay curled close to the glowing coals, and a big dog put a friendly paw into my lap when I had taken a seat in one of the homemade chairs.

The simplicity and gentleness of the old man charmed me at once. Whatever awe I was prepared to hold him in, melted away into sympathy—almost affection—as I saw him lift up one of the kittens and stroke it to sleep against his breast.

He was not only willing, but eager, to talk. In response to my questions concerning the origin of Andorra he chatted away for a half-hour telling me how the son of Charlemagne having expelled the Moors from the Pyrenees in the eleventh century proclaimed the independence of the people of these valleys in return for their valiant assistance. In 1278 the tiny country, for protection, came under the joint guardianship of both France and Spain, and this dual responsibility has continued to exist up to the present time. Thus protected by her two great neighbors, Andorra has drifted along through the centuries, history-less. She has had no wars, no enemies, no social upheavals, no heroes, no dominating figures, no change. She has been protected by her weakness, her isolation and her poverty. No one would gain anything by gaining Andorra.

"What share do these two guardians take in the government?"

"Really very little, though disapproval of a measure from either is sufficient to block action. But that never happens," he added with a shrug. "Our government is so simple and so old an injudicious act is most unlikely. We have nothing to legislate, you see. While our twenty-four congressmen are convoked four times a year, they sit for only two days and often there is not enough to do to occupy them that long."

"Your people seem supremely content."

"Yes, it is true. It is true because we have nothing with which to contrast what we think is happiness. There was never a greater adherent to tradition than the Andorran.

"A civil war was almost precipitated by the progressive party wishing to introduce the violin and cornet for our féte dancing in the place of the age-old musette and tambourine. We have no art, no industry, no literature. Few of us have ever seen a railroad or a moving picture. But after all, what have we to do with progress? Look at the barren rocks and arid mountains! There is only one life for us—pastoral, and from that we must get what joy we can in loving the melancholy charm of our country and in worshiping the God that speaks so clearly on such a day as this has been."

"What of your population? Has it increased through the centuries?"

"No, Monsieur, it has fluctuated not two hundred people in six hundred years. We have between fifty-eight hundred and six thousand now, always have had and always will have. There is no hope of industry to attract outsiders. We are destined never to expand. It is a struggle to live even now, compressed as we are between two mountain walls."

"Have you traveled in Europe much?"

"Yes, a good deal," he replied, and I had to struggle to suppress a smile when he added naively: "I've been to Barcelona once, and into France as far as Toulouse. Of course I do not count Ax and Urgel. Some day, when my term is over, I hope to visit Paris and Madrid."

Our conversation then turned to America, concerning which he had a few ideas, all grossly mistaken; so that it was midnight when I felt they had all been corrected, and made ready to depart.

"If you will come back to-morrow I will show you the Capitol," he said, holding a candle to guide me out of the door.

I walked home across the deserted Place de la Concorde, lit by a fading moon half eclipsed by a snowy mountain-top, and thought what a modest and delightful gentleman was the president of the republic of Andorra.

When, after several days I began to make my plans for

departure, I felt there was only one thing lacking to the complete success of my visit and that was a picture of the president, on whom I had called several times after our first meeting. So, taking my camera, one sunny morning I set out to hunt him down and photograph him if possible. In fact I was so absorbed in resolving not to be denied this last favor I should have passed him in the street had he not spoken to me. He was dressed in his working-clothes and slippers, so that but for his celluloid collar and untied string cravat which distinguished him above his fellow-countrymen he might have been mistaken for a muleteer—which is exactly what he was before interests of state called him to the capital.

"Good morning, Mr. President; this is a fortunate meeting. I am leaving to-day, and was looking for you that I might take your picture as a reminder of my pleasant visit in your city."

Though greatly embarrassed at having so much attention centered on him, he finally agreed, since it was not in his kindly nature to be unaccommodating.

"But not now," he pleaded. "Come to my house in an hour, and I will have my robe and hat of office ready to put on. I am not the president dressed like this—only a farmer."

I readily agreed to wait, and on going to his house at the appointed time found a change in his appearance nothing short of miraculous. He was arrayed in his Sunday suit; his leather shoes shone from fresh polish; he had had a *hair-cut*, and he made me wait ten minutes longer while his daughter straightened his new tie and brushed his coat. At last, he stood on his sunlit veranda, with the gown of office hanging from his shoulders, and while the daughter with her smiling infant tucked under one arm held the clothes-line out of the way of his face I took the picture—which, thanks to my violent prayers, did not disappoint me.

He was the last person to whom I bade good-by.

"Adieu, Monsieur," I said as we shook hands. "*Vive Andorra et vive son Président!*"

"You are very kind," he replied, "but we are a simple people unaccustomed to any glory. I hope you have received a courteous reception in our country, and regret that you must go so soon, but if you must, adieu, *et bon voyage.*"

A native son of the mountains, he stood in the doorway as I untied Hannibal from the White House hitching-post, and watched us until we had crossed the square and turned on to the south-bound trail.

My mule and I soon reached the southern gate that leads on to the nearby Spanish town of Seo d'Urgel, and as I turned to look back once more at the magnificent panorama, the sun broke from the clouds and the wind blowing from the north brought the graduated rumble of the distant cataracts. A wave of sadness swept over me as I beheld for the last time the green and happy Valley of Andorra, and there was a sigh in my voice as I gave the mule a prod and cried:—

"Spain, Hannibal, Spain!"

# VII

# Spanish Dancing

*I*T was an extraordinary introduction. I had gone to bed on Friday night in a Barcelona pension, more dead than alive from the three devastating days of travel by foot and train from Andorra, and by Sunday morning was still sleeping off Pyrenean fatigue when the piercing nasal whine and drumbeats of an Algerian orchestra, beginning suddenly to rend the heavens in a near-by square, brought me back to consciousness. Before I was fully awake the lilt and wild rhythm of the Oriental bagpipes had set my toes to dancing. Such stirring music was irresistible. I waltzed out of bed, horn-piped to my bath, boleroed into my clothes, fandangoed to breakfast, cancaned out the front door, and mazurkaed down the street in search of those mad, mad pipes. I found them playing furiously on a platform in the Plaza de la Paz, sur-rounded by circles of Spanish idiots doing the most ridiculous dance I'd ever seen. A circle consisted of from three to thirty dancers, holding hands shoulder-high, and revolving with a slight dip of the knee four steps to the left and then four steps back again. The groups moved with perfect unity, every member reversing direction on the same note, and bobbing up and down at the same instant. I laughed out loud at such an inane spectacle. Nevertheless something must be done about that tantalizing music. I simply couldn't stand still, so, looking furtively around to be sure there was no other American on hand, I jumped into a stepping sextet and soon caught the simple movement.

It was a most ludicrous sensation. The very seriousness of the dancers was absurd. There was not a word spoken or a smile smiled as the thousand people, not a twentieth of them women, stepped and dipped to the right, stepped and dipped to the left, with oppressive solemn dignity. Entire circles, including my own, were made up of men, all holding hands and all wearing their hats. Although I was continually uneasy for fear some one I knew should catch me doing this, I was as disappointed as any when the music stopped.

As my circle broke up, I saw the young man next to me reach into his pocket and pull out a fiery red English edition of *Baedeker's Spain and Portugal*. Minerva's owl! What was a dancing Barcelonan doing with *that*! The horrible truth dawned upon me—He was not a Barcelonan; he was an American examining his guide-book.

"Didn't you feel silly doing that fool dance?" I asked him abruptly.

He almost dropped his *Baedeker*.

"Why—why, of course," he said, looking unutterably sheepish. Then with an afterthought, he added: "But see here, my lad, you were doing it *too*!"

We agreed never to tell.

"Name and occupation?" he demanded with mock officiousness.

"Halliburton—horizon chaser. Yours?"

"Paul McGrath—Chicago—architecture student."

Evening found the architecture student and the horizon chaser celebrating their Terpsichorean meeting, appropriately in a music-hall, and shouting "bravo" at Gracia, and showering her with centime pieces and coffee spoons. Gracia! Never was a girl named so appropriately—Grace. Never did a girl dance with such joyousness. She was about seventeen, a true rose from Andalusia, seemingly unspoiled and uncoarsened by her Barcelona music-hall environment. When she first walked before the footlights there was supreme indifference and aloofness in her manner, as if to say: "I do not know whether I shall condescend to dance or not." A noisy ovation from the pit encouraged her. Yes, perhaps she would. Her castanets were adjusted; she stamped the floor scornfully with her heels. There was a burst of music, and Gracia threw herself into the wildest, most spirited dance abandon ever seen on the Iberian peninsula including Portugal. Her flashing black eyes and superbly agile limbs would have melted a slug of pig-iron. This young Spanish flower took the music-hall by storm. Every one cheered and applauded and showered her, as is the Spanish custom, with coins, caps, cigarettes, coffee spoons, while one man from a box above, in a delirium of delight, took off his coat and dropped it at her feet as if he had been Sir Walter Raleigh and she Queen Elizabeth. We had never before seen so electrifying a dancer. Perhaps she was Salome come back to life—at least we could find out by visiting the adjoining ballroom, where after the entertainment was over, she acted as one of the hostesses.

She was there, but, oh, how changed. Her glistening black hair had been freshly frizzed. She wore a severe tailored suit becoming a woman of fifty. A stiff ugly hat, pulled low over her forehead completely hid her expressive eyes. We groaned to see our Rose of Andalusia turned into a would-be-chic Parisian.

We were to groan many times again during our succeeding six weeks in this country as the Spain of our dreams was brutally supplanted by the Spain of reality. I had thought of Spain as a land filled with art, lilting music and romantic adventure—the Spain that used to be. Disillusionment began with this first glimpse of Gracia in a Sears-Roebuck street dress.

But we could not surrender our first impression of her without a struggle. The music-hall proprietor introduced us and by the closing hour we had learned that her sophistication was only costume deep. She was really as naive and ingenuous in manner as we had hoped. She spoke not a word of English, and while Paul chatted away in the most fluent Castilian, I was confined to expressions out of my "How-to-speak-Spanish-in-five-minutes" book.

The next afternoon it was agreed that if she would leave her Paris hat at home and wear a mantilla—oh, yes, and bring her castanets—we would take her for a drive in the park.

Afternoons such as that happen only once in a lifetime. We three had a victoria open to the sky and sunshine. Paul brought his mandolin (which, like Irvine's dumb-bell exerciser, he carried everywhere), and I a basket supper from my pension. We found a shady spot in the municipal park and dismissed the carriage. Gracia was in the gayest humor: she sang all the songs she knew, while Paul supplied the music, playing everything from Chinese hymns of the second century to Irving Berlin's latest jazz-time. She spent an hour teaching me castanet technique, and ended by contributing her own clickers to the cause of my musical education. Once I had mastered them our artistic unity was complete. Gracia danced, Paul played, I clicked. We grew more and more confident as darkness began to hide us from amazed spectators. Gracia gave an imitation of a colorature soprano, Paul stood on his head and I juggled three lemons. It was unanimously agreed that we should form a company and become wandering minstrels, and perhaps we should have, had Gracia not suddenly remembered that she was due at the music-hall in ten minutes.

Depositing our charming friend at her dressing-room, we bade her a sad farewell, went to the railway-station, and, to compensate for the victoria extravagance, bought our tickets for Valencia third-class.

One who has not traveled third-class in Spain has yet to experience the uttermost depth in discomfort. The twelve hours' ride on the galloping, oscillating coach would have proved fatal to both of us had Paul not had his inseparable mandolin and I my castanets. All through the weary night he tinkled away his variegated repertoire while I accompanied him with the clickers.

Valencia is the very breath of Spain. The view from the bell-tower of the huge cathedral makes one forget the mud and decadence in the streets. Here December is a brilliant month. There is never a wisp of cloud to be seen. Close about us the ancient white walls glittered, nestled beneath the myriads of exquisite towers, red and gold and gray. Acres of green orange and olive trees stretched to the blue Mediterranean, breaking on the Gibraltar-like Cape of St. Antoine, which rose behind the fleets of white specks sparkling and scudding before the southern breeze.

The glitter of forty Madrids could not have lured Paul away from his golden towers, and so, as I was impatient to visit the capital, I had to go on alone, planning to meet him later at Granada. Twenty-two hours more of third-class travel had to be endured, and without any Paul to while them away on his mandolin. However, my fellow passengers were not bad substitutes. For a part of the journey, a father and his three daughters, aged four, ten and twelve, sat across the aisle and supplied me with a three-ring circus. Getting out the "Five-

Minutes" Spanish book I made an attempt at conversation with these chatter-boxes, and thanks to my amazing mispronunciations, succeeded.

"*Que preciosos son los aretes que Usted ostenta,*" (What beautiful earrings you are wearing) was the initial attack, having first looked it up.

"Black Eyes" the eldest sister, put her dainty hand to her bobbing gold pendants and naively admitted the fact.

"*Usted es también muy bella, Señorita,*" (You are very beautiful yourself, Señorita).

"*Creo que tengo el cabello bonito,*" (I think I have pretty hair), she replied artlessly.

"*Le daría una peseta por él,*" (I'll give you a peseta for it.) My offer was not accepted, but it made us fast friends.

Then we explored my camera, and since it was empty they could wiggle everything to their heart's content. Remembering the castanets I dug them from my knapsack, whereupon ten-year-old "Brown Eyes" clapped her hands in delight, slipped the strings over her fingers, and, unable to resist the stimulation of their click, jumped into the aisle. Father and I began to stamp the proper rhythm, and daughter, with a broad grin on her face, threw back her curls and fandangoed and boleroed till she was out of breath. Here was another Gracia in the making. She twirled and swayed; her castanets rolled and syncopated. She had not had a lesson in her life, but what sense of rhythm she had not inherited from centuries of fandangoing forebears she had assimilated from ten years of association. Such grace deserved recognition. I gave her the clickers Gracia's clickers—and had the pleasure of seeing before me the happiest child in Spain.

"*Adios, Princesita,*" I said to her, as she led Butter-Ball off the train at their station.

"*Adios, Señor Americano.*"

Then as they disappeared across the platform they turned and waved, and from that hour their country was to me a new place. I rode on into the capital in my frightful third-class coach with a light heart. I had fallen in love with Spain.

# VIII

# New Tales from the Alhambra

ℳADRID disappointed me. It was beautiful to be sure, in a grand metropolitan way, but about as romantic as Indianapolis. Anglo-Saxon civilization lies heavily upon it. There are no Valencia golden towers, no Granada Alhambras, no Seville cathedrals. In fact it is hard to find anything about Madrid that *is* Spanish, if one overlooks the bull fights, the eccentric hours, the cafés packed with idling men, the army of beggars, and an occasional mantilla worn by some cranky old-fashioned woman.

After a week's residence I gave Madrid up as hopelessly disenchanted, and determined to return south to storied Granada where Paul awaited me, and where, surely, in such December moonlight as was then flooding Spain almost anything of a mad and beautiful nature might happen. As my funds were now reduced to thirty dollars I felt it wise to forego the luxury of a railroad ticket, and in consequence spent most of my time during the twenty-four hour journey dodging conductors.

The sun was almost down when we approached Granada, striking with its last shafts the snowy summits of the Sierras, and beating upon a ruddy cluster of castellated battlements crowning an eminence above the town. Anticipation told me that I beheld no commonplace Spanish ruin in this haughty fortress, but the shrine of endless pilgrims, an Oriental palace in the Occident, the most romantic monument in Spain—the Alhambra.

Our pilgrimage could not have been chosen at a better season, since the flood of tourists ebbs in December and leaves one to worship in peace and solitude. Why the Christmas season should be out of season in the "Red City of the Moors" is difficult to explain for the sun pours its rays over the ruddy battlements day after day, and the sky remains blue and brilliant, admiring itself in the unfrosted pools of the gardens where the flowers and orange trees fill the air with fragrance.

During the last fortnight of the last month of the year the fortress belonged to Paul and me. No door was closed to us, no restrictions imposed. All but the sleeping hours, we passed within its walls, where I was allowed to roam at will, leaving Paul, surrounded by beauty, industriously sketching some pool-reflected portal or graceful colonnade.

Every detail of this justly famous castle has been so fully described by writers qualified for the task that I shall not burden these pages with the attempt of an horizon chaser to subdue the terms of Arabian architecture. Even so, since it was soon to prove the scene of an extraordinary adventure, I can not resist dwelling for a moment on the pool in the Court of Myrtles, where the graceful peristyles before the Comares Tower cast their images in the water with such perfect likeness that in a good photograph one can scarcely tell which is which, and I was determined to get such a photograph. But success depends entirely on the mood of the goldfish which animate the sky-blue basin, for if they are in a playful humor the reflection is rippled beyond recognition.

One sunny morning, I adjusted my camera for a picture, and was on the point of congratulating the fish on being in such unusually calm temper, when the splash of a handful of bread thrown by the warden to his piscatorial pets interrupted me. The instant the bread struck the surface a miniature hurricane agitated the water and completely destroyed all signs of reflection.

A long wait for more settled conditions availed nothing, except to convince me that I was being mocked by a school of insignificant goldfish. So I decided to assert my rights, and, declaring war, began to gather in with the assistance of my tripod, all the scattered crumbs, supposing that the enemy deprived of his food would retreat sulkily to the depths. The campaign was progressing splendidly—only one more crumb remained; but it was so far away I had to seize a myrtle bush for support and lean out over the water. Ah, treacherous myrtle! Never again will you be trusted as an ally in wars with the goldfish. I placed confidence in you, poor weed, and you broke, and down came myrtle bough, tripod, photographer and all, with a great resounding splash into the historic fishpond which, in all the vicissitudes of fortune, had perhaps never before received an amphibious unbeliever beneath its mirroring surface.

My cry of distress as I took the plunge, brought Paul hurrying to the scene from an adjoining courtyard. On finding me spluttering in four feet of water, clutching half a myrtle bush in one hand and a tripod in the other, he was too convulsed with laughter to rescue me. Finally getting his hysterics under control, he thought to seize the tripod and drag his ignominiously thwarted companion out of the enemy's territory.

Once we had reached our lodging (a long mile away), and I

had changed my dripping clothes for an extra outfit of Paul's (since, with my submersion my entire wardrobe was likewise submerged), we deemed it wise to take a brisk walk as a means of reviving my chilled circulation. The gardens of the Generalife, a summer palace of Moorish kings, located just across a ravine from the Alhambra, was chosen as a destination. However, being without the necessary passes, the gatekeeper, a decidedly choleric old Spaniard, bruskly refused us admittance. But I was not going to be disappointed, having come this far, so while Paul was arguing with him, I slipped through the pearly gates and once inside, broke into a run, in an effort to get a glimpse of the dilapidated Moorish heaven before the celestial bouncer should drive me, as Adam was driven, out of the garden for having committed the unpardonable sin of disobedience. Needless to say the conquest soon met with fierce opposition from St. Peter who removed his obstructing presence from Paul's path and turned to pursue the impudent intruder with all the indignation of an irate farmer after juvenile apple thieves. Up one path and down another I raced, with the guardian angel swearing and panting close behind, as McGrath, dancing with excitement, urged us both on with lusty cheers. All records for rapidity for sightseeing in those gardens were broken that day, for to say Paul and I were within the enclosure five minutes would be a gross exaggeration.

As we made our precipitous and undignified exit, the solid oak gate closed behind us with a furious bang and rattle of chains that might have made one suspect another Moslem assault was anticipated.

"What we saw was scarcely worth the trouble, was it?" said Paul, recovering his breath.

"Then we shall see more," I retorted, angered by the new

insult that had been added to my aquatic injury. "We're going to get back into that garden again though it be Gethsemane."

The gate was obviously out of the question, but by systematic exploration we discovered a pass over the surrounding wall, and by dropping through a clump of rose-bushes, from which we plucked a boutonnière apiece, trod once more on the forbidden ground.

The gate-keeper was still smarting from the lack of respect shown his position when he heard familiar voices behind him, and, on investigating, beheld his ancient enemies strolling peacefully near the very spot from which he had catapulted them shortly before. Astonishment overcame him. Surely they were devils sent to haunt him, but devils or not, they were not going to stay in *his* protectorate without a ticket; so once more, sputtering inarticulate Spanish, he rushed upon us. The rose boutonnières suggested the route by which we had entered, and amid a volcano of threats the guard shook his finger in the direction of the rose-covered obstruction. Ah, yes—Paul understood—the warden was outraged because two poor little flowers had been plucked from their bush. To appease his wrath, McGrath made a respectful bow and with an expression of seraphic innocence extended his purloined bud toward its guardian. Such imbecility was more than this Spaniard could stand. He howled wildly, clutched at his temples, and fled back to his cell, where he remained until the two diabolic fiends, after a leisurely visit, had left the garden.

Christmas Eve was at hand, and all Granada was preparing to attend the special midnight service being held in the cathedral. It seemed a peculiarly inappropriate moment to seek the Alhambra, yet I felt that on Christmas Eve more than at any other hour, the irreconcilably infidel personality of the Mohammedan temple would manifest itself. High Catholic services could be attended any time; I would perhaps never again be present to watch the captive Alhambra, on the night it most detested, defy and mock the religion and the race that held it in bondage. And so, an hour before midnight, Paul, who preferred the animated Cathedral to the deserted Moorish ruins, separated from me—he to consort with living Christians, I with dead Mohammedans.

There was not another person to be seen within the walls. Wardens and visitors alike had shunned the intolerant fortress and left it in haughty solitude to look down upon Granada blazing in holiday lights.

But how lonely it was, how cold and forbidding. On that evening the pagan palace with its scornful attitude had not one friend other than myself, for its uncompromising aloofness repelled even those who hold beauty to be above theology, and drove them into the very arms of the Christian church, which was only too ready to profit by its rival's lack of hospitality, and to welcome each and all into its radiant wide-flung portals.

Alone I stood on a wall and listened to the carnival in the streets. All about me the towers, so ruddy and sparkling by day, stood black and ominous, silhouetted against the starry sky of the December night. Unbowed they were by their centuries of captivity, proud of their glorious past, disdainful of the unwar-like Spaniards, unconverted by their Christian surroundings, and as all Granada moved in the direction of the Cathedral to celebrate the nativity of Christ, the Alhambra, infidel to the core, drew itself to its supreme height and mocked all this pitiful yet amusing festivity of unbelievers. The wind blowing through the empty halls whispered past me, taunting and deri-sive. I sought refuge in the Court of Lions. Here the fountain, in disdain, spat its spray upon me. "Hypocrite," it seemed to say, "go to your infidel priests, go sing your foolish psalms: the Alhambra, the abode of kings, needs no sympathy."

Such ridicule, such arrogance, was unendurable. Unconcerned with creed and sect I had come here to worship beauty—I was being driven away. An overwhelming revulsion and a fierce desire to escape took hold of me. I hurried from beneath the shadowy entrance arch and fled down the hill, followed by the mocking laughter of the echoing walls.

Immediately, eagerly, I sought the Christian cathedral and, casting one challenging glance back at the contemptuous Alhambra, entered the welcoming doors.

## ◡ IX. ◡

# The Sirens of Seville

"*I* DON'T understand what the señoritas see in *me* to inspire so much coquetry," Paul remarked before we'd been in Seville twenty-four hours.

"You!" I exclaimed. "What brazen egotism! It's *I* they smile at, cross-eyed one."

As a matter of fact both of us had been peered at from beneath secretive mantillas by more than one pair of exotic eyes—eyes whose shocking behavior somewhat surprised us, since no one could have been less conspicuous than we. In Barcelona and Granada whenever we looked lonesomely at a heavily chaperoned maiden we were usually met with glances as icy as soft brown eyes can give, and though it is true that sometimes the soft brown eyes looked first, it was from curiosity which might have been bestowed with equal significance on a pink and blue elephant or any other strange animal strolling about town. But in wanton Seville there were glances that were unmistakably flirtatious, and this gave us the smug feeling that comes of being misogynous from preference rather than necessity.

Our initial encounter with a Seville siren was on the third-class railroad coach en route from Granada, a few days after Christmas. She first arrested our attention by laughing at us when we climbed into her compartment, loaded down with mandolins, cameras, sketching boxes, knapsacks, and "Alfonso XIII," the friendless Heinz dog (fifty-seven varieties) that had become attached to us in Granada and refused to be left behind. She was so exceedingly pretty, however, Paul and I both found it very easy to forgive her for this mockery of our impedimenta. She had eyes filled with roguish good humor, and a red dress that accentuated the high coloring of her dimpled cheeks. But her amusement soon changed into amiability as Paul extracted his mandolin and began to play a stirring Spanish song which set her toes to twitching and her curly head to bobbing. She finally smiled at him shamelessly, right before my eyes, and by the time our destination was reached, had demoralized him so completely with her flirtatious glances that he left my walking-stick and his own cap behind in the coach as we dismounted with Alfonso XIII at the station. Of course the brazen creature was only five years old—but she was typical just the same of her sex in Seville.

The harvest of smiles continued to meet us every time we left our pension, until Paul's vanity became inflated to such a degree that he made the remark about not understanding what they saw in *him* to inspire coquetry. When I insisted it was *I* they smiled at, he in turn excoriated *my* egotism and sarcastically reproached me for believing that just because a few people, usually street urchins, stared at my funny blond hair, I had all the hypnotic allurements of a Brigham Young. But I was so sure of my position I challenged him to a duel of philandering in which we would keep a strict account for twelve hours of the smiles that each could inspire, and in this manner settle our dispute like gentlemen.

He agreed readily, and thus began the most disgraceful contest ever heard of in Spain.

We had difficulty at first in determining rules for the game, and in deciding what constituted a foul, out of bounds, disqualification and other limitations. A "foul" we concluded was a look of scorn in response to our smiles and should be *heavily* penalized, while an "out of bounds" was any one over forty.

Paul gained an initial victory by grinning pleasantly upon the hospitable proprietress of our lodging, who returned the greeting with equal friendliness. I contested the decision on the grounds that the lady in question was out of bounds, so to decide the argument we asked her if she were over or under forty.

"I am thirty-seven," said the señora, who naturally would not have admitted more.

It was my inning next. When a comely young woman with a basket of bread under her arm passed on my side of the promenade, I beamed upon her like August sunshine, until with a contemptuous toss of her head she spurned my amiability. Paul chortled with laughter:

"Well, Romeo, you get penalized one point, making you to date one below zero."

The succeeding encounter rallied my drooping spirits. Upon overtaking a veritable Spanish rose accompanied by her equally attractive mother, the daughter smiled at me, and the mother nodded a pleasant "good morning" to Paul. I insisted that the choice of the charming señorita was significant enough in itself to settle the affair decisively, but Paul was uncharitable, arguing (not without effectiveness) that the gracious mother, owing to her more mature mentality, had naturally chosen with greater intelligence than her impetuous daughter. Grudgingly he agreed to call the incident a tie.

The contest raged up one street and down another, in and out of cafés, even into the cathedral, continuing with increasing violence as night approached. It was not waged without numerous heated disagreements over the proper distribution of spoils, since it was not always easy to decide who was the beneficiary. We should have been arrested, and would have been in any other city than Seville.

Needless to say, Paul won the match with an overwhelming score. The final count showed thirty-six points for him and only twenty-one for me. But he minimized the glory of his victory, good sport that he was, by attributing it to the fact that he was five years older than I, and had had that much more time in which to acquire proficiency in the subtle art.

## ꙅ X. ꙅ

# The Jails of Gibraltar

ERE this a guide-book, which it is not, or were it a travel book, which it is only incidentally, the author would state that any one traveling in Spain who did not visit Gibraltar would miss the last word in interesting places; because among other things, it is a British colony, the headquarters of the Ninth Army Corps, an important fortress, lies opposite Algeciras, is the seat of an archbishopric, has an indifferent harbor, and consists of jurassic limestone overgrown with cactus and infested with monkeys.

Strange to say, it was none of these intriguing facts that aroused my intense interest in the Rock. I sought it for less prosaic reasons. When the road to romance crossed the Pyrenees, Gibraltar was its ultimate goal—Gibraltar, the ancients' "Pillar of Hercules," beyond which they dared not sail lest they come to the edge of the world and fall off; Gibraltar, the place where Tarik, the first Moorish chieftain, landed for the invasion of Spain, and the point from which the last of his race returned to Africa, seven hundred years later; Gibraltar, the scene of fourteen dramatic sieges dating from Phoenician times to the Napoleonic wars; Gibraltar, the Lion of Rock, the impregnable lord of the Mediterranean, the universal symbol of indomitability; Gibraltar the *romantic*.

For three days in Cadiz, whence we had come to recuperate from Seville, I poured its praises into Paul's ears. He heard none of it, so captivated was he by the once queenly city's decaying but still seductive architecture. Unable to restrain my impatience longer, I embarked alone on the Gibraltar boat, having first wrung from my stubborn companion a sacred promise to follow within a week's time.

That same afternoon we approached the Bay of Algeciras, and there before me, rising abruptly across the water, I saw the majestic Rock, entirely devoid, to my great disappointment, of the Prudential Life Insurance advertisement I had always seen emblazoned upon it in picture.

As I ferried across the bay just at twilight what should rise serenely from behind the massive head of the Lion but a full moon. Pale and mysterious, it seemed to roll for a few moments caressingly along Gibraltar's ridge, and then gently take flight into the fading heavens. I began to wonder if here, in such moonlight, on one of the world's most dramatic stages, some delightfully indiscreet adventure was not awaiting me. Prophetic instinct whispered that there was.

The Gibraltar air seemed unusually inviting that January night. Having located inexpensive quarters on the top floor of a hotel obscure enough to satisfy my dwindling funds, I ate a late dinner and strolled out into Main Street, leaving my hat and topcoat behind. Not meaning to wander far away, I started climbing aimlessly along the drive that zigzags up the town side of the Rock. There was an unusual clarity of vision that night, for the winter moon had been developing brilliance with every passing hour, and now, high above, it illuminated the conflict between the marshaled myriads of stars and the thick cluster of the colored lanterns hanging from invisible tug and battle-ship that dotted the Bay of Algeciras. This exquisite view of sea and city fulfilled every expectation, and made me glad that for it I had braved the elements. My purpose accomplished, I was on the point of yielding to the cold and lateness, and turning back, but on such a night there was madness in the moonlight...a sudden and intense desire to reach the sacrosanct summit of the Rock took hold of me.

My suspicion that strangers were not allowed to wander about the upper reaches after dark was confirmed when I bumped into an iron-spike fence fifteen feet high, that said in very eloquent terms: "Thus far, stranger, and no farther. Below this point there is only an international seaport; above—the greatest and most significant fortress in the world." The gate through which the road entered forbidden ground was guarded by a sentry-box and a small but, where a light shining through the window gave evidence of a guard. However, the gate was wide open, and I walked up to it. The box was empty, but I could see the British soldiers in the hut through the open door. It was a tense moment. Should I try to slip by, or should I do the timid commonplace thing and wait until to-morrow for official passes? While I debated the subject, the moon poured its evil gleam upon me. "Yield! Yield to this exquisite temptation," it whispered.

I plunged. There was no challenge. I was safe inside. With my heart pounding in my chest I raced up the winding road until it came to a branch path before which there was a faintly legible sign: "Positively forbidden except on call of duty." Surely *this* path led to something interesting! I followed it as it climbed another five hundred feet, and led me, breathless from exercise and suspense, to the very flagstaff atop Rockgun Point, the northern peak, one thousand three hundred and sixty feet above the sparkling Mediterranean. In this soaring eagle's nest I found a camouflaged nine-inch fieldpiece. I jumped upon it, stood on tiptoe at its muzzle, and reached up into the star-strewn sky, feeling that I needed only to leap out into space in order to sail away as the moon had sailed at twilight from this very pinnacle. I wanted to give a wild intoxicated shout. The winter wind swept angrily against my hatless head. But the wind—the wind—let it blow! It filled my lungs; it drove me to deride a force so contemptible. Was I not enthroned on the very symbol of invincibility? Was I not dominating two oceans and two continents, and consorting with the planets in the sky? For those moments of ecstasy I was no longer an earthly vagabond—no, no—I was almighty Jove, commanding the universe from the summit of this British Mount Olympus.

And oh, what a glorious universe—Africa and Europe and the Atlantic and the Mediterranean, flooded in starlight at my feet—the tiny blazing ships far below creeping east to Suez—the sleeping sloping city on one side; on the other a sheer precipice from the top of which I could drop a stone into the phosphorescent breakers nearly one thousand four hundred feet below—northward was Spain and the Sierras; southward the jagged crest of this wonderful Rock as it sagged and rose once more to a point even higher than my own. The Straits of Gibraltar were turned to silver by the moon. The African Pillar of Hercules, so clear and so close, rose yet another one thousand feet above me. The stars in the heavens met the stars in the harbor. It was Paradise enow even without the jug of wine.

The temptress moon had counseled me wisely for, after all, what did prison matter now? Unable longer to endure the cold I hurried down the forbidden path, and arriving at the gate found the sentry not in his box but leaning comfortably against the doorpost of the guard-house. I posted myself in a shadow and waited patiently for over an hour for him to disappear inside. At last about two o'clock, the unsuspicious soldier became restless, paced idly up and down, and presently sauntered into his hut, giving me an opportunity to escape. Once more I slipped stealthily through the wide open gate, feeling sure at last of a fact long suspected—that I was the devil's pet protégé.

Next day, armed with a pass, I retraced my steps of the evening before, was duly halted at the gate, and after much signing, stamping and checking was allowed to visit the galleries with a military guide.

"Is a stranger ever allowed up here after the evening gun?" I asked my companion, still unable to fathom my experience of the previous evening.

"Indeed not!" was the emphatic reply. "This is a fortress, you know, and the military authorities are very strict. It's a pity, too, for the view from Rockgun Point in the evening is wonderful."

"It must be," I said non-committally. "But what would happen if one *were* caught on top at night without a pass?"

"Oh, he would never get by the sentries."

The wonderful pictures made by the views of land and ocean very quickly caught the eye of one as interested in photography as myself, and then and there the germ of rebellion against the anti-camera law was born, a rebellion which led to an adventure such as few American visitors in Gibraltar have ever been so ill-starred as to experience.

Of course I knew that photography on the Rock was rigorously forbidden. Nevertheless I wanted illustrations for the story I meant to write about my midnight adventure, and as it was impossible to buy them, the only alternative was to take them with my own camera.

Hidden in my raincoat pocket, it was a simple matter to

smuggle the infernal machine past the sentries, dispense with a guide and enter the galleries, where I took pictures to my heart's content. Finding St. George's Hall, hewn out of solid rock, deserted, I maneuvered for a time exposure and photographed whole rows of cannon. Hurrying out again and up the forbidden path to the top of Rockgun Point I saw in my finder, reflections that would have delighted the heart of any amateur photographer, and needless to say quickly used up my stock of films.

The sentinel was wholly unaware, as I surrendered my pass and rushed out again how eager I was to get to the developer's and learn if the camera had done its duty. Long before the negatives were dry, I was back to inquire after their health, and found, to my delight, that all eighteen were models of what photographs should be.

Next morning I went back for more pictures, but finding the sun obscured, abandoned photography for the moment and paid a visit to the signal station on the ridge. The officer in charge greeted me with the greatest hospitality, and over a cup of tea talked to me for an hour about the Rock, its history, and its significance. As he escorted me to the door, I pointed to the harbor way below us seen through a rift in the pine trees, and remarked what a fine photograph it would make.

"Yes, it would," he replied, "but I fear it never will, for, as you know, photography above all things is forbidden. It is the unpardonable crime in Gibraltar—and heaven help the person caught at it."

I turned a bit pale. I had a roll of photographed cannon in my pocket that very moment.

How many successes are plunged into failure by not letting well enough alone. That weakling policy of "just one more" all but wrecked my quest for romance and all but led me to an inglorious end. With thirty splendid photographs taken from every possible point, I returned for just one more expedition. Climbing up to a position near the signal station I was on the point of opening my camera, saying to myself that after this picture I would pay my respects to the commander and bid him good-by, when I looked up to find that very gentleman standing about thirty feet behind me with a look of indignation on his face.

"Young man," he said coldly, "I can't understand how one who has been warned so repeatedly against the act you are committing could be so stupid as to commit it. I hope you will understand that it is my duty to arrest you."

To deny that I had taken the picture would have been contemptible, and only half true, for others had been taken. So all I said or could say was: "Yes, sir, I understand."

More curious than fearful of the consequences of my indiscretion, I descended the road unaccompanied, and, to my surprise, was not detained by the sentries. However, I suspected that this was only the calm before the storm. On reaching my lodging-house, I thought the situation over and decided that if I met the charges in a straightforward way the authorities might consider the affair of small importance and allow me to make the freight boat, which, sailing the next day, was to take me to Marseilles. Had I foreseen the harsh temper of the Gibraltar courts, I should not have been so optimistic. Photographs I knew would be demanded and my room searched. I could not deny having any pictures for the proprietress of the shop was sure to be questioned. But only I knew of the two undeveloped rolls and they could be secreted without involving any one. These, under the cover of darkness, were placed in the gutter which ran along the eaves near my window. The eighteen negatives I left carelessly on the bureau.

Not till next morning did the inspectors call. They had

delayed, thinking perhaps I might try to make a break for safety, and thus compromise myself by being arrested at the military border attempting to escape with the pictures. But I was not so foolish. Without any preliminaries they quietly, seized all my belongings—including the conspicuous negatives—and invited me to accompany them to the police station. Here I faced a very blustering but thick-witted chief whose mind had already been made up for him by the excited military authorities that I was a German spy and that my United States passport, two marine passports and two seamen's discharge papers were all forgeries made in Berlin. As a trap one of the English officers addressed me in German, assuming, I suppose, that in my surprise I would forget my role and lapse into my native tongue. The officer, stumbling and blundering, asked me to tell him in that same language how I got the passports. So I did, floundering even more awkwardly than the officer, until our conversation became a burlesque and the entire court broke down in a roar of laughter because every one knew that no German on earth could have spoken his language as badly as I.

I answered the thousand foolish questions that were asked and made every effort to clarify my case, sticking to all the truth except that I did not mention the two rolls in my hotel gutter. Naturally I said nothing about the midnight expedition through the open gate to Rockgun Point for fear the shock would be too much for the officers and the court-martial too much for the accommodating sentry.

They sent me up before the judge that afternoon at six. When I heard the military representatives begin to describe me as an arch spy and a suspicious character who "traveled with only one small brown knapsack," I began to get alarmed. The prosecution asked for a four-day postponement of the trial in order that they might collect more evidence. The judge granted it, and I, realizing that my social career was blasted, was led away to jail in the old Moorish keep.

The warden was ordered to take every precaution in guarding the prisoner who, while harmless-looking, was really very dangerous. My clothes were minutely searched; I was weighed, numbered and conducted to a six-by-six cell, lavishly furnished with a mattress of the Queen Anne period in one corner and a canned tomato packing-box, Louis Quatorze, in the other. A guard brought me two semi-washed sheets and tossed them at me. "Get to bed—lights out in ten minutes!" he said curtly, as he walked away.

"But wait a minute, guard," I called after him through the bars. "I've had no lunch and no dinner. How do you expect me to live till my trial?"

"Oh, you'll get food to-morrow," he said consolingly.

Next morning before daybreak an electric bell awoke me with such suddenness that at first, unable to comprehend what I was doing in a cell, I began to wonder if I'd lost my mind and murdered some one. In a moment the much less interesting truth dawned. Presently an inspector came into my apartment and nearly expired when he found it was still disheveled.

"The maid is out this morning so you will have to tidy your own bed," he said with withering sarcasm.

"But I do not know how this prison wishes it done," I replied truthfully.

"*This* prison! And how many prisons are you acquainted with?"

"Oh, many."

"What for?"

Realizing I was on the downward path, I decided to make a good story of it, and confess to really interesting crimes.

"Train robberies and bigamy."

From that moment his respect for me was profound.

However that did not keep him from ordering me to do so many disagreeable things that I finally went to the warden with my indignation.

"I have been found guilty of no crime; no sentence has been passed on me. I am merely here in your keeping until found guilty or innocent, and I refuse to be treated as a convict." My harangue had instant effect.

"You are quite right, my boy. You will not have to work till you come back after your next trial." This was rather an ominous statement.

Before breakfast, about thirty of us were lined up and made to walk for half an hour about the circular path in the courtyard. The morning had dawned crystal clear, and as the sun and pedal exercise thawed my half-frozen limbs, I began to whistle as though God were really in His heaven and all was right with the world, whereupon the slave-driver told me to "shut up."

"Shut up what?" I asked.

"Shut up whistling."

"May I sing?"

"NO! Can't whistle, can't sing, can't laugh, can't talk, can't do anything. You're in the *jib*, son."

"Oh—that's right!" I said, straightway forgetting the fourth prohibition.

As the morning wore on, the warden, on learning that this was my twenty-second birthday, granted me more and more privileges. In response to a request for something to read he opened up the "library," a shelf containing some twoscore of dusty books, and invited me to help myself. The first volume I picked up was *Lives of the Saints*. The next was *Moses. Catholic Theology* proved the prize and pride of the collection, for it was bound in red leather. There were nearly a dozen Bibles in both English and Spanish, and had there been an essay on excommunication or transubstantiation the library would have been the most perfect illustration of inexcusable stupidity ever perpetrated against a prison full of helpless convicts. I resolved then and there that if I ever got free again I was going to send these fellow-sufferers the sort of literature that would make them glad they were in jail—the *Police Gazette*, or my first book, for example.

There was just one little volume in the collection, *Short History of Gibraltar*, that attracted my attention. It contained a splendid picture of my cell, so, desiring a souvenir to remind me of this penal experience, I pocketed the volume; and when I departed from the prison, the *Short History of Gibraltar* departed with me.

By this time Paul had arrived from Cadiz. After a prolonged search, he found me, much to his surprise, enjoying the hospitality of the city, and had the audacity, on peering at me through the iron bars, to laugh. He came at a very opportune time, for I was growing uneasy about the fate of the two gutter-hidden rolls of negatives, and needed him to report whether or not they had been discovered by the police. Positive of their safety, I could stand firmly by my defense. Paul promised to establish himself in my old room, if possible, to search the gutter, and to greet me as I entered the court room with a smile if the rolls were safe, but with a frown if missing.

On the fourth day the police called for me. I was more than willing to go, for the novelty of cell-dwelling had worn off and this life of passivity become a bore. The warden bade me farewell and wished me success in my trial.

Meanwhile Paul had played his rôle with great skill. He met me in the corridor, and there was a smile upon his face that reached from ear to ear. There was no mistaking its meaning—the films were safe. I was immensely relieved.

After much swearing on all sides to tell all and nothing but the truth, the trial began with a rehearsal of facts by the military authorities, who accused me of magic powers because I had slipped past their infallible sentries with my camera; of designs against the safety of their fortress, as my pictures of the fortifications which they had so cleverly seized (all but the rolls hidden in the gutter) showed; of being an insidious character in general because a small *brown* knapsack was my only baggage. So they advocated a heavy sentence in punishment of my great crimes.

Having no counsel, I was allowed to defend myself.

"I plead guilty, Your Honor, of taking photographs. They were merely to illustrate a magazine article about the Rock. I have surrendered my pictures. (How bold I could be with Paul's smile to back me up!) You found from the shop that developed them that eighteen were left there. All eighteen are in your hands. The American Consul has assured you that my five passports are authentic. I admit I knew photography was forbidden in Gibraltar, but seeing *five* supply shops doing a thriving business, I concluded the law was not to be taken seriously. As to my suspicious small *brown* knapsack, I am surprised that my accuser (whose powers of criminal analysis are so penetrating) should find the color and diminutive size of my baggage proof that I am a German, when four days growth of beard on my face argues so much more eloquently that I am a Bolshevik!"

Then the judge had his turn.

"Young man, this court is no place for your ironies. They are quite inappropriate, coming from one in your dangerous position. I am convinced you are not a spy, but I think it dishonorable of you to have taken photographs when you knew so well that they are forbidden."

"But there is a utilitarian side to this question, sir," I replied. "The publication of these pictures, taken against your law, would in no way have harmed your fortress, but would have interested thousands of readers who have not had the pleasure of visiting Gibraltar."

"I do not agree with you." The judge was emphatic. "And as a warning to all others who have your contempt for the law, I sentence you to a fine of ten pounds *or* a month in *jail.*"

I gasped at the weight of the sentence. Thirty days more among that undernourished gang of rogues was unthinkable, yet at that moment I could have paid a fine of fifty thousand dollars as easily as fifty dollars. The English officers then showed what gentlemen and good sports they were, for the very man with whom I had held the brilliant German conversation, learning I did not have the amount of the fine on hand, *was the first to offer me whatever sum I needed.* It was not necessary, however, to accept this favor, for Paul came to the rescue and provided me with the necessary funds.

The fine paid and felicitations exchanged, I left the courtroom somewhat purged of my photographic ardor, yet not entirely. It would never do to leave Gibraltar without a picture of my dungeon, so, I seized my camera, which the authorities had returned to me, and climbed the familiar trail to the old Moorish keep. Gaining admission, I persuaded its friendly warden to pose before the door of the very cell that had caged the notorious German spy.

"You'll come to a bad end yet, young man, unless you throw away that camera," he admonished paternally.

He grinned into its finder nevertheless.

That night, under cover of darkness, I rescued my gutter-hidden films and fled to Algeciras, armed to the teeth with a first-class Spanish railroad mileage book, a seven-hundred-mile remnant of which had been given to me in Gibraltar by a philanthropically inclined American woman who was leaving Spain and had no further use for it. Paul's skilful fingers steamed off the donor's photograph and substituted my own. With it I traveled de luxe to the French border, and aided by a loan from Paul, reached Marseilles.

Shortly after, I sat in a café, smiling triumphantly over the copy of a letter that I had sent to the Gibraltar Military Censor:

"My dear Sir: You may remember the case of an itinerant American journalist who was arrested and tried at Gibraltar a week ago for espionage. I am he, and as a memento of the tempest you raised over this teapot affair, I am enclosing twelve excellent photographs of your picturesque fortress, the negatives of which I saved from the gentle treatment accorded their companions. Realizing how rare such pictures as these are, I am sending one duplicate set, autographed, to the jail warden, whose considerate treatment I appreciate; and another set, artistically mounted on cardboard, to the judge for court-room decorations.

"Please do not concern yourself with any letter of acknowledgment. I know how busy you are apprehending spies. Anyway my address is very uncertain. Kindly present my compliments to the detective force and my homage to the Rock.

> Very cordially yours,
> RICHARD HALLIBURTON."

## ꗚ XI. ꗚ

# The Count of
# Monte Carlo

*A*MONG the three months' accumulation of mail that
awaited me at Marseilles were several small checks
from editors—naturally not one-fourth as large as I
had expected. My Matterhorn story had been accepted by a
travel magazine, and the Germany masterpiece had been broken up and consigned to newspapers. Disappointing as it was,
the hundred dollars coming at this critical time was most
acceptable. And yet, now that I had it, what was I going to do
with it?

"Get to Monte Carlo, of course, and double it—and then
go to Egypt," hissed temptation. "You haven't much to lose by
the venture, and you've a great deal to gain. What if you do go
broke? Monte Carlo is a charming place to starve in."

Temptation began its insidious whisperings about ten
o'clock one morning. By eleven I had redeemed my bicycle,
shipped from Carcassonne, and by twelve was pedaling furiously along the Riviera coast headed straight for Nice from
which city I planned to commute back and forth to Monte

Carlo, ten miles away. The road was smooth and hard. It flirted with the Mediterranean, now beside it, now far from it, but always returning for another glimpse. It writhed over pine-clad granite hills, past wildly beautiful capes, and red rock-islands where the surf drew the line of eternal struggle between the waving evergreen and the restless everblue. The only thing I needed on this bicycle journey I did not have—a box of paints.

A muddier outfit than mine never rolled into Nice, for a period of rain had descended upon me and sloughed the roads. I went straight to a hotel which I remembered from a previous visit two years before had been unpretentious. In the interim it had added a few palms to the lobby, and in consequence increased its tariff to a figure that prohibited one in my financial condition from remaining there long. I was so disarrayed from the bicycle journey it was necessary to register nevertheless for at least one day of general cleaning.

"I've only one room in the house available now," I was informed by the clerk, "and it's promised to another party, but you may stay here temporarily until we change you in the afternoon."

It was all the same to me, so I made myself at home and turned the chamber into a laundry, personal and sartorial.

On returning from luncheon I crashed carelessly through the door—and as precipitously tumbled out again. Magic had been wrought in my absence. Where I had left muddy apparel draped over the furniture, a fluffy colorful shawl hung; where I had left shaving implements strewn about the bureau, ivory toilet articles and silver cosmetic jars lay in tidy rows; where I had left an unsightly knapsack on the table, a great cluster of roses in a vase draped themselves over a small gallery of rich photographs. In short what I had left in a wrecked state, a woman had touched and made beautiful. Indeed, the woman herself—a young and charming woman—with Chinese jade dangling from her ears, a book in her lap, and an expression of startled astonishment on her face, reclined on a chaise longue by the window, looking exactly like David's picture of Lady Rècamier—without the bare feet.

My impetuous return had landed me well into the room before I could stop.

"*Oh, Mademoiselle, je vous prie pardon*"—and fell back into the hall.

"*Monsieur, monsieur,*" she called, coming to the door and handing me my bicycle pump, which the maid who had moved my belongings had left behind, "*voici quelque chose à vous.*"

"Thank you," I said absent-mindedly, so disconcerted was I from the unexpected encounter.

"Oh, you're not French?"

"N-no, I'm American. And you're not?"

"Not very. I live in New York."

I apologized for my rude intrusion: "This room was mine an hour ago, and I didn't know they had changed me."

"I half expected you back to get the pump—but not so abruptly."

The pump had to be explained, which led to the bicycle trip, and that to a suggestion that she accompany me (not on the bicycle) to Monte Carlo, where I was bound that afternoon.

"Why—that's very kind of you, but I—I don't know who you are."

"Oh, that's right. Well, I'm Richard Halliburton, Princeton graduate last June—out in quest of the pot of gold at the foot of the rainbow. I've just heard it's to be found at Monte Carlo, and want to investigate. And you?"

"I'm Pauline ——, graduate of Miss ——'s School, New York dèbut in 19——. I'm a social parasite—a spoiled and wilful daughter who left a wonderful home to study art in France. I'm looking for sunshine at present. I've not seen it for weeks."

"Now that we are acquainted, won't you please come with me? It will be much more interesting if we both go. I've an infallible system that will break the bank."

"Well, I suppose so—but I know I shouldn't."

"If that's the case, we're sure to have a good time."

At the Casino the authorities hesitated to grant me permission to enter, as my passport issued nearly a year before gave my age as twenty-one, and no minors or near-minors are allowed inside. But as at the Trocadéro, the lady's smile, abetted by my struggling mustache, saved the day.

So confident were we of our "system" that each of us bought two hundred francs' worth of plaques, exchanging almost all the money we had brought along. Pauline, seated at a table, placed our chips, as I, with pencil and paper, directed. We placed only a five-franc chip at first, until, winning steadily we became so bored with such miserable wagers we jumped to twenty francs, likewise winning.

"It works!" I exclaimed, and began to have visions of yachts and luxurious second-class travel. "Let's play faster—play one hundred on black; it's come red twice now."

She did, when click!—the pointer again stopped on red.

"Oh, we can't win all the time. Play black once more with one hundred."

It came red a fourth time.

"This run won't keep up always. Black *must* come now. Another one hundred."

Pauline backed black—and lost.

"Five times! It certainly can't go six. Put *two hundred* on black."

The sixth successive time red came. We began to lose our nerve.

"Oh, it's coming red—red—red," I said disgusted. "Play red! Put on everything we have left."

"*Faîtes vos jeux, messieurs*," cried the croupier. Pauline, her hands trembling slightly, stacked up fifteen twenty-franc plaques on red, and clenched her fists in apprehension. We both held our breath as the little ivory ball was spun in the opposite direction from the wheel.

"*Rien ne va plus*," cried the croupier as the marble began to lose momentum.

Pauline's head was turned from the table. The suspense was agony.

"ZERO!" called the official, and began to rake in hundreds and hundreds of francs from "combinations" and "squares" and "12's" and "columns" and "impair" and "manque," etc., regardless of the clever mathematical precision with which the plaques had been placed, for when this "Ami de la Maison" comes, the Casino gleefully seizes everything but the stakes placed on colors. These are put on the "dead line," and if your color wins at the next spin you get them back, but no more. If the other color wins you naturally lose.

So our three hundred francs were pushed on to the line and once more we had to endure the terrible wait.

"*Faîtes vos jeux, messieurs.... Rien ne va plus....*"

"Come red—*red*—RED!" I prayed.

"*NOIR!*"

Together, in a dazed state, Pauline and I slunk over to the nearest divan and sank down upon it. Eight hundred francs we had owned together a moment ago; eight hundred francs—sixty-five dollars—more than I had spent during my entire visit to Spain—we had lost in three minutes.

"Why *didn't* we stop when our money was doubled?" I groaned.

"Why did it have to come red *all* the time?" wailed Pauline, whose loss of two hundred francs did not embarrass her nearly so much as the loss of almost half my fortune embarrassed me. "I suppose there's no use worrying over it, though. Remember, we have our return tickets to Nice; that's some consolation."

"Let's see what else we have," I said digging into my pockets. "Two francs in coin—one safety-pin—two matches—one key—three cigarettes—one Lincoln penny—one button—oh, yes, and one gold tooth-filling. What have you, Hetty Green?"

Pauline rummaged in her bag: "Ten francs in paper—one gold vanity case—one powder puff—one glove—and my jade earrings."

This inventory taken, we walked slowly past the tables surrounded by eager crowds struggling to lose their money, and once in the fresh twilight air wondered how we could have been so downcast. Close to the Casino there is a de luxe candy shop before which we stood like orphan children until Pauline, seeing a platter of creamy chocolates in the window, could resist no longer.

"We've twelve francs and one Lincoln penny still left; let's spend it on candy."

"How much is a pound of chocolates?" I asked the salesgirl.

"Twenty-four francs."

"Half a pound, please."

Then our candy jag began. Munching ravenously, we reeled past the rich display windows of Monte Carlo, scorning all but the most extravagant jewelry shops where the three-pound diamonds sparkled contemptuously at the destitute couple on the other side of the pane. We were equally disdainful of the diamonds, for, as Pauline said: "What respectable person would wear such vulgar jewelry?"

Finding diamonds very boring, we sat on a bench in the Casino Gardens overlooking the sea, and there surrounded by great banks of flowers we finished our inadequate box of candy, realizing how much better it was to drown our desolation in this form of narcotic than to do the commonplace thing of shooting bullets into our skulls.

Not until the last morsel had been divided between us did we realize it was past six o'clock and that we had not had tea. Such an oversight must be remedied at once. We chose an outside table at a near-by café and ordered *deux thés et gateaux*, but any pleasure we might have received from these dainties was rudely shattered by a sudden remembrance that we had spent our last sou in the candy shop.

"Pauline!" I exclaimed, "We can't pay for our tea; we've no more money."

"Oh, what are we going to do?—and we've eaten four cakes apiece! Let's run!"

So run we did, straight for the railroad station, and not until we were safe on the train did we stop to worry over the damnation that awaited us for the theft of two cups of hot water and the cookies.

My bicycle was worthless in Nice, where shop after shop refused to buy it at any price, so using this as an excuse to get back to the Casino I rode it to Monte Carlo and received eighty francs there. Hurrying straight to the tables, I played with such extreme caution this time that nearly two hours passed before the last of my eighty francs was swept away.

"You play too conscientiously, son." Some one next to me was speaking in unmistakable American.

"Beg pardon?" I was not accustomed to being addressed as "son" and was not sure the rather paternal old gentleman was speaking to me.

"I say you play too conscientiously. No one ever wins if they sit all day at one table and worry over it as you do. You should move about. I've been too long here at this table myself and am going to the next one. Why don't you come along and play as I play? I've been winning all afternoon."

"Thank you very much, sir. I'd like to, but I've lost all my stakes. I'll watch, if I may, and learn how you do it."

"Oh, here, hold your hands." Before my incredulous eyes he reached in his bulging pockets and handed me two fistsful of mixed chips.

I was his shadow the rest of the afternoon. He played "twelve's," that is, he wagered that a number in the first twelve or middle twelve or last twelve, of the total thirty-six numbers would win, and by placing a plaque on two of the three columns he had twenty-four out of thirty-six chances to win two plaques on one of the bets, losing the other, and only twelve out of the thirty-six to lose both. Every spin I placed two small stacks of chips beside his two big stacks. The first three spins we won in a row, to lose the fourth.

"Enough of this table," he said. "Let's try another."

We continued the process table after table, sometimes losing, oftener winning, until by five o'clock my pockets were crammed with chips, the value of which I had long since lost track of.

"Mr. 'Midas' (I did not learn his name till next day), would you please wait a minute and let me count my money? I can't postpone it any longer."

"Why, certainly," he laughed. "I've an appointment for tea and must be going anyway."

TEA!—when he was winning all the money in the Casino and aiding me to secure a good share of it! But that was his strange way, so I thanked him, and realized as never before how inexpressive words can be.

"If you come back, remember it never pays to stick long at one table. Good-by and as good luck next time."

I rushed to the exchange booth and emptied handfuls of plaques before the perfectly unemotional clerk. Fifteen hundred—sixteen hundred—seventeen hundred—*seventeen hundred and forty francs*—one hundred and forty-five dollars—had I been handed the Standard Oil Company for a present I could not have felt myself as rich as when, with one thousand seven hundred and forty hard-earned francs, I walked on air to the café Pauline and I had robbed, and, finding our waiter, handed him forty francs in payment of our stolen tea and cakes.

I never dared go near Monte Carlo again—except to take Pauline to luncheon at Ciro's where we celebrated our financial renaissance by dining on peacocks' tongues, and wining on Paul Roget, and by wearing a new green gown and the jade earrings, and pearl gray spats and gay cravat and Malacca cane and the largest carnation in France.

## ⌐ XII. ⌐

# Camped on Kheops

*a*N opening remark in one of Professor Rogers' lec-
tures at Princeton on Ancient Oriental Literature was
that "The land of Egypt is five thousand years and
five thousand miles away." I recalled this statement when, near
the end of the eight-day voyage, the white walls of Alexandria
began to peep over the horizon and I realized that Egypt was
only ten miles away and not five thousand.

Nor was I at all unwilling for the voyage to end. Eight days
of deck-passage across the Mediterranean in February were
quite enough—especially since the waves insisted on breaking over the deck. Then, too, such a harsh life contrasted
painfully with the languorous respectability so abruptly left
behind in Nice. Pauline was really to blame for my inglorious
passage. She began to intimate after ten days of sunlit inertia
that my vagabond career was degenerating into futile sloth-
fulness. I was so stung by her contempt that in a moment of
rashness I hurled my cane into the Mediterranean, flung my
new derby after it, ripped off the pearl gray spats, snatched

the boutonnière from my coat lapel and ironically bid good-by to an astonished Pauline. Piling my scanty possessions pell-mell into my knapsack, I checked out of the pension, and jumped upon a train just departing for Marseilles. There I booked deck-passage to Egypt for twenty dollars on a French freighter, partly because I could not afford to expend my limited capital on anything better, and partly as a gesture to convince myself of my own tenacity of purpose. Another case, Monsieur Dumas, of "*Cherchez la femme*."

The steamship *Harvraise* left Marseilles February twenty-fifth—not an ideal time of year for a deck passage, one might think. Yet I found it endurable. The days were sunny, and the nights made fairly comfortable by spreading my blanket in the hollow of a coil of rope, and by piling rope as well as blanket over me. Then every evening on "retiring" I could lie there with only my face exposed to the stinging wind, and after reciting all the poetry I knew by heart, look for the Great Bear, Cassiopeia's Chair, the Pleiades, and all the figures imagination can find in the stars.

What vagabond could have asked for more—the boat almost to myself, enough water to keep clean, enough food to keep nourished, enough sunshine to keep warm? Again and again as I lay on the deck under the brilliant sky, dividing my time between reading Voltaire and watching the seagulls, the lines came to me:

> "Sun and wind and beat of sea,
> Great lands stretching endlessly.
> Where be bonds to bind the free?
> All the world was made for me."

And so I voyaged for eight days on to "the land of Egypt."

The price of a second-class ticket from Alexandria to Cairo rudely awakened me to the fact that I was no longer in a country of debased currency, and that the rigid economy, practised so heroically on the *Harvraise*, must not be modified in the least if I were to "do" Egypt on my remaining one hundred dollars.

In keeping with the necessity for frugality, Shepherd's and the Semiramis Hotels gave way to the Y.M.C.A. dormitory, where comfortable quarters were mine for next to nothing. With the living problem solved I was ready to meet whatever was in store for me.

I knew that something stirring awaited, for two lunar months had passed since Gibraltar, and now again the moon illuminated the city and flooded the Nile. Night after night, with only a flash-light, a dagger-like knife, and a few piasters, I prowled about the Arab quarter, exploring the mosques, visiting the hashish dens, trailing through the narrow alleys and into evil-looking corners—seeking, in short, the adventure that I had always supposed lurked in Cairo. These nocturnal excursions were packed with novel sights and amusements, but offered nothing really dramatic. I was never robbed of my seven piasters, nor was the dagger once drawn from its case. In fact the only stirring moment was caused by a parade of Nationalists swarming down the street in front of the Continental Hotel, consisting of a thousand yelling hoodlums throwing rocks through the shop windows and then running like mad. Cairo obviously had become too well ordered to be interesting any longer.

About ten o'clock on the fourth night of this vain search for blood and thunder, I gave up in disgust, and returning to the "Y" sought the roof of the rather high building. The period of moonlight was fast waning and still no good had come of it. I berated my guardian devil soundly for this failure to provide me with romantic entertainment—and in Cairo, too, where it should have been abundant.

Evidently this denunciation had immediate effect. A mental picture of the moonlit Pyramids (which I had not yet visited) was presented to me for consideration. At once the idea captivated my fancy, and I strained my eyes beyond the rim of the sprawling city, across the Nile, to the edge of the Libyan desert, where I knew they lay deserted.

Deserted! How lonely they must be at this hour. No doubt they needed company. I did anyway, so I decided to go out and sleep with them.

It took but a moment to drag a blanket from my bed, seize my camera, and by the last tram-car head for Kheops, on top of which I was determined to spend the night.

The trolley terminal showed no signs of life; the motors and donkeys and camels, which I had always heard swarmed about the station, were nowhere to be seen. Splendid! I would not be annoyed by importunate guides. Greatly relieved by this discovery, I set off in search of the Pyramids, which were not difficult to find, especially on a night such as this, for they rose above everything and shut out a great slice of brilliant heaven with their acres and black mountains of stone. In the dim light, however, I failed to locate the well-beaten trail which I knew led up one corner of Kheops, even though I examined all four sides, two of which were intensely illuminated by the moon and two deep in shadow. But for an armed guard here and there scarcely another person other than myself was to be found within the entire area of this awesome graveyard. In making a reconnaissance I stumbled upon the Sphinx mysteriously reposing in the moonlight, and departing from my immediate plan of climbing, halted to pay my respects to Thomas Cook & Sons' greatest asset. As I stood before the old statue, blue and shadow-haunted in the moonlight, I tried my best to assume an air of supercilious indifference, but my effort was a miserable failure. The inscrutable face profoundly impressed me.

Returning to the big Pyramid, I saw little to choose from by way of route to the top, so started up the side facing the Nile, lifting the blanket and camera one block ahead and then climbing after them. Some five millenniums ago the surface of these gigantic tombs was smooth—triangular blocks, long since removed, having fitted into the angles between succeeding steps. The condition of the surface to-day does not differ greatly from the original condition. The decaying stone and accumulated debris have again filled the angles, so that in another few thousand years this hewn stone monument will be only a symmetrically shaped hill of sand and gravel. As I clambered from ledge to ledge, this waste matter was frequently dislodged and sent clattering down the slope, making such a noise that I expected to have the police from Cairo rush to the spot, fearful that someone was trying to steal their prize Pyramid. Later I found on the northeast corner the clear and stair-stepped trail used by all tourists, but I was now determined to blaze a virgin track since it added novelty to the adventure.

Twenty minutes, climbing, and I stopped for breath, to find myself only four steps from the summit. A scramble and a jump and four steps were three—then two—then one—and then behold, I stood on top!

Many, many pens have described the panorama seen at midday from the peak of Kheops; few have described it at midnight. The desert that lay behind had lost all distinctness of outline and had become a floating sea of sand, a stretch of indefinite softness. The line between arid waste and tropical verdure might have been cut with a knife; there was no gradual shading of one into the other. The prolific vegetation along the river-bank tolerates no fraternizing with the desert.

Although historians say King Kheops built the Great Pyramid as a glorified tomb, it is my belief that he built it as a throne to sit on during starlit nights in order that he might find peace and tranquillity in the sight of his flourishing domain, in the sight of velvety fields of grain and grass dotted with clusters of stately palms, traversed by silver streaks of canals, ornamented by glittering pools and cleft in the distance by the brilliant Nile.

Without several lion-skin overcoats, however, the king could not have tarried long on this lofty throne, exposed as it is to the sweep of the night wind. Only by heroic use of the blanket could I keep warm, and as for sleep, that was impossible. But who would have cared to sleep with mystery and antiquity hovering around? The droves of annoying guides had gone to bed; the droves of tourists were safe at Shepherd's; five-thousand-year-old Kheops was mine alone.

About four o'clock the moon dropped behind the Second Pyramid, and, hidden by three million cubic yards of stone, turned this mountainous pile into a black triangle with two glowing edges. An hour later this soft light disappeared entirely, leaving the triangle an enormous bulk without shape or significance.

Not long after, from a tiny village far below, a cock crew, indicating that the eastern horizon was clearing. Once more the hamlets and palm trees began to take shape as the light gathered strength and color; the vast patch-work of tilled land lay hidden under a purple earth-clinging mist; the two needle-like minarets of the Mohammed Ali Mosque at Cairo pierced the sky-line. A rainbow would have departed in shame could it have seen the sunrise colors on city and river and garden and desert. A long caravan of fifty camels, stealing a march on the early dawn, crept noiselessly inland from a distant oasis; a hawk launched forth into the air from his perch not far below me; the shouts of the donkey drivers broke the stillness; a red sun rose over the Nile. It was day.

Thus for the one million seven hundred and fifty thousandth time the pyramids watched the break of dawn. "Centuries look down upon you," said Napoleon standing at the base. Far more than mere centuries, say civilization, say the history of the world. Three thousand B. C.! It is incomprehensible, and yet they stand and will stand for as many ages yet to come. They are not a perishable work of man; they are an element, a part of the earth to bide its time until we and all our civilization and our monuments and languages and manners shall have been lost and forgotten. And when London and New York are known as is Troy, only by legend, that future era will look upon the pyramids just as we look upon them to-day, with wonder and admiration.

About nine o'clock the heat of a blazing sun assisted me to detach myself from these thoughts and hastened my retreat from the ever-changing panorama that I had looked upon for nine hours. As I descended along the clearly marked corner trail, ascending tourists stared in amazement at the strange apparition passing them—a solitary hatless man with sleepy eyes and disheveled hair, dragging a blanket behind him. Had they watched this odd figure they would have seen him clump wearily down to Mother Earth, wander over to a grove of trees beside a grassy-banked lagoon, spread his blanket in the shade and fall asleep beneath the sheltering palms.

## ๑ XIII. ๑

# The Nile Merman

OOK's de luxe steamer-ticket from Cairo to Luxor costs three hundred dollars; third-class on the railway, three. Unable to decide which to take I discussed it with my pocketbook and was won over, after a heated debate, to land transportation.

It was an interminable all-night ride. The crowds of Egyptians with their babies and baggages were such poor company I fled to a first-class coach, and refused to move or pay or get off, all the way to Luxor. As ready as I was for sleep by morning, I was more eager for the local attractions, so dumped my knapsack at a disreputable Greek hotel and walked the two miles out to see the celebrated Karnak Temple—one of the first wonders of the ancient architectural world.

From nine o'clock till tea-time I wandered through Karnak's forests of gigantic columns and acres of prostrate magnificence, feeling myself an earth-clinging ant amid such enormous blocks of stone. Not till mid-afternoon did I turn back along the Luxor road through the blistering sunshine.

Hunger and a parching thirst began to assail me as I tramped along, and an uncomfortable conviction that, between the train ride and the clouds of Karnak dust, I had accumulated half the dirt in Egypt. With a little stretch of imagination I could have seen mirages of the Princeton swimming pool—so clean and cool and crystal clear, and of the exhilarating, frothing surf surging against the rocky coast of Maine. Water! Water! What a beautiful death drowning suddenly seemed.

"Why not have a swim in the Nile, if you want a bath so badly?" My guardian devil was always ready with evil suggestions.

"It's so dirty," I remonstrated.

"Not half so dirty as you are."

"And so full of crocodiles."

"Nonsense! The natives swim in it all the time."

"Oh, all right."

So I found an ideal little cove, shaded, sandy and secluded, a few hundred yards above the up-stream extremity of the city, and removing my grimy clothes, splashed into the luke-warm river. But even so the water was refreshing, after the heat and dust of the baked streets. One stroke inspired another, until before I knew it there was little choice between banks. At this dry season the river was scarcely a third of a mile wide, demanding no great effort to swim across. I easily fell for the temptation to reach the opposite bank, not noticing until I got there that during my aimless splashing I had been carried down-stream past the Winter Palace Hotel and was stretching my spent length on the shore, like one of Mrs. Malaprop's Nile "allegories," just opposite the Luxor Temple, a third of a mile below the starting-point. Then, to my consternation, the delicacy of the situation dawned upon me. It was impossible to get back up-stream the same way I had come, and before I could even reach the side my clothes were on I would be carried several hundred feet farther down the river. A group of donkey-boys were approaching to investigate the curious merman, and as the merman was in no state to be investigated it was necessary to do something. Calling on Allah and all the water gods to preserve me, I again plunged into the stream, and going north about twice as fast as I went east, finally approached the home bank beneath the front porch of the Savoy Hotel, where a group of Europeans (no doubt easily shocked) were in plain view. So I drifted on down, farther and farther, landing at last when exhaustion demanded it beside a moored sailboat—to the great astonishment of the boatman. There was a crowd of native stevedores near by, but I was so alarmed at my rapid Mediterranean-ward progress I would have beached there had it been in the midst of a Presbyterian Sunday-school picnic. Several moments of accustoming themselves to the strange apparition passed before the master of the boat addressed me in Arabic, not a word of which I understood.

Under the circumstances it must have been: Where on earth did you come from, and what *could* you be doing?

Between gasps for breath I pointed to his garment, then to myself, then to his boat, waved my hand up-stream indicating that was where I wanted him to take me, and said "Piasters!"

He understood, and laughed uproariously.

Again jabbering Arabic he pointed to his crew (one man) busy carrying sacks of grain from the bank to the boat, and shrugged his shoulders in a way that eloquently explained his inability to accommodate me until his craft was loaded—perhaps next week.

I groaned over my dilemma. There remained only one thing to do—wait till darkness. I asked the boatman for his "crew's" pink cotton nightgown (the conventional Egyptian garment) and enveloped in its folds sat, a most idiotic spectacle, on the gunwale praying for darkness and deliverance.

About eight, protected by nightgown and obscurity, I summoned up courage for the dash. Some one had to go along to recover the garment, and the boat owner, feeling it was bad enough to have a white man at large clad only in pink cotton without being accompanied by the "crew" in his loin cloth, decided he himself was the best person to go. Grinning from ear to ear he followed close behind me as I crept furtively, barefooted, barelegged, bareheaded, past the town to the cove, where to my complete surprise and unspeakable relief, my clothes were found intact.

At the hotel, Hassam, the boatman, who had followed me to get his bakshish, asked the Arabic-speaking Greek proprietor to ask me if I were going to the celebrated Temple of Horus at Edfu, sixty-five miles up-stream, and if so would I not care to go next Sunday (this being Friday) via the Nile in his "butterfly" boat. The idea had great merit and I agreed immediately.

This plan gave me a day in which to visit Thebes, which, having come to Luxor, I would not have missed for a dozen Edfu temples. Early on Saturday I was rowed across the Nile in a small skiff. The same donkey-boys and dragomans that drove me back into the river on the previous afternoon awaited us in marshaled phalanxes, pouncing upon the huddled tourists with savage cries. One officious Arab seized me bodily as I disembarked, gaining in consequence a whack over the head with my cane and irrevocably binding my sworn oath to avoid each and all of his profession.

Following my map I struck out along the road to the Valley of the Kings, rejoicing in my independence. I had not gone a hundred yards when a portly Englishman and his more portly wife, part of a Cook's conducted party, passed me riding on donkeys being driven by two of the very same drivers I had treated so bruskly at the landing. Realizing their destination was mine, I resolved to keep them in sight, to make doubly sure of maintaining the right road. The two donkey boys emphatically disliked to be of service, especially free service, to so bitter an enemy as I, and in order to rid themselves of my unwelcome presence they beat their poor animals into a breakneck speed, running and shouting behind them and frequently looking around to see if they were losing me. It was difficult to keep up with this flying squadron, but just to teach them proper respect for a white man I swore by Allah to follow all day at their heels.

The endurance test lasted scarcely a hundred yards. The Englishman's wife, weighing all of two hundred pounds (or about twice as much as her little mount), had never won fame as a horsewoman back home and was in no manner qualified by weight, figure, experience or disposition, to be jockey for a galloping donkey. The unfortunate lady soon lost one stirrup, then the other. Her hat fell over her eyes, but she did not dare take her hands off the saddle pommel to right it. Strands of hair and fat limbs began to trail forth and from the general ensemble rose a frantic cry of "Stop him! Stop him!" By way of stopping him the malevolent driver, seeing me still trotting close behind, rained upon his plunging animal a new series of particularly vicious blows, which sent him bounding forward more furiously than ever and made the poor woman give herself up for lost indeed. Her husband, flying ahead, finally managed to halt his mount, though he lost his white helmet in doing so. When the trailing donkey caught up he, too, stopped, with a suddenness that almost threw overboard the precariously-seated, disheveled, terrified, unspeakably angry lady. Having rescued the helmet, I had a good excuse to approach the panting red-faced couple, who were busily engaged in reviling and threatening the guilty drivers. Try as I might I could not suppress the laughter which this crushing victory over mine enemies inspired. A withering glance from the wife suppressed it for me—and immediately. She saw nothing amusing in this indignity. In fact laughter was emphatically *défendu.*

The helmet returned, and peace declared, I accompanied them throughout the tombs tour and joined their luncheon party at Cook's rest-house. Immediately after, though there was much more to see, the one great aim of my jaded friends became to get back to the hotel as fast as possible, so we parted. Poor browbeaten tourists. It takes the physical constitution of a gorilla and mental equanimity of a mud-turtle to last through a conducted tour of Egypt, especially when the sand and sun and flies are doing all they can (which they always are) to destroy the satisfaction of visiting these ribs in the cradle of civilization.

As I approached the river, covered with dust and parched with heat, the muddy tepid water looked like mountain dew. Another swim after such a blistering day, in spite of previous disasters, was a necessity. Having profited by the lesson of the day before, I engaged a skiffman to accompany me across and transport my clothes. Half-way over he aimed the camera in my direction and took a picture of the Nile with a semi-submerged head in the middle of it.

Wouldn't it be a great surprise to Hassam, I thought, to call on him again from out of the depths? It was easy enough to trace the familiar down-stream course and once more clutch at my friend's craft as I sailed past. He was on board and nearly expired at the sight of me. The crew fled, fearing another appropriation of his nightgown; but it was unnecessary this time, as my companion had hovered beside me through the entire voyage, and at the bank handed over everything from boots to helmet.

Next morning at dawn, with a supply of food, I was back

again on the *Hassam*. As the sun glinted through the columns of the Luxor Temple, we cast off for thirty-six as beautiful hours as I've ever spent. What combination of delights could be so thoroughly romantic as a sailboat on the palm-lined Nile, blue-canopied by day, star-illumined by night? It took little imagination to picture Cleopatra on her flower-decked barge floating past these very banks, surrounded by sensuous, indolent Egyptian luxury. It came as a rude shock when, straight upon the heels of my impersonation of Cleopatra, Hassam asked for transportation payment in advance.

There being a propitious wind we did not tie up with the approach of darkness, but sailed on as sunset glazed the water and turned it from brown to gold, as the twilight calm deepened into evening and burnished the spangles in the heavens. I had hoped to draw Hassam into conversation under the spell of the tropical night, and would have done so had his English not been confined to "mon-ee" and my Arabic to "imshi!" (be off!), limitations which caused us to refrain from debating the superiority of Mohammedanism over Christianity.

That evening spent on the sailboat was one replete with such romantic charm that when my thoughts drift back unguarded to Egypt they rest not on the sunrise seen from Kheops, nor on the mountainous Temple of Karnak, but on this night of beauty on the ancient river where the butterfly boat bore me half dreaming between its wind-filled wings up the rippling, twinkling pathway of the Nile—and all for a dollar and ten cents.

As Hassam was not returning to Luxor for two days, I went back by train, having explored the superb temple at Edfu to my satisfaction, and, being rather bored with temples, hurried on past to Cairo, feeling I had checked off Egyptian antiquities with a very heavy check.

Cairo, on April first, found me wrestling with the question of "Where next?" The Isles of Greece, Mount Olympus, and the Dardanelles tugged hard at the left arm; Benares, Agra and the Vale of Kashmir tugged just as hard at the right. For years my secret passion had been to swim the Hellespont, yet no less consuming was my adoration of the Taj Mahal. While I had only sixty dollars, that fact did not enter into the argument one way or the other, as I could not see where either continent had any advantage over the other as a place in which to be destitute.

Two days of inward debate elapsed before I thought of my good-luck Lincoln penny, brought from America and first mentioned at the Monte Carlo Casino, as a safe means of coming to a decision. The problem of destination could be settled oracularly by the turn of a coin—a coin that surely would not betray me. Heads championed the course of Greece; tails, of India. Greece won the first toss, then India, then Greece, then India, and then—what tremendous adventures lay in the dictatorship of that fateful fifth toss—*tails*!

This decision having been made, I spent three more days increasing my capital from sixty dollars to one hundred dollars by acting as special guide for two middle-aged American husbands who wanted to be "protected from mosques, and bazaars, and cemeteries." Then lest I waste my precious funds in gold-digging Cairo, I rushed for the coast, carrying an omnipotent personal letter from the American military attaché to the consul at Port Said.

The very day I arrived the steamship *Gold Shell*, a fine big American oil tanker, bound for Calcutta, entered the Suez Canal, in need of a seaman. I was immediately signed on, and sailed away with the ship across the one hundred miles of desert into the stirring months ahead—months that were to provide the royalest romance of all in this romantic history.

## ﹌ XIV. ﹍

# The Garlic-Eaters

OUR passage through the canal was made on a Sunday, which, being a holiday, gave me nothing to do except get acquainted with the crew. The other nine seaman were Greek to a man, likewise the bo's'n and several of the "black gang." Only the officers were first generation Americans. If I had any initial distrust of the attitude of my fo'castle mates to their new member it was quickly dissipated when, on their learning that I had no proper working clothes they vied with one another in supplying me with the necessary articles from their own limited wardrobe. One man offered me a cotton shirt, another a pair of khaki trousers, another repaired my locker, another helped me arrange my bunk. We were comrades from the first.

True to form, they had such unpronounceable polysyllabic names I was forced to simplify matters by reducing "Dourateliasinous" to "Slim," and others of his countrymen whose names were even more tongue-tying to "Louie," "Shorty," "Jack," etc. They found "Halliburton" no less difficult and retaliated by abbreviating it to "Boy," thereby humiliating me into a place of proper respect for Greek nomenclature.

The hearts of the Hellenes were better than their table manners. At the approaching odor of food they lost all self-control, dropping their rust-chippers and paint-brushes as if these tools had suddenly become red-hot, and with eager eyes crushed one another in the mad race to our mess-room. At first I tried to set a good example and maintain some pretense of dignity at the table, but I almost starved in consequence and soon abandoned my idealism for a leading part in the fight for the survival of the fittest. From necessity I was forced to invention, and my solution of the problem for getting my share of the food was nothing short of a *coup de maître*. Oh, a college education is a great thing—otherwise I should never have thought of foregoing the soup as a strategic measure. Since none of the Greeks could ever bring themselves to so great a sacrifice, I had no competition in being the first to seize upon the meat and vegetables.

While there was always quite enough food to go round, these sons of Epicurus piled their plates with such quantities that often nothing was left for the last man. Having mixed all the elements together and drowned the whole with olive oil and vinegar, as a final triumphant addition they would bring forth from under lock and key the rarest delicacy of all—a piece of garlic, and having cut this morsel over the assembled goulash eat perhaps a third of it.

There is nothing like food to animate the Mediterranean tongue. At our mess-table one was in constant danger of immediate death from wild knives and forks when in their excited conversation the seamen gesticulated furiously without the least consideration for the safety of those near by. They raised such a din one had to allow five minutes to get a dish one asked for. A quiet "Would you please pass the bread" was worse than futile. One had to make a megaphone of one's hands and howl down the table: "Hey—BREAD!" but even then, since some of them knew almost no English, one was sure to get pickles or the indispensable toothpicks.

The mortal enemies of our mess-boy were the engine-room men, who immediately after he had scoured our tables and benches, would come forward to pay us a visit, bringing with them their grease-dripping clothes which stained whatever they touched. The greatest offender in this respect was "Micky," a gigantic Irish fireman, whose twinkling blue eyes and smiling countenance simply exuded affability and good-will toward his fellow-man. "Micky's heart is as big as a wash-tub," the chief engineer remarked. One had but to look at him to know it was true. He had run away from home at sixteen to become a coal-passer on a steamship, and for fourteen years had stoked so many fires that much of his intelligence had been literally burned out of him and gone to brawn. Yet with all his enormous powerful frame there was not a more serene-tempered man in our crew of forty-five.

This gentle Hercules and I became friendly at the very start of our long trip to India. He showed me his box of letters and grinned boyishly when we came to the photograph of his Providence, Rhode Island, sweetheart. There were three unmistakably Irish girls in the picture, and, of course, on his suggestion that I guess which of the three was the mistress of his heart, I chose the prettiest one—a dreadful faux-pas, as I should properly have chosen the huskiest.

Before we had made our exit from the Red Sea into the Indian Ocean one of the quartermasters drank too much paregoric, and the chief mate, realizing I was not a demon rust-chipper, proposed that I should stand the watch of the incapacitated one.

"Ever steered before?" he asked me. (I never had, but thought it high time to learn.)

"Well, rather, I'm the original rudder."

"Then take Louie's place till he gets well. Your watch is eight till twelve. You and Slim can arrange your time at the wheel to suit yourselves."

"Slim" Dourateliasinous was my special friend and champion among the Greeks. He was twenty-five, and, with a slightly superior education and finer sensibilities, far above the mental and moral level of his countrymen on board. He was recognized as the best sailor on the ship, the most intelligent and trustworthy. Was there a particularly delicate piece of work necessary on the top of the mast? Send Slim!—and up he would go like a scampering monkey. He comprehended every emergency as soon as the bo's'n, and was on his way to meet it before the rest of us had been told what was to be done. He tutored me in splicing and rope craft; he taught me how the stars are used in navigation, and a little modern bootblack-Greek. Of all the men on the *Gold Shell*, our tormented feline mascot, "Sweet Caporal," loved Slim the best; and no wonder, for this kindly sailor showered his affection on that grouchy old English-born tomcat, fed him pie, condensed milk, flying-fish that blundered on board, scratched his furry neck, and in affectionate caressing tones heaped upon him every insult and every evil name in a seaman's amazing vocabulary: "You lazy, lousy limeyuicer (the universal term among American seamen for anything British), you damned old Liverpool bum, who let you sign on this American boat? You've not done a lick of work—just lie around and drink up our condensed milk. So the skipper caught you sneaking up on his canary-bird, did he? You better keep away from that old——! And don't you get mixed up wit' no females in Calcutta and miss the boat. Those cats don't speak limeyuice, you dash, dash, dash, dash."

That was Slim.

And now when the steering of the *Gold Shell* faced me I confided in this man that the only things I had ever steered before were a motor-car and a dancing-partner.

"Oh, well, it's a big ocean, and there's lots of room," he said consolingly. "You'll catch on in a minute."

When my watch came I managed to take the wheel with such outward indifference that the mate seemed quite confident of my ability and sauntered into the chart-room.

Our course was due east. In half a minute the indicator began to drift toward port—I gave the wheel a terrific yank to star-board—no immediate effect—half a turn more—the needle began to waver again in the right direction—but once under way it raced past the home plate and ten degrees beyond. If this kept up I would soon land us back in Suez, so I threw the wheel two complete rotations to port, hoping to check this reckless driving, only to send us another ten degrees too far off the course. For quarter of an hour the *Gold Shell* charged back and forth, on the straight and narrow path only when she was crossing it.

Unfortunately, the captain was swinging merrily in his hammock behind the wheel-house and thus was in a position to notice (who wouldn't have?) the serpentine wake zigzagging behind. He came storming into the wheel-room amid a shower of damns and hells and demanded what dash dash lunatic was trying to dodge submarines.

"I am, sir."

He looked at the compass—it was ten degrees off. Then he squinted his penetrating eyes at me:

"Did you ever steer before?"

"Often, sir, but this is my first turn at this wheel. I have to get the hang of it."

"You should hang *for* it," he exclaimed unsympathetically. "Mr. Bond," (the mate had shared in the general damnation) "see that some one stands over this man and keeps him from running off the ocean. We'll be a week late if this continues."

Thereupon Slim was called up from his deck work to superintend. In a quiet way he told me to keep my eyes on the forward mast which responded to the wheel several seconds before the compass, and immediately when the *mast* began to shift, to give a turn of only two or three spokes (not three rotations) to check it. In a short while the light touch began to straighten out our wake, though for several days after the captain said he could always tell when I was at the wheel by one glance at the trail the ship left behind.

The two hours from ten till midnight spent on the lookout were always enjoyed as a pleasant duty. Where in all the world are the stars so brilliant and the night wind so caressing as on the Indian Ocean? From the bridge one looked down upon the deserted decks, so animated by day, so quiet now. Eight untroubled seamen slept like the dead in the airy fo'castle, with no pains, no nerves, no responsibilities, no vain regrets, no anticipation of gathering difficulties, no family cares, no financial problems to disturb their hard earned slumber. The ocean swells lifted them gently up, then let them gently down. The rush and foam of the cloven waves rustled like the sound of a waterfall. Neurasthenic, would you sleep? Be a seaman!

Of all the men on board, our chunky sawed-off bo's'n had the most years and the least sense. Although he had been at sea forty-two years and was but fifty-two at the time, he had never learned to read or write or navigate or speak more than a crude score of English words. His orders to me were such jargon, especially after being strained through a bushy mustache, that I understood only enough to make a wild guess at what he wanted.

For some reason he chose me as handy-man around the ship and when I was not on watch kept me busy turning the grindstone for him, holding this and fetching that. He took a grandfatherly interest in my comfort and safety which would have been amusing had it not been so illogical. When he drove the other men on to the scorching iron deck to chip rust in the fulgor of withering sunshine, he carefully kept me away from it, offering as his reason that the "sun make you seek," but in the next sentence he would send me down into the suffocating, sweltering stores hold and have me lug around one hundred-pound iron pulleys and five-gallon cans of white lead until I had to climb on deck to seek relief in the comparatively cooling sunshine. It was his firm policy to forbid my working along the edge of the ship for fear I might fall overboard and be eaten by sharks, yet he hesitated not at all to send me up the mast with a paint bucket twenty feet above the crow's nest where the ladder ceased to have rungs and only by grasping the bucket-handle with my teeth could I manage to move at all. Whenever the old bo's'n began to shield me from dangers and discomforts I immediately said my prayers and resigned myself to the worst.

One twilight when we were some five hundred miles off the coast of Ceylon a dozen of us were lounging under the awning of the fo'castle head seeking relief from the sun which, having been exceedingly fierce all day was now sinking below the horizon, fiery to the last. A band of lavender softened the entire sky-line and only endless schools of flying fishes disturbed the viscous stagnant ocean. It was a time for smoking and story-telling, nor was the opportunity lost for either. Every member of our crew, down to the youngest mess boy or engine-oiler, were adventurers whose sense of ethics was, to put it mildly, indelicate, and whose tales of violence, of prisons, of escapes, of bloodshed, of sordid romance, and of deprivations made one fully believe the saying that truth—if such it were—is stranger than fiction. Always during our twilight story hours some member of the group would dismiss each bit of narrative with an inevitable: "Oh, that ain't nothin', why, I seen…" and the telling of what *he* seen would occupy the next few minutes.

Well after dark on this particular night we got on the subject of swimming, and "Old Ed," a seaman of twenty years' service whose stories were more trustworthy than the others, told us a yarn which, while he may have read it an hour before in a fiction magazine, held our attention closely.

He claimed to have been on a Nova Scotian schooner from which a comrade named McAlister was knocked overboard by a boom nine miles from port. Their ship was racing with a rival craft and the renegade captain rather than lose his head, left the seaman to drown, not knowing that nine miles was no more than this particular man could swim when his life depended on it. McAlister actually reached the dock unassisted and with a gun set out to hunt down the captain. They met on the street—"Mac walked straight up to him, called him a damned murderer, and right before everybody…"

Old Ed never finished his story. At this point the sun seemed to fall from its course and switch night with terrifying suddenness back to day. A radiant, blinding light glared over sea and sky that had been wrapped in utter darkness a second before.

But it was a mechanical, not an astronomical, phenomenon. A roaring, blazing volcano of fire was leaping from our stack and rising one hundred feet into the air, illuminating heaven and earth with its flames. Our cargo was crude oil and gasoline, so the eruption had only one significance—the tanks were burning, and our time had come.

The jangle of fire-gongs roused us from our consternation—everybody leaped aft toward the engine-room, which, judging from the magnitude of the fireworks, must be a furnace. With the others I tumbled down the fo'castle ladder on to the deck; half-way some one grabbed my shoulder and held me back. It was Slim.

"You wait!" he cried, "too many get mixed up."

"Let me go, Slim—the ship is going to explode."

"And when she does everybody back there get killed."

There were shouting and uproar everywhere. The geyser of burning oil was drifting back down upon the canvas awnings and setting them on fire in a score of places. Yet after the first quake there was no disorder—fire drill had been rehearsed too many times. With Slim following, urging me to wait and see if the sudden flames were going to prove too great a strain on the boilers, I got aft to find the pumps and half-dozen hose already in action. The conflagration subsided nearly as quickly as it had arisen, to the indescribable relief of every one. Instead of the explosion we had feared, there had been only the ignition of fuel-oil gas, which, deprived of air in the fire boxes by a careless attendant, had ignited in the stack on finding oxygen there and then been swept violently skyward by the sudden release of the compressed air. So great had been the glare that other ships, some of them miles away, believing a catastrophe had taken place, sent out alarmed inquiries by wireless. Our operator replied that things were not so bad as they appeared and that their appreciated assistance would not be needed.

Nevertheless during the remaining few days to Calcutta we could not forget that we were living on the lid of a tank holding thousands of tons of gasoline, a fact that had concerned us not at all before.

On Easter Sunday, with the thermometer hovering around one hundred and ten in the shade and the wind burning one's skin like a blast from a furnace, the *Gold Shell* docked at Budge-Budge on the Hooghly, a dozen miles below Calcutta, and the seamen, confined to the boat since they left Texas, fifty days before, hurried to dock her in order that they might put their feet on dry land once more. According to agreement I was discharged, with forty dollars added to my capital. The other seamen, allowed half their accumulated wages, emerged from the captain's office waving a handful of rupee bank-notes apiece and dancing about singing at the top of their lungs in that state of supreme happiness that only a sailor, liberated from the sea and supplied with funds, can experience. The peg-top trousers, the green silk shirt, the heavy red tie with brass stick pin, the squeaky tan shoes, the checked cap cocked on one ear, the hair close-cropped by each man for his neighbor, and the *Gold Shell* crew was arrayed in all its glory, prepared to sweep noisily upon the seaport, paint it red and leave it enriched by their hard-earned, easy-spent wages.

But that I was going along to partake of the night's revels never entered my shipmates' heads, and several hours' debate with myself on the question had left me undecided. The negative argued against going, only to be met with derisive howls of "piker!" from the affirmative, which in turn faltered before the opponent's whispered admonitions such as: "You'll be sorry," and "No good will come of it."

In the end the affirmative won, though it was a questionable victory. I left behind all but five dollars, consoling my conscience with the indisputable argument that no one is going very far toward hell with only five dollars.

Thus it was that in the doubtful company of Slim, Micky and the bo's'n, I found myself in that swarming, uninteresting, half-caste city of Calcutta. Several rounds of whisky and soda began to have effect on three of our quartet, especially on the bo's'n whom I had persuaded with small difficulty to consume nine-tenths of my orders. Passing through the Chinese quarter we came upon a rickshaw stand, and as three of us had never seen this vehicle before, we felt inspired to have a ride immediately. Each rickshaw carried two, but no, we must have one apiece, since to spend as much money as possible was the chief purpose of our shore visit.

The ride that followed would have made Paul Revere gnash his teeth with envy. The excitement began immediately, for the coolies pulled us away in single file, and each of us, unwilling to drop behind the other three, spurred on his coolie until with a shout of victory he forged ahead into the lead. There could be but one consequence—a mad race. Down the congested thoroughfares we galloped, urging on our terrified man-motors with threats and shouts and bribes. Micky, being the heaviest, soon fell behind, and with his cap took to beating his coolies furiously in an effort to catch up. Seeing how effectively this method worked, the rest of us followed suit, and resorting to blows nearly doubled our speed. Over curbs and cobbles, pursued by urchins and policemen, we dashed, dodging bullock-carts, bumping together and leaving a wake of astonished and prostrate natives all along the way. The intoxicated whoops from Micky and the bo's'n could be heard a block, and I am sure my laughter carried as far. The poor coolies, wheezing for breath and dripping perspiration, galloped on, darting into any opening that presented itself in the labyrinth of crazy streets, regardless of destination. Such violence could not long continue. Slim's coolie, who had managed to keep him in the lead most of the time, brought the race to a sudden close by running straight into a bamboo scaffold-support. He tumbled head over heels, with the rickshaw on top of him, into the gutter, and precipitated poor Slim into the dust, where in great disarray he sat cursing his dazed uncomprehending Chinaman.

"Get up, Slim, before the rest of us are jailed," I urged as we drew alongside.

He responded, and with our half-dead rickshaw men well compensated for their ordeal we proceeded on foot to break through the dense crowd that had gathered around us.

In the course of time Slim and the bo's'n became detached from our quartet, leaving only Micky to keep me company. Feeling, about midnight, that we had seen enough, I thought it time to steer my joyous companion to the Y.M.C.A. where I had procured a room for the night. This goal was not to be reached without great difficulty. The most serious obstacle was a tattoo shop, whose façade was festooned with alluring sample designs of the artistic masterpieces that could be sketched decoratively on one's flesh. There were anchors and eagles and crossed flags, butterflies, crucifixes, girls in tights, bleeding hearts, snakes and all the other familiar objects designed by the tattoo needle. Micky was fascinated by the array, and could not be dragged away.

"I've always wanted some of this thing," he said. "Every man that goes to sea *oughter* be tattooed. You and me are the only ones in the boat with no pichers on our arms. Now's our chance."

"Micky!" I said, horrified, "you *are* drunk! Come on away before you get yourself pumped full of red ink."

He was obdurate, and all my admonitions failed to keep him out of the shop. The proprietor, a spectacled Chinaman, just on the verge of closing his establishment for the night, on seeing an intoxicated seaman enter, knew business was in the air and came to greet the late customer. Micky could not decide which of the hundred designs was most appropriate to his style of beauty. A mermaid appealed to him, but I vowed

I'd tear up the shop before I allowed him to be disfigured with that. Then he resolved upon a six-inch gory crucifix. This was worse than the mermaid.

"Then you choose one for me," he exclaimed, exasperated by my scoffing disapproval of everything he wanted.

"If you must submit to this degradation, Micky, why not have your initials, as a sort of identification tag, put in very small letters some place where it won't show?"

While that did not strike his fancy it gave him an idea: "Not *my* initials—*Mabel's*—my Providence girl I got a picher of. That's it—M. M. C."

Uncontrollable from enthusiasm, he ordered the "artist" to bring out his needle. It was a very questionable compliment to Mabel, but the Irishman thought otherwise.

"Where'll I put it?—I know, here!" he cried, tearing open his shirt and drawing a finger across his chest, "here in big letters."

I groaned. "Not big ones, Micky—small neat ones."

"Naw, big M. M. C. like these on the paper— M - M - C."

It was all over in a few minutes. Micky was branded for life, yet he bore the crude lettering with great pride and complete happiness. I prayed no one would be in the Y. M. C. A. lobby as I entered with my boisterous shipmate, and my prayers were answered; it was quite deserted.

Next morning Micky awoke with a bewildered expression: "Where am I?"

"You're in the Young Men's Christian Association."

"In *what*!"

I repeated—"And it's no place for a drunkard like yourself. You'd better get out and back to the ship before you're docked a week's wages."

"What happened last night?" he asked, trying to establish vague recollections. "I remember beatin' a Chinaman who was ridin' me in a cart."

"Is that all you remember?"

He nodded his head slowly.

"Well, look at your chest."

He could not believe his eyes. There in magnificent inch-and-a-half letters sprawled "M.M.C."

"Who did that to me?"

"That's tattoo, idiot."

"Will it come off?"

"*Never!*" I said triumphantly.

"They ain't my initials."

"No, they are Mabel Somebody's."

Then it was his turn to groan.

"Now you've *got* to marry her," I continued consolingly. "At least you can't marry anybody else unless she has initials M.M.C."

"Why have I gotta marry her?"

"Why! Do you think a girl with initials C.O.D. or F.O.B. or P.D.Q. will live with you when she finds another woman's name scattered all over her husband's *chest?*"

Another groan was his only reply.

That same morning I left the *Gold Shell* for good. Not until the hour of separation did I realize how attached I was to that clumsy old tanker and her blasphemous crew. Slim and the bo's'n were not aboard, so I didn't get a chance to say good-by to them. However, the very next day a letter from Slim addressed to the Y.M.C.A. reached me and I reproduce it verbatim:

"Burg-Burg (Budge-Budge) April 20. Dear frend Boy [despite my advancement to quartermaster this mortify-ing *sobriquet* had endured]. I arrived on the Gold Shell well. I am not drung but in my happy feelings. Where you go lass nite. Micky said he woked up in Y.M.C.A.

with tatood chest. If you got tatood I beat you up. The short legged animal [his name for the bo's'n] is ashore today hisself so nobody work. They say the ship is going to take six cargos to Ramgoom [Rangoon] and I see you maybe when you come back from the Himmalyammas [Himalayas.] Sweet Caporal [the tomcat] was ashore lass nite but came back today not drung but grouchy. Take care of yourself. I close my letter wishing you the perfect of health—Frendly.

Slim Dourateliasinous."

A postscript from Micky was scrawled at the bottom:

"Hello Boy—This is just to bawl you out for letting me get tite last night and that damed tatoo stuck on me. Slim and me have laughed ourselfs sick over the cart race. The bosn aint showed up yet but I'm back on me durty job. Wisht I was going out in them jungles with you Boy—I aint never seen no canabells. By-By matey,

truly and sincerely—Micky."

# Tiger Tales

ALCUTTA in April is one of the four hottest places in the world, the other three being suburbs of the same city. Though I had been repeatedly warned that the climate of India was typical of the country's eccentric character, and that April, May and June were the most disagreeable months, it was impossible for my inhibited brain to comprehend that "spring" north of the equator could be anything but a time of showers and melting snow. Thus it was that when a scorching blast greeted the *Gold Shell* as she steamed up the Hooghly, I exclaimed with Shelley: Oh wind, if this be spring, shall I ever live through the summer?

Arriving then in the height of the hot season, the blue-serge suit acquired in Monte Carlo would soon have caused hydro- phobia had it not been quickly shed. After considerable hag- gling with a native merchant in the city market I exchanged my European raiment for a pair of Boy Scout "shorts" such as are worn by the British soldiers in India, a khaki shirt, a black bow tie, a pith helmet, six handkerchiefs, a pair of golf stockings and a box of soap. Native-made brogues, a pipe and walking stick I had to buy, as the merchant refused to include these articles in the exchange. Feeling like a palm-tree with my bare knees and abbreviated pants, and expecting every minute to be arrested for immoral attire, I sneaked home to the "Y" by the back streets to avoid meeting any of the men from the *Gold Shell* whom I knew would excommunicate their erstwhile shipmate for wearing such unseagoing clothes.

After the departure of the ship I was more than ready to leave commonplace Calcutta in favor of a visit to the general manager of the Tata Steel and Iron Company, at his home in Jamshedpour, five hours west of the seaport. With my host's wardrobe and an army of servants at my disposal, I was introduced into the British-American colony which has grown up with the gigantic steel plant. This change from the *Gold Shell* garlic garden was decidedly welcome. Wop culture had begun to pall. It was not without some effort, however, that I cast off the rôle of Greek seaman, and renounced the gesticulative self-preservatory table deportment in favor of the more dainty manipulation of the teacup. Once or twice only providence saved me from howling down a formal dinner-table at my hostess, "hey-BREAD."

It is a far cry from Jamshedpour sophistication to Mennonite missionaries, yet not so far but that in twelve hours I could speed the one and greet the other. I was not at all unwilling to accept an invitation that came to me at Jamshedpour to spend a week at the Christian settlement (especially as my host there had written that it was in the very heart of Hindustan and teemed with big game) for, even though I had parted from the *Gold Shell* ten days before, I was seriously in need of a relapse to righteousness after the month spent with forty heathen sailors.

To reach the village of Dhamtari, my destination, it was

necessary to plunge five hundred miles deeper inland, and this brought me face to face with the old problem of transportation. Even second-class travel for one with my limited means and ambitious program (already I had dreams of reaching Kashmir) was too extravagant, while third-class, given over to the natives, was, of course, out of the question. These two being eliminated there was nothing left to take except first-class, which, by means of a small bribe to the native conductor, I managed to keep all the way to the Dhamtari junction, forty miles from the mission station.

At the end of the last century, Doctor J. M. Lapp and his wife came to this province of India in search of a wild, unexploited, jungle-wrapped spot where they could found a mission which, because of the very barbaric conditions surrounding it, would be able to render the greater service. Starting with nothing but courage this self-sacrificing couple has built up a mission that is one of the greatest sources of benevolence in the territory. For twenty-five years Doctor Lapp has shepherded his flock of converts, acting not as a soul-saver only, but also as physician, surgeon, judge, pastor, carpenter, policeman, representative, until now he is all-powerful in his community—a veritable white maharajah.

On arrival I was led around on a tour of inspection. In the girls' quarters, under the chaperonage of two missionary ladies, I had a very jolly time, being saluted everywhere as "papa," their affectionate term for Doctor Lapp and consequently all other white sahibs. Any one who believes that Indian women are of inferior order of beauty should have "inspected" with me that afternoon and been agreeably disillusioned. The Hindu poets who sang of their maidens as "little lotus blossoms," etc., knew what they were talking about. Judged even by our Western standards of beauty many of these children of semi-barbarous jungle dwellers, with their soft deep eyes, their glistening hair, their fine features and slim graceful figures, yes with all their dark coloring, were undeniably, alluringly exquisite.

Scarcely had we got inside the compound when these siren children, much too pretty to be sequestered from appreciative eyes, were the cause of shocking behavior on my part. Never before having seen a sahib (much less a "papa") without long gray Mennonite whiskers, they were consumed with curiosity, feminine, of course, and watched slyly from behind posts and doors as my chaperons and I moved in close formation about the compound. Several times I caught the eye (seek and ye shall find) of some overbold maiden who, entirely indifferent to my good name, would laugh shrilly and hide her head beneath her green or yellow scarf. I almost choked trying not to laugh myself, hoping just the same that the bright-eyed little observer would show herself again, which she always did for a yet more reckless round of ocular hide-and-seek. My irreproachable companions, seeing the sinful trend of our inspection, led me firmly by the shortest route to the exit and thus delivered me perforce from temptation.

Dhamtari is backed by three hundred miles of jungles, though in early May because of the withering heat, they were very different from what we commonly imagine jungles to be. There were open glades, little underbrush and a great lack of vines and tangles usually found in the tropics. This enormous uninhabited forest half-way between Calcutta and Bombay affords ideal shelter for swarms of wild things ruled with a tyrannical hand by his imperial majesty, the Tiger. The natives who live along the edges, averse from religious scruples to taking any form of life and unprepared to attack anything more ferocious than a rabbit, have allowed the jungle dwellers to live on and increase in numbers and daring.

A month before my arrival a notorious tiger had waited by

the side of the highway not a mile from the station for a long line of bullock carts to pass and, choosing the fattest bullock of the lot, sprang upon it, in broad daylight, broke its neck and dragged it from the cart's harness. Though the natives were twenty and the tiger only one they did not dare attack him, but allowed the bandit to carry his victim to the roadside and, according to tiger etiquette, depart in peace until the flesh had cooled and twilight announced the proper time to dine.

Meanwhile Doctor Lapp had been acquainted with the situation and accompanied by a Mr. B———, a visiting missionary, whose innate dread of tigers made him a poor hunter, established themselves with rifles in trees close to the slain bullock. Though the tiger may have been aware that human enemies awaited him, he was either so hungry or so indifferent to the menace of man that he did not refrain from returning to the anticipated meal, passing directly beneath the very tree where the trembling Mr. B——— was secreted.

Creeping and cautious the wary assassin crawled toward the carcass. As silently as possible Doctor Lapp raised his rifle and aimed for the shoulder; the notch, the sight, the animal, were in line; in another second the jungle would have echoed with the report of the gun. But fate had preordained this to be a dramatic moment.

Crack! It was not the rifle—it was the limb to which the unhappy visitor was clinging. In his attempt to get as far up the tree and as far away from the conflict as possible he had put his weight on a limb too frail to support him, and it broke. With a crash and a despairing cry he tumbled through intervening foliage to the ground, and fell not a yard from the nose of the astonished beast. The tiger, recovering quickly from his surprise, suspected an enemy in the prostrate form, and not stopping to reason why sprang at it with a roar. But Doctor Lapp had not lost his presence of mind. The delayed rifle crack sounded and the huge charging cat collapsed on top of his intended victim—dead.

Several days after I reached Dhamtari, Doctor Lapp left the mission on one of his rounds of medical inspection. Seeing him depart, and realizing that I was now the only danger to be faced, every beast in the jungle felt this was a most auspicious opportunity to run amuck and commit all manner of depredations. That very twilight a panther dared to come within a stone's throw of our house, slaughter a calf and drag it into a glade half a mile away. Immediately panthers were exceedingly unpopular in the community and requests for vengeance, in Doctor Lapp's absence, were made to me. Here was my chance to assume the rôle of a great defender of the weak, even though I had never before wielded any firearm more deadly than a bow and arrow. Not knowing one from the other I chose Doctor Lapp's elephant gun, since it was the most ferocious-looking in the collection, and accompanied by the owner of the calf, about eight o'clock staggered under my weapon's weight out to a tree that stood some three hundred feet from the carcass. Nine o'clock came, but no panther. The moon (what strange things I was to see before this period of moonlight faded) emerged from behind the clouds and lit the glade with a faint illumination;—still no panther. The cramped position in the tree was becoming unendurable, and I was just on the point of abandoning the hunt when the bearer seized my arm and stared into the dim edge of the jungle. A shapeless black form emerged, and slinking close to the ground moved serpent-like toward the bait. I aimed carefully, as I supposed it should be done, and followed the panther with my sight. Once beside the body he paused to reconnoiter, and I fired. One could have heard the rifle's roar in Calcutta. The recoil knocked me completely— along with the native—out of the tree. I thudded to the ground on one side, the bearer on another, and the elephant-gun on a third. In three terrified leaps the panther was back in the jungle. I had not killed him, and my self-condemnation knew no bounds. To investigate the possibility of a blood-trail the bearer and I walked over to the carcass, and found that instead of slaying the panther in the best accredited Daniel Boone style, I had shot a large hole straight through the ample side of the dead calf.

My humiliation was so touching Doctor Lapp on his return arranged for a real hunt with the idea of giving me a chance to redeem myself. Some ten miles deeper into the jungle lay a water-hole where, in this dry season that was parching all pools of lesser magnitude, animals of every description were sure to come to drink. Five-inch tracks of feline paws about the edges of the water-hole and mysteriously disappearing children in near-by villages gave eloquent evidence that at least one of the reservoir frequenters was a tiger of unusual size and boldness. In fact, during the last fortnight natives had repeatedly brought reports of his crimes to Doctor Lapp, who had resolved before this to hunt him down, and was just waiting for an opportunity such as my visit afforded to go on the warpath. All afternoon I practised with the powerful rifle (not the elephant-gun) I was to use on the hunt, blazing away at a target until a black-and-blue shoulder forced me to desist. Two hours before sunset my host and I, each accompanied by a bearer, left the mission and plunged into the seared jungle in pursuit of his Honor, Mr. Stripes.

As we tramped through the trees the setting sun inflamed the western sky and the fiery heat of the day began to retreat before the evening breeze. From some native village the noise of a tom-tom came clear, perhaps four miles away, perhaps ten. There was a wedding being celebrated, for now and then the shrill notes of a native fife accompanied the syncopated beat of the drum. The ceremony would have been interesting to watch had there been no more exciting sport.

In my enthusiasm for the impending adventure I walked impatiently ahead of the party, and when some hundred feet away from Doctor Lapp passed under a tree that bore an unfamiliar kind of green fruit. Then a most startling thing happened. Without warning a tremendous monkey fell from somewhere over my head and planted himself with bared teeth and angry snorts three feet in front of me. From the foliage above a pandemonium of growls and monkey noises broke loose, as thirty or more of these beasts leaped from the tree and began to scatter, reluctant and hesitating, in every direction. The tree seemed made of monkeys—long-bodied, long-tailed, forty-pound hanamans, big ones, little ones, some clutching frightened babies, all growling and squealing at once in anger at my intrusion. At a safe distance they sat on their haunches in a wide semicircle to watch the encounter between me and their big chief, who as leader of the colony had appointed himself to dispose of me and who at the moment was doing it very successfully.

"Be careful there," shouted Doctor Lapp, "don't annoy him."

"Don't annoy him!"—my word—and there I was about to be torn to pieces by the vicious brute. Remembering now a late king of Greece died from the bite of a monkey I retreated from the field with the loss of only my pride, which, after the conflict with the dead calf, was nothing much to boast about. As I left the monkey in complete possession of the path, his retinue, supporters, harem and camp-followers applauded the prowess of their lord and jumping up and down chortled in derision at my ignominious retreat.

"No one concerns himself with these big monkeys," my friend informed me. "They are sacred to the Hindus and even protected. Now and again they get obstreperous and require severe handling. A short time ago a certain Mr. Monkey observed that the mission cows were milked at the same shed every afternoon and decided to try the milk diet. After easily routing the dairy maids, by making ferocious faces, he proceeded to wallow in lacteal delight, drinking himself almost to death and overturning what he could not consume. I finally had to shoot him."

At the banks of the reservoir a naturalist would have found material for many books, for there at the twilight hour the birds and tamer jungle-dwellers were holding a water carnival in celebration of the passing of a trying day with its scorching heat. Cool gray doves in flocks of a hundred or more fluttered restlessly from grove to grove. Numberless pairs of rock pigeons came swiftly from the forest, veering as swiftly at the sight of man. Giant crows, as familiar and as numerous in every part of India as sparrows in America, waddled awkwardly over the cracked mud edges of the pond and filled the air with their noisy cawing. Great numbers of strange birds with brighter plumage than I had ever seen before flew about to add color to the pageant. Indeed it was one vast aviary.

It did not take us long to arrange ourselves on the bank. The only access to the pond not leading across a hundred yards of treacherous mud was down either side of a sharp hillock abutting on the water. Knowing nothing about tiger hunting, with one coolie I fortified myself behind a pile of rocks near the water's edge at one base of the hillock, and Doctor Lapp, knowing all about tiger hunting, climbed a tree with his bearer, at the opposite base. While neither could see the other because of the intervening mound, both our rifles commanded its top.

As darkness approached the animation about the water subsided. The ridge to the west was lined with palms standing in black relief against the fading sky. A straggling flock of belated crows flew noisily to their mangrove rookery. Then the silent jungle enwrapped us, dark, mysterious, forbidding and all-pervading. As if out of the very air came the faintly audible *tom-tom tom-tom tom-tom* from no recognizable distance, from no positive direction. From the tree-tops the young moon of the night before rose and with it our expectations, for now we could distinguish one animal from another and aim with fair accuracy. The feeling came to me that I was in the midst of the truest picture of aboriginal India that could be found, in a region where man has not conquered nature, where only the fittest survive and where great misery and violent death are accepted as the established order of things.

Seven o'clock passed in complete quiet. Toward eight two small deer approached within gunshot, but Doctor Lapp had instructed me to shoot at nothing except tigers for fear of frightening away the particular villain we sought, so I merely watched them move stealthily to the water's edge, and, clear in the moonlight, drink without the faintest sound. Several wild pigs emerged from the blackness, sensed danger behind my pile of rocks and approached the water close to Doctor Lapp's tree. I wondered if he would shoot. He did not. Nine o'clock came, and with it the distant crack of dry underbrush several hundred feet in the jungle. It grew more and more distinct, and seemed to come straight at me. My bearer could scarcely control his excitement, holding his arms to his head in imitation of branching antlers. Certainly from the crush it made in the underbrush it was something large. The sound came cautiously just to the edge of the jungle and then turned back.

Ten o'clock passed. The moon was well up now and flooding the pool. My bearer, who from long familiarity with the jungle usually saw and heard things before I did, suddenly registered extreme agitation and opening wide his penetrating eyes stared before him up the hillock. I followed his gaze, and saw nothing but black shadows; yes, one of them moved, and took shape—the shape of a tiger. He moved a few feet, waited, looked about. I began to appreciate how exposed was my position. Even if it were my opportunity to shoot I might not kill, and then the small pile of stones would offer little protection in case I became the prey. However what could be a more novel and heroic death than to be vanquished in hand-to-hand battle with a tiger? That is the most sportsmanlike way to meet tigers after all. Perhaps my chance was at hand to revenge myself on the animal kingdom for the two humiliations I had suffered recently at its hands. So I prayed hard for the black shadow to choose my side of the ridge as its route to the water. In this method of attracting the beast I met strong competition from Doctor Lapp, who could see the shape silhouetted against the sky no less than I could and who was doubtless praying with equal fervor that his side be favored. It was a contest between vastly unequal powers; what chance did I, who never *had* learned the Presbyterian catechism and whose patron saint was obviously the devil, have against the eloquence of Doctor Lapp, a man who for thirty years had preached the gospel and by actual count had saved two thousand and forty-one heathens from eternal damnation? Naturally the tiger turned up his nose at my puny spiritual power, and, overcome by the missionary's invocations, turned and walked directly under the deadly tree. There was a moment of excruciating suspense, then a flash of fire from the branches, the crack of the gun and a piercing snarl from the tiger. Mad with terror and pain the beast no doubt glared about for the source of the murderous assault. Flash, crack; flash, crack. The mortally wounded tyrant of the forest struggled twenty feet from the shadow of the tree into the moonlight, and with a hoarse moan fell dead.

The next moment I was hurrying over the hillock, eager to be the first to tweak his whiskers.

"Wait there," Doctor Lapp shouted from the tree, on seeing me appear on the ridge. "He may still be alive."

A rock or two tossed at the motionless form failed to draw any sign of life. His sleek and striped majesty would terrorize the vicinity no more. He had been done to at last as he had so often done to others. The slaughtered cattle, the butchered deer, the human victims of this tiger's blood lust were avenged now. By violence he had lived and by violence met his end.

Doctor Lapp and I stood over him in the moonlight. What a magnificently beautiful superbeast he was, yet what an outlaw, what an assassin, what a black criminal. Hated though you were, Tiger, we profoundly respected your courage and your power, and to have killed you made us the two proudest men in Hindustan.

Back home with our spoils, the natives from near-by villages came in droves to gaze upon the notorious beast that for over a month had been the terror of their lives, to stroke his glossy coat, to pull his tail, to pay homage to the great sahib that had conquered the tyrant. Each mother took special care to bring all her children along in order to familiarize them with the appearance of the dread enemy they must avoid above all other. One mother walked a two-year old baby girl up and down the ribs of the carcass, to the laughing delight of the infant, and was quite ready in response to our request for a photograph to balance her, clutching a bouquet of honeysuckle, on the shoulder of the fallen giant.

Just before I bid good-by to my hospitable missionary friends, my native bearer, who had been so ignominiously knocked out of the tree-tops by the recoil of my elephant-gun on the occasion of the panther hunt, presented me with one of the tiger's tusks, which he insisted would be a good-luck talisman of magic power.

"Will it protect me from railroad conductors when I haven't a ticket?" I asked him.

He solemnly assured me it would, and I was half inclined to believe he was right when after a thousand-mile-roundabout journey back to Calcutta and up the Ganges Valley to Benares, I reached Agra, the city of the Taj Mahal, with only one rupee's expenditure for railroad transportation.

## ‿ XVI. ‿

# The Garden of
# Immortality

*I*T was almost night, and the first shy breeze we had felt that day came from the Jumna. Across the river, through the twilight haze, a huge and swelling dome could be dimly distinguished from the dark sky behind. Soaring from the tree-tops into a bank of clouds, it seemed a Maxfield Parrish picture come to life.

"What's that?" I asked of Ahmed, my Punjabi companion.

"That the Taj Mahal."

Had it been the post-office or the mission church he could not have spoken with less enthusiasm, yet it would be impossible to describe how deeply I was stirred by this casual reply. It was as if Columbus on his first voyage had asked Roderigo: "What's that dark line over there?" and Roderigo had answered: "Oh, that? That's land."

The Taj Mahal had been deified in my mind ever since that childhood day when I had first looked upon an oil painting of the fairy tomb and read the immortal story of its creation. It had always been a dream castle to me, something so fabulous it could not have dimensions and weight and location; something so lovely it could not exist outside of picture-books. Poring for hours at a time over these very books I had come to revere this building above all others, and had made a divinity out of Arjemand, the Mogul princess who became the Empress Mumtaz Mahal, whose beauty and perfection it commemorates. All my adventures in India up to this time I had known to be only preludes to the great final adventure—the actual sight and touch of the Taj.

Facts and legends came to me now in a jumbled mass, as I stood in the fortress tower and watched the great dome disappear into the night. The follies of the Emperor Shah Jehan, who built the Taj, were forgotten; what mattered the number of his crimes—his genius as a builder, his fame as the greatest lover in history, were more worthy of memory. In the marble poetry of the Taj this greatest lover has immortalized the object of his passion. Arjemand, favorite among a thousand wives, is embodied in its stones; her chastity is carved into its spotless walls; her exquisiteness reproduced in every delicate line; her majesty reflected in the aereal grace of dome and minaret that floated and faded there above the river side.

We had been silent for some moments, enjoying the coolness of the night that now had blotted out the distance. Ahmed was the first to speak:

"You know Shah Jehan?"

"Yes." I said, "I 'know' him."

"He die here in balcony."

"What, Ahmed! Is this the *Jasmine Tower*?"

He assured me it was, and that we were treading thoughtlessly on stones numbered among the most hallowed in India, for this was the point from which the emperor last saw his beloved wife's memorial. For her shrine he had squandered the wealth of an empire, until his subjects, led by his own son, revolted and imprisoned the "King of Earth" here in his own palace, on the banks of the Jumna. Dethroned, disgraced, held captive, for seven years he had only the memory of his lovely Arjemand to comfort him. At last, when he felt his end was near, the old and broken man pleaded, not in vain, to be carried at dawn to the Jasmine Tower, where his dying eyes might rest upon the distant minarets of the mausoleum. There his heart and soul already were, there he knew his body was soon to be, beside her for whom he had created the one perfect thing. Through fading eyes he watched the eastern horizon brighten with light, watched the first beam of sunrise strike the dome. Then the heavy weary gates closed forever—and the Taj passed from view.

"You stay here all night, *Sahib*?"

"No," I said, my reverie broken, "I am ready to go now."

We descended from the tower, threaded our way out of the unlit corridors, found the grim entrance-gate, and hurried homeward through the animated streets. But I saw neither the swinging lanterns, nor the shops, nor the crowds. My thoughts were of Mumtaz Mahal, whom, on the morrow, I planned to meet, at last, face to face.

Early and eagerly the next morning I set forth alone. I passed beneath the ruddy arch that commands entrance to the gardens of the Taj, and there, behold!—beyond, in the blinding summer sunshine I saw it, a miracle of sky and verdure and ivory, beckoning to me through the framing gateway. My dream castle had come to life.

I answered its call with absolute surrender, moving almost without volition down the marble pavement that led straight and glittering into its very heart. I was unaware of the fountains at my feet, or of the indigo sky above. I saw only my long-sought Taj awaiting me, harmonious as music, lovely as the face of the immortal woman it commemorates.

The entire day I remained beside the snowy temple, enchanted by its serenity, forgetful of time and self. I wandered about its polished corridors, climbed upon its roof, descended into its crypts. Attracted by a myriad of colors I drifted about the gardens that enthrone the monster pearl, tarried by the lily pools reflecting dome and minaret, and loitered along the avenue of stately cypresses.

Noon came, and afternoon. From a shaded bed of grass I looked up at the shimmering walls. Built of cold stone they are, and yet how ethereal; erected by man, yet touched by the gods. "Make it as beautiful as she was beautiful, as delicate, as graceful," commanded the grief-striken emperor of Ustad Isa, his greatest architect. "Make it the image and the soul of her beauty." And in a dream Ustad Isa visioned a finished tomb that was as lovely yet withal as majestic as the moon-faced empress. Though two hundred and fourscore years have passed since this dream was realized and Mumtaz Mahal laid to rest, to-day the Taj appears to have been built but yesterday. There it floated above me, not only a symbol of matchless feminine beauty but an expression of the adoration the Shah-in-Shah felt for his chosen favorite of all the palace. Even in building, it was marked by the passion that distinguished the idyllic union of the emperor and the Lady Arjemand, for he spent upon it not only his treasures, but his grief and his tears. Thus it has come to pass that the sepulcher has a soul, which, so legends tell, has been known to manifest itself on summer nights, and in the image of the queen emerge in radiance from the tomb, dissolved to mist by moon-beams.

Twilight came, and the wind ceased. The tropical dark blue background of all this beauty was fading into night. About me the deserted gardens were hushed except for the faint splash of falling water. Twilight faded into starlight. Still I clung to my veiled Taj, and no duty or need could lure me away from this glimpse into Paradise.

The summer moon had reached its zenith a week before, and now, rapidly waning, rose nearer the hour of dawn than darkness. Yet at midnight every visitor must depart from the gardens, so I would have to leave without seeing the palace melt beneath the flood of moonlight. Already guards were closing the tower gates; sentries were gathering before the threshold of the tomb. A few belated stragglers were being hurried to their waiting *gharries*, and as I saw them go the thought came to me: "Why not try to stay?—then I could possess the Taj by myself alone!" The romantic possibilities of such an adventure captivated my fancy. Quickly I hid in a darkened grove. The watchmen, carrying their lamps, came close to me—but passed on. Not for a kingdom would I have surrendered, with this opportunity before me to remain through the night by the side of my marble mistress.

Then from the entrance I heard the ponderous iron-bound doors groan as they were swung laboriously into place. I heard the clank of fastening chains, and their ominous echo, reverberating from wall to wall across the breathless garden, filled me with sudden dread, for I, a mortal, was now imprisoned with a pale pearl ghost—I was alone with the Taj Mahal.

For an hour, and an hour more, waiting for the moon, I lingered patiently beneath my willow grove, enraptured by the dim beauty of this dreamland and by its hovering mystery. Then with the tolling of two the shroud was lifted from the sky, as the moon glinted through the boughs upon the sleeping garden.

Utter silence had reigned till now; but all at once from a

top-most branch came the herald hooting of a sentinel owl, commanding the myriad invisible inhabitants of the garden to awake from bush and vine and flower, to acclaim their lady of the night. Straightway a cricket orchestra began to chirrup forth its homage; flying-foxes tumbled through the air. From flame-of-the-forest and banyan bough, from clematis vine and honeysuckle tangles, came stirs and flutters of awakened doves and the faint woodnote of the hoopee. Only the guardsmen at the gateway slumbered on.

Then, as I watched, the moon floated upward from the trees to commune in secret with the phantom Taj, while all earthly worshipers were far away and the union safe from the disenchanting gaze of mortals. Silvered, the mausoleum emerged from shadow, and hypnotic in new radiance beckoned to me once more. Heedless of consequences I crept from my green grotto;—there was no sound. On tiptoe I mounted a stairway to the dais;—there was no challenge, for the sentries had been touched by magic too, and slept profoundly.

Higher rose the moon; fairer gleamed the Taj, a harmonious pile of masonry in the sunshine of the morning, a specter underneath the stars, now transfigured to a gleaming gossamer, an airy bubble that might evaporate into ether while one looked upon it.

Unaware of the passing moments, I watched the shadows move in the deep recesses of the façade, until unable to resist the lure of the interior, I turned to the main portal. Stealthily I crept around the sleeping sentries, softly crossed the threshold, and entering stood beside the faint-lit tombs of the Shah-in-Shah and Arjemand. A bronze lantern hung by a chain from the obscurity of the dome above, and the light shining through its perforated sides cast fantastic shadows on the carven walls. Forgetful of sentries, I whistled a subdued note and listened to it ringing and reringing in slowly dying echoes far up in the blackness of the vault.

The fourth hour came, and found me standing pensive beside the Empress' grave. A pilgrim to her shrine, she had blessed me with protection. With sudden shame I realized I had brought no offering. Neither gold nor silver did I have, not even a flower; but in a recess of my wallet, kept for memory's sake, there withered a twig of myrtle, plucked six months past from some courtyard in the Alhambra of the Moors, amid whose storied battlements I had sought romance on such a night as this. From one Moslem monument in Spain it had come to another in India, directed perhaps by the hand of Allah. Reverently I placed these fragile leaves upon her tomb. The wind brushed gently through the vaulted corridors, and slowly swung the hanging lantern to and fro; and I was filled with happiness, fancying that her spirit had sent this murmured benediction.

No one was awake to see me creep forth into the balmy night, or to watch my shadow as it left the marble platform and moved again across the moon-blanched park. Streams of water from the Jumna flowed upon the thirsty gardens, so that a glittering film covered lawn and bed and pavement. Barefoot, I waded in the flowered ponds. How cool and refreshing was the touch of flooded grass—how far from the realities of earth I felt myself. On a marble bench I sat beside the deepest lily-pool and looked at the great white blossoms drifting among the reflected stars of an Indian sky. And as I looked there seemed to come from its depths a call, the same that had twice drawn me powerless into the Taj: "Come to my caress, oh, mortal—bathe your body in my coolness—float upon my tranquil mirror—wash your mind of consciousness."

Only an insomniac owl watched me remove my clothes, or

heard the faint ripple as I dropped into the alabaster pool. This was a page from the *Arabian Nights*, a reversion to the fabled luxury of ancient emperors—this, at last, was Romance.

It was but an hour before dawn. The moon had reached the peak of its course and was shining with unearthly brilliance. Alone, in all this supernatural beauty, resting by the pool before the phantom Taj, I felt myself transported to some previous existence that knew neither time nor space nor substance. I and all that I beheld was myth. The subconscious mind was master, linking me with previous incarnations in the dim past.

A strange ecstasy came to me. I heard myself laugh deliriously. A giant lily floated on the unruffled mirror, and as I leaned over the alabaster rim to tear it from its stem—whose eerie face peered back at me from the water, whose queer slant eyes, whose horns? In terror I leaped to my feet. Was it this that I had been in the beginning, or was it to this that I had come, distorted by some avenging spirit for profaning with my touch a sanctuary of immortality?

Caw—caw—caw! A crow in a near-by grove mocked my bewilderment. Twice startled, I glanced up to find day streaking the east. There was a rush of wind, a rustle of leaves.... Suddenly I was aware of being bitterly cold. Realities began to emerge before my eyes. The gardens lay about me, stark and tangible. The Taj—had turned again—to stone.

In a fever of dread and perplexity I flung on my clothes, hurried to the tower gate, surrendering myself to the sentries, and besought them to liberate me from this realm of the supernatural.

As I passed, with a guard on either side, underneath the vaulted tower, I looked back through the arch-framed opening to find the sky in amber hues, the park dew-pearled, waking to the matin song of lark and oriole. I saw the Taj, reflecting the rose-and-gold horizon, still tenderly beautiful, still beckoning, and as I turned to her for one last, farewell glimpse, the first beam of sunrise struck the dome. Then the heavy weary gates closed behind me, and the Lady of my Dreams passed from view.

## ~ XVII. ~

# Adventure in the Punjab

STRAIGHT to the bungalow of the British superintendent I was led. He got out of bed to investigate the cause of the disturbance raised by our approach, and was in none too amiable a mood when I was marched before him.

"What were you doing in the garden at such an hour?" he asked sternly on hearing my captors' report. "It is forbidden and a punishable offense."

As at Gibraltar I pleaded my own case, explaining as frankly as possible my position, and emptying my pockets to disprove any suspicion of having stolen the Taj.

Assured that my infringement of the rules was harmless, and too sleepy to care one way or the other, he dismissed me and went back to bed.

Through the early morning I tramped back to the ugliness of Agra, beset by the depression that always follows intoxication. The terrific morning heat, the dust, the hunger, brought my thoughts brutally back to stern realities, and to the realization that with all the enchantment of the previous night I was still a frail-pursed vagabond, walking homeward from Paradise because I could not afford a vehicle.

On reaching my lodging, the English proprietress had good news for me.

"Last evening, during your absence, another American, named David, came to visit us. He's about your age and seems to be 'bumming' just as you are—said he was on the lookout for a companion and right away I thought of you. He's here now."

David proved a made-to-order comrade, globe-trotting from east to west on the proceeds of a year's work in central Alaska. He was twenty, a good sport, and a clever vagabond whose youthful appearance and manners persuaded his creditors to cancel his debts, railroad officials to wink at tickets, and chance acquaintances to supply him gratis with food and shelter.

With this companion I "did" Agra and moved on, ticketless as usual, to Delhi.

David and I will not soon forget the first night we spent in the capital (since 1910 Delhi has been that). True, it was spent mostly in our beds, but they were out in the lilac garden of our pension, where the flame-of-the-forest trees in full bloom interlocked so thickly overhead that only a few of the billion stars hanging like lamps in the heavens could be seen through the branches. Close by a band was giving an open-air concert and the music blown to us by the breeze made the night doubly beautiful and peaceful.

For a long time I lay awake laughing at the past ten months. How amazing they had been and how crowded with sensation. Delhi was a sort of terminus, a relay station, where one reoriented one's self and began again with new destinations and new enthusiasms. What was to come now? Whither would the road to romance lead me?—to Kabul, as I hoped?—or to

Argentina? It gave me no small satisfaction to realize that this question could not be answered, and it was just as well, for had I known then what adventures I was to have in another ten months I should not have slept a wink that night.

Somewhat to our disappointment we learned that most of the interesting places at Delhi were at a distance from the city. Determined to miss nothing we started before sunup one morning, and during the day made a complete tour of all the "sights."

There was so much to see on this sunrise excursion that the seven miles out to the famous Kartub Tower passed very quickly. The tower is the solitary minaret of a mosque long since destroyed, belonging to a former city. Its great height and odd conical shape cause it to be visited by every tourist that comes to Delhi. From its two hundred and fifty-foot summit one can see the ashes of all seven of the great capitals of all the seven empires that have risen one after the other on this plain, only to meet obliteration. It would seem that the British, with their traditional stubbornness, were courting disaster by daring to ignore the writing on the wall and building yet an eighth Federal City on the very graves of its ill-fated predecessors. But after all, Delhi is the capital only five months in the year for the climate is so trying that the entire government must remain away seven months of the twelve in Simla, a little out-of-the-way mountain village eight thousand feet up in the Himalayas.

In the center of the mosque-ruins rises a fifteen-foot solid bronze pillar dating back to distant civilizations. A local superstition is that if one stands with one's back to it and can make the fingers touch on the other side any wish made in this position will come to pass. The circumference is such, however, that unless a person has an unusual reach it is impossible to accomplish the requirements. Having succeeded in bringing my middle fingers together only after several attempts I wished violently that we would get to the Afghan consul at Simla (who alone had the power to grant us the passports to Kabul) without being required to pay the forty-five rupees which we had learned was the price of a first-class ticket.

David followed me at the wishing-post, but though he struggled heroically his fingers missed connection by an inch. I tugged at his arms till he howled for mercy—without avail. Half an inch of column still intervened.

"Oh, make your wish anyway," I said, discouraged. "You'll get all except half an inch of it."

So he wished that we would not have to pay the forty-five-rupee charges *back* from Simla.

Perhaps it was the mysterious power of the post, perhaps coincidence, but we had reason to recollect our respective wishes the very next day, when, after an eighteen-hour ride, we descended at Simla from our first-class compartment without one *pice* paid for transportation, while on our return trip an emergency made it necessary for us to hand over two rupees of the fifty on a ticket to Lahore. Two rupees! That was caused by the half-inch which prevented David's wish from coming entirely true.

Simla is a pleasant little town. No wonder the government spends most of the time there, shaded by its pine-trees and cooled by its mountain air. All the rigid formality of Delhi official society is transported to Simla, all the heavy emphasis on rank and social position and proper costume. People stared at our hob-nailed boots and our khaki shirt-sleeves; speculation was rife as to just what "those two peculiar young men" were and what right they had in exclusive Simla. Haughty wives of commissioners whirred past in rickshaws pulled by four coolies in spectacular uniforms, and glared at us through supercilious lorgnettes. We retaliated by bowing and smiling with Pollyanna affability at these rude women, and some of the outraged expressions resulting were all we could have wished for. Even at the Y. M.C.A. (where we lived almost free of charge) the assembly of faultlessly-dressed young Christians nearly expired from shock when we swept in to dinner wearing Boy Scout pants and no coats.

The Afghan consul shattered all our hopes for Afghanistan almost before we expressed them: utterly impossible—recent murders in the Khyber Pass had put a stop to all visés—many regrets—good morning! We really didn't care much. Kashmir *was* accessible, and that was much more important and *far* more romantic than Kabul. And so we plunged back into the railroad struggle, headed for Rawalpindi, the gate to Kashmir.

As we drew near Lahore next morning David awoke with such an attack of internal pains that I felt sure, judging from his groans, he must have at least cholera. This deadly disease is the great hobgoblin in India, and well it may be, for it strikes with sudden and awful violence, and irrespective of color or station claims its victims in a very few hours unless antidotes are administered immediately. The remedy, as well as preventive most commonly used is strong alcoholic drink. When cholera rages the drunkard is absolutely safe; when one is infected whisky is his best friend.

Knowing this, I pushed the unhappy David into the railroad buffet, and, ordering enough whisky for six men, made him drink every drop of it. This intemperance was immediately successful. The stomach-ache devil was driven out by the purge of fire, but the cure proved to be as bad as the disease, for Bacchus himself could not have remained sober under such a draught.

Another change of trains was necessary at Lahore, and another strategic maneuver for a first-class compartment. In obtaining free rides heretofore, invisibility had always been our greatest asset; now, with me half-carrying, half-dragging the reeling, stumbling alcoholic down the crowded platform our movements had all the subtlety of a brass band on parade. Regardless of consequences I pulled David into a first-class compartment, and on to one of the deep leather seats, where he was soon sleeping off the effects of cholera cure.

When the conductor came our way the flushed face of the prostrate youth proved a blessing in disguise. With tears in my eyes I pointed to my mortally afflicted brother (both being of a decided blond type, and only two years apart we were invariably mistaken for brothers), and explained that though he was burning with fever and too ill to raise his head, I was taking him to the cool valleys of Kashmir in a desperate effort to save his life. I asked for the cooperation of the railroad in carrying my penniless and invalid brother and my penniless and distracted self, away from these mortal plains of the Punjab.

The conductor's heart was touched to the core. He looked at David's face—it was *very* red; he felt his forehead—it was *very* hot.

"Poor lad," he said sympathetically, "I understand. Ride as far as you like. I've a bottle of brandy in my locker. A bit of it might be of use to you."

When it came—a tumbler-full—the poor invalid was not the beneficiary, but the poor invalid's companion, for after the strain of the deception a stimulant was absolutely necessary. Anyway one should discourage cholera in India at every opportunity.

Dismounting at Rawalpindi we found that Srinagar, the fantastic metropolis of the Vale of Kashmir, and our goal, lay two hundred miles away and was accessible only via a single long and tortuous highroad. The price of overland transportation proved entirely beyond our capacity to pay, but that didn't stop us. All our lives we had been attracted to this poetic vale, this Paradise of Asia that had always seemed as intangible as heaven itself, and now we were too close to the realization of our dream to allow a little thing like two hundred miles to interfere. Shouldering our knapsacks we started up the Kashmir road on foot, trusting that by some means or other we would be delivered from our difficulties. As usual, we were. A heavy freight-truck lumbering behind just at the outskirts of the city halted in response to our waving, and with a rupee and package of cigarettes the native driver was bribed into a state of such amiability that he made room for us on his leather seat and drove us over the famous Jhelum River high-road as it bored and writhed and bridged its way along the one hundred and sixty spectacular miles to Baramula. Here the canyon opens wide and the most beautiful valley in the world is at hand.

## ↜ XVIII. ↝

# Into the Vale
# of Kashmir

THE year was at the spring, the day at the morn, the morning at seven, when David and I began to tramp the last forty miles to Srinagar. The walnut trees that shaded the road through Baramula shut out the sky and withheld from view the surrounding landscape. Suddenly the branches stood aside, and there, before us, stretched the Vale of Kashmir. Far and away we beheld a sea of green, the fresh lush green of sprouting rice paddies, the springtime green of waving poplar trees, the deep dark green of pines and deodars that climbed the slopes. Green, green, green, all overflowing with water and radiant in the spring sunshine. Ten miles to each side the towering mountain walls wrapped in unbroken snow extended in parallel lines the length of the valley. Not mere Sierra Nevadas, these, not mere Mount Blancs and Matterhorns, but *Himalayas*. Eighteen thousand, twenty thousand, twenty-two thousand feet, breaking the sky-line as far as the eye could reach. What else could the poets through the ages have called this valley but an emerald set in pearls?

We had chosen well our season. It was May. On every hillside branches of white pear-blossoms dipped into the fields of wild poppies that splashed the landscape with scarlet. The river soon to begin its impetuous dash through the Jhelum gorge, here flowed as the gentle Avon, between banks rioting with royal iris. This brilliant flower seemed like a plague, smothering every other plant that crossed its path—every other save the belligerent wild rose, which dared defy even the iris and struggled for supremacy in a battle of pink and purple blossoms.

In our first day's tramping we stopped often to drink at bubbling springs or to climb into roadside mulberry trees to dine upon the large and luscious fruit. Greatly astonished at our lack of dignity the local population gathered around to stare into the branches at the two unconventional white *sahibs*. They were justified no doubt in their astonishment, for almost the only foreigners who visit Kashmir are British Army majors and lady missionaries, and neither is in the habit of scrambling up mulberry trees on the public highway in search of food.

These distractions came so frequently that by tea-time we had progressed no farther than Petan, a picturesque hamlet less than twenty miles from Baramula. Here we sought shelter in the travelers' rest-house, a comfortable little cottage nestled in a flower garden. All that day the sun had shone with true tropical ardor, but with twilight came a drop in the temperature that made us remember the six thousand-foot elevation and regret that khaki shirts and shorts were our only protection against the chill. On the scorching plains of India the very thought of more clothing had been unendurable. "Going to bed" had consisted simply of removing our sunhelmets and lying down on the barest possible canvas cot. Such cold and stoic beds here in the mountains, at a season which by no means had blossomed into summer, made it impossible to sleep, so we commandeered the carpets and red cotton draperies in both rooms for comforters. Thus wrapped in vast bundles of red and rugs we thoroughly enjoyed the cold night, and recalled that with the exception of Simla it was the first David had experienced since China, and I since Madrid.

I wondered, on seeing occasional tourists rush past in motor-cars, how they could afford to treat the vale so lightly. In time I learned. It was to get to Srinagar for in comparison with the interest of the capital the sights of the country are secondary. Not only has this strange metropolis great natural beauty, but also a setting amid waterways and bridges and gardens that makes it rival Venice itself in charm. It is, in fact, a picturesque, tumble-down replica of the Queen of the Adriatic, divided by the river Jhelum, which glides under its seven bridges and bears a fleet of gondolas as graceful and swift as ever floated down the Grand Canal.

So much did the novelty of our first glimpse of this fantastic city appeal to us we blocked traffic standing on the footpath of First Bridge and looking down-stream past the other six at the panorama of picturesque water-craft and quaint houses that lined the banks.

No visitors ever reached Srinagar knowing less about their plans for staying than we did. Seeing a sign over a doorway marked in English: "Civil and Military Agency," we went in to inquire if there was a Y. M. C. A. in town where we could sleep.

Our knapsacks and travel-worn appearance naturally aroused the curiosity of the Englishman behind the counter.

"Are you missionaries or 'Y' workers?" he asked, looking at us quizzically.

"We are colonels in the Salvation Army," we replied.

"I asked you," he said, "because the only Americans I've ever seen here have been one or the other."

But we assured him we were a completely new species.

"Where are you going to live? Srinagar has no Y. M. C. A." The agent began to take an interest.

"We are in hopes the Rajah will invite us to the palace when he learns we're in town."

"Have you brought a tent along in case he doesn't?"

"No."

"Have you any bedding or equipment?"

"No. About all we have are two cameras, and we've no films for them."

"Well, there's a tent erected near my camp. It's all equipped and waiting for a Doctor Barnard whose arrival has been delayed. He could have no objection to your using it for a day or two."

"Oh. I'm sure he would insist upon it." David and I replied in one breath.

So to our well-ordered camp we went, and in truth it was faultless in its appointments.

Residing in Srinagar at the time was a Mr. C—— of New York, a man of benevolent spirit and understanding heart. When he heard from the English agency that there were two new Americans in town, he at once invited us to dine. We called at the given address and found a palatial houseboat, with a roof-garden, a gay gondola alongside, and several immaculate servants to admit us. Our host immediately became interested in our vagabond careers and insisted that we make use of his establishment and stay as long as we liked, since he had three spare bedrooms and an extra bath or two. We were very happy to accept his hospitality, and that same night were at home on the *Lucky* houseboat, feeling our craft had been well named.

The days that followed stood out in bold contrast to the days that had preceded. It was no longer necessary to appropriate the red curtains for comforters or climb mulberry trees for food. A vagabond life is the logical life to lead if one seeks the intimate knowledge of the world we were seeking, yet an occasional reversion to luxurious respectability was very welcome nevertheless. The houseboat seemed doubly delightful right on top of the long weeks of stern economy David and I had been practising. On the *Lucky* it was necessary only to clap one's hands to have slaves rushing in all directions. One clap brought our valet; two, our boot-boy; three, our bath-boy; four, the gondola. Mr. C——'s well-stocked wardrobe was at our disposal so that we could enter into the pleasant social life the Srinagar foreign colony enjoys. Such an Occidental sport as golf was the last thing on earth I should have expected to find in the Vale of Kashmir, yet a splendid course awaited us in the heart of the capital, and we played almost daily. It was rather difficult however to keep an eye on the ball, for soaring in a ring all about one the snowy giants caught and held the attention that should have been centered on the stroke.

Golf in the midst of these peaks was a novelty; riding through the flowering countryside a delight; dinner coats and club life, a welcome change, but of all the happy hours the happiest were spent in our gondola. It was a graceful little craft, lithe as a canoe, canopied with bright cretonne and cushioned with soft pillows. The three of us floated about Srinagar's waterways hours at a time. There are almost no streets in this Asiatic Venice—a network of canals serves the purpose. They wind between grassy banks and under groves of walnut trees that arch above and make cool green tunnels for the gently-gliding craft to travel. Here a Hindu shrine framed in branches casts its shining image in the still mirror, and there through a rift in the foliage one sees the hoary Himalayas glittering in the sunlight of another world.

Mr. C—— was one of those rare individuals who, try though they may, can never spend all of their incomes. Even with our gallant assistance there was always a big surplus. On several occasions we made tours of the art-shops that overhung the Jhelum River, buying for a song the most exquisitely carved furniture pieces, the rarest Oriental rugs, and Kashmir shawls so soft and flexible that they could be pulled through an ordinary finger-ring. In one shop the Mohammedan proprietor as a special favor displayed to us his most prized possession—a twenty-four-foot peacock-blue Persian rug made of pure silk and of ancient weave. Here was an unmistakable masterpiece, and Mr. C—— immediately began negotiations to purchase it. The merchant, much to our astonishment, emphatically refused any price—an experience unique indeed in the Orient.

Finding me staring reminiscently at a picture of the Taj Mahal upon his wall our shopkeeper brought forth ivory miniature portraits of Shah Jehan and Mumtaz Mahal, the very things that I had looked for and longed for ever since the romantic night I had spent within the marble mausoleum. At last I could see what the "Lady of my Dreams" looked like. The portraits, yellow with age, were so delicately beautiful, I could not resist them and offered the merchant half my capital. This was not nearly enough, and I would have had to go without, had not Mr. C—— realizing how *very* much I wanted the miniatures, secretly bought them for me, and left them at my breakfast plate next morning.

Our four gondoliers rarely rested. After a day spent moving up and down the Jhelum, we often turned at twilight to Dal Lake, there on cushioned ease to float till the glow of sunset faded upon the flaming water and the moon waxed above the amphitheater walls. Then down a glittering path, our gondoliers would take us on to the gates of Shalimar. I had heard songs sung about this famous garden all my life and pictured it as a little paradise. For once there was no disillusion. Built by a

Mongul emperor for his favorite queen, it combines all that is beautiful and best in nature with enchanting artifice to make a poem in verdure and falling water. It is sensuous with heavy perfumes and musical with splashing fountains. On any summer night one will find young lovers from Srinagar stealing across the lotus-covered lake to disembark upon the garden's marble shores. They are fortunate Kashmiri who have such a romantic spot as this wherein to pursue their love-affairs.

After our first moonlit night in the playground I found new beauty and new poignancy in the most famous of Laurence Hope's *India's Love Lyrics*—the lament of a broken-hearted lover, who, abandoned by his faithless mistress, cries out in his distress:

> "Pale hands I loved beside the Shalimar,
> Where are you now? Who lies beneath your spell?
> Whom do you lead on Rapture's roadway, far,
> Until you agonize them for farewell?
> Pale hands I loved beside the Shalimar,
> Where are you now? Where are you now?"

## ʚ XIX. ɞ

# Outlandish Ladakh

HAT one should ever have tired of such a luxurious and beautiful existence seems incredible—and yet before two weeks were gone the majestic Himalayas, so cold and pale and challenging, were beckoning us away from our enchanted valley. The call of the wild from those far-off sky-soaring icebergs began to drown out the murmur of the Shalimar fountains. Our eyes rested less and less on the poetry that encompassed us, and more and more upon the dreamy giants that glittered in the distance.

"Hither! Hither!" they seemed to say. "Come away from your incensed breeze and fill your lungs with the blasts from our glaciers. Exhilaration and adventure await you on our slopes of snow. Come away!"

And in the end we surrendered. We resolved to divorce the Garden of Eden and woo the Himalayas. Mr. C—— thought us mad to give up the lavish hospitality we were enjoying and plunge into the hardships of the mountains, but our hunger for new sensations, new scenes, new dangers, was too strong to deny.

We sought our English agency friend and asked what spectacular mountain expedition he had to offer.

"The caves of Amernath is a good trip," he suggested.

"Nonsense," I scoffed. "Every tourist goes there. We don't want a conducted tour. What have you that's difficult and high and dangerous—something up there among those wild mountains?"

"Oh well, of course there's Ladakh, but that's out of the question."

"What's Ladakh?" David and I asked in unison.

"It's a province of Kashmir on the Tibetan side of the Himalayas. Most amazing place. So far as I know, the only country in the world where a woman has plural husbands."

"*What*—!" I exclaimed.

"It's true. Polyandry you know."

"Oh, wonderful!"

"But it's two hundred and fifty miles there—straight east of Srinagar—and two hundred and fifty miles back—and only one narrow mule trail that climbs as high as the Alps. Even that's buried under ice and snow most of the time."

"Superb!"

"And you have to cross three mountain ranges at thirteen thousand feet and more."

"Oh, beautiful!"

"It's the highest inhabited country in the world—three miles high in places, and the temperature varies eighty degrees every day, and every third man is a monk, and only twelve foreigners a year can go, and—"

"Wait! Wait!" we shouted. "Only twelve foreigners a year can go? Then *we're* going, so be a good boy and tell us all you know about this Ladakh place, and don't jump around so."

He was most accommodating, and with a map of Asia before us, he talked for an hour about this weird bit of the world.

On the map we saw a great bulge rising from the northern side and thrusting itself in between Afghanistan and Tibet. The upper part of this hump is Kashmir. Running from north to south across this state, and dividing it into equal halves, is a series of high and almost impassable mountain ranges which have always formed a natural boundary between India and China. A hundred years ago, however, the Sikhs, a warlike tribe from the plains, penetrated the mountain barrier and extending their conquests to the east annexed the western end of Tibet. This is now Ladakh. But isolated as it is from Kashmiri influences it is to-day as Tibetan in appearance, society and religion as it ever was in its history. The people have slant eyes and high cheek-bones. They even wear pigtails. In short they *are* Chinese.

Since this country is reached only after many days of arduous travel, by pony, on foot, through snow, across deserts, the number of foreigners who visit it is not legion. Also because of the strain this unproductive region must undergo to supply them with food and transportation, only twelve white visitors are allowed each year to make the trip. That is the chief reason why Ladakh, replete though it is with extraordinary geology and inhabited by an abnormal race unique among the peoples of the world, has escaped the attention and investigation that are its due.

Leh, the capital city, built eleven thousand feet in the clouds, differs from Rome in that only three roads lead to it. Since these three, however, are serviceable only to mountain ponies which can climb, swim and slide, the title of "roads" is too dignified. One route comes from Yarkand, which was inaccessible to us; the second leads from Lhasa in Tibet, which is forbidden to all foreigners; so the third route, beginning at Srinagar in the Vale of Kashmir and riggling its way to Leh along a quarter thousand miles of cliffs and canyons, we would be forced to take as it was the only one left. But as we were residing in Srinagar already this would cause us no inconvenience.

While we could have learned much more than this it was not necessary. Our minds were made up to visit Ladakh as soon as the agent mentioned polyandry. The five-hundred-mile walk there and back at eleven to fourteen thousand feet altitude did not weaken our determination. We needed exercise after our conscientious languor on the houseboat. Nor did time concern us. We had more of that than anything. Expense was the only factor to be considered.

"By traveling cheap and fast, you might make the trip for seventy-five dollars each," the agent informed us.

David and I gasped. I did not have nearly that much. We offered an idea instead.

"We are journalists," I admitted, "and wish to take this trip in search of copy. Our accounts will be published in several newspapers so that we are in a position to advertise 'Civil and Military Agency' to a large number of readers in America—that is, if it were worth our while." (This was indeed a bold stroke, because, so far as I knew, though I had been sending articles to the States spasmodically, and had received checks way back in Marseilles for "Rhine" and "Matterhorn," I had about as many readers as the Greek Testament.)

The manager, being an intelligent young man, saw the value of our good will, so he agreed to outfit us with utensils and staple food supplies, free of charge, cutting the budget squarely in half, in return for a mention in this book. So let me say right here that—

"CIVIL AND MILITARY IS THE MOST REASONABLE AND MOST

ACCOMMODATING AGENCY IN KASHMIR. PATRONIZE IT IF YOU WISH YOUR VISIT TO THE VALE TO BE A COMPLETE SUCCESS."

By serving ourselves, we reduced our personnel to one cook; by walking and by making use of the ground for sleeping-quarters in place of a tent, we made two pack-horses suffice, and by resolving to barter for the necessary food along the way, we further diminished expenses until we struck an irreducible minimum of sixty cents a day each for fifty days. Even this, however, would take more than half of what I had left, but what of it! Providence had always been my friend. Anyway, Kashmir would be a delightful spot to starve in on our return.

All the cooks in the city seemed to know about our decision to visit Ladakh as soon as we did, judging by the dozen that had lined up outside the office to mob us as we came out. We chose the one who spoke the best English and who said he could make corn muffins. His name was Mohammed, which we soon abbreviated to "Mo," later expanded to "Moses," and finally, thinking that this might have some weight in converting him from the crescent to the cross, to "Holy Moses." Under his experienced guidance we secured a goodly supply of jam, spices and olive oil, forgetting the meal for the muffins. For ourselves we purchased a blanket, an extra bottle of ink, and a new tooth-brush apiece. Thus armed against any event we were all ready to undertake the five-hundred-mile tramp trip over the Himalayas and be gone six weeks.

By the light of the moon we loaded Holy Moses and our few supplies into a small barge in which we were to reach Ganderbal, the first stage of our journey, by water. Then we set sail.

The memory of other poetic nights has come and gone, but the memory of this will never go. As David and I, weary from the day's work, lay on the floor of the barge, two tireless rowers propelled us under the seven bridges of the Jhelum, past the fantastic, moonlit houses, more jumbled and grotesque than ever in the dimness. A wedding-party, singing to the music of native instruments, sailed by in a huge gondola, pushed forward by twenty gondoliers whose twenty heart-shaped blades flashed with every stroke. Their craft was ablaze with paper lanterns, and decorated with garlands of jasmine and chains of dahlias which drooped into the water and trailed behind on the wake of glittering ripples. In a hubbub of song and revelry they swept past and sped beyond, sending back in ever fainter tones the strains of music and of laughter, till distance deadened every sound and left the lake to stillness—and to us. Then quietly through the night we floated on across the cool calm surface of the Dahl, where the wind and the lotus-leaves brushed so gently as we passed that we were lulled to sleep.

At the head of the Scind Valley up which we moved toward the crest of the first range to be surmounted, we entered the Zogi Pass, which while it is only eleven thousand five hundred feet, is one of the most notorious defiles in India. The tropical rains from the peninsula turn to snow upon its heights, and a trail of animal carcasses and human graves bears witness to its bloodthirsty disposition. In fact the very day we made our crossing the corpse of an unfortunate coolie, lost the winter before, was just emerging from a snowdrift. This in itself would have dampened the gay spirits David and I had enjoyed for weeks, but to make life a completely dreary affair the enveloping clouds, for sixteen miles over the pass, poured sleet upon us. Nor did that night spent at eleven thousand feet bring relief. Rain fell in torrents upon the cooking-fire; the wind blew our blanket-tent down on top of us; the cold penetrated to the very marrow; and only a large bottle of brandy bequeathed by Mr. C—— saved us from total extinction.

Next morning the arctic storm rumbled away into the

mountains, and a true June day dawned in its place. How contrasted was the nature of things on this side of the range! The ascending slopes had been all forest and flowers, the descending were only barrenness and desolation, as it continued to be all the way to Leh, with only a patch of oasis here and there to prevent the country from being a veritable desert. Our pass soon narrowed into a canyon with sheer rock sides and a seething thrashing torrent roaring at the bottom. Day after day we followed the mule-trail along the face of such a gorge, stopping noon and night at the tiny villages that came from ten to twenty miles apart at places where the walls opened wide enough to permit them.

On the tenth day the summit of our trail to Leh was reached—fourteen thousand feet! From this commanding point we saw the Himalayas spreading for a hundred miles in all directions. Fourteen thousand, the top of things in most mountains, is in this region often only the plateau from which the peaks begin to rise. All about us snowy pinnacles reached to twenty-five thousand feet, and one, endless miles to the north, was Godwin-Austen, twenty-eight thousand two hundred and sixty, topped in the entire world by Everest only. There was not a tree or a blade of grass to be seen in this vast sweep, since it seldom rains. In their places were colors of an astonishing prodigality—vertical veins of brilliant orange and red and purple, streaking upward until they met the inevitable robe of clouds and diadem of snow.

Snuggled against this third and highest range, we came upon our first Tibetan village, Lamayuru; and at the sight of this amazing community, felt we beheld another world. The contrast of sterile granite that we had seen for days with the sudden fresh verdure of irrigated rice paddies gave us a distinct shock. Stuck on a cliff straight above the canyon floor appeared the huts and caves of the citizens, while on the very brink of the highest rock perched a good example of the "gompa" or lama monastery, where dwells the only spiritual or civil authority the country knows.

No sooner had we halted at a cleared space that lay in the shadow of the overhanging village than the greater part of the male population came down from the cliff-tops to surround us—all real Ladakis, with Chinese faces and long loose clothes of gray wool. Each of the men was resplendent in jewelry, with silver ear-hoops dangling to his shoulders and colored necklaces reaching to his waist. Even the poorest muleteer possessed a bracelet or two. The average citizen of Lamayuru, however, was such a symphony of dirt and gray that not even these jewels could give him much of a swagger appearance.

They had seen few white men, and none at all who traveled as we did, with only one servant and no mounts. An exclamation of surprise went up when they saw us unpack the ponies, extract the cooking utensils and assist in the preparation of a meal, which, when served in our own quaint way, attracted the circle of staring citizens to very close range where they sat spellbound by our strange manipulation of scrambled eggs. Next morning we awoke to find every window and roof sprinkled with curious villagers, who from their superimposed seats could look down upon the making of our toilet. Never before or since have I dressed so publicly. As they seemed fascinated by the spectacle, David and I obliged them by an extravagant employment of tooth-brush, soap and comb.

The monastery roof was packed with dozens of red-gowned monks, perched three or four hundred feet above, who scampered out of sight when they saw us begin the climb to their stronghold. We stumbled through black tunnels, up ladders and precipitous steps, through a mystic maze of passages, emerging, under the guidance of a priest, into the innermost shrine. Here the images of Buddha, in gold, wood and bronze, sat leering fatly down at the burning incense and at the rows of dull brass bowls, filled with oil and grain, placed before them as offerings. The light was just strong enough to give the gaudily-colored and elaborately-carved room a fantastic, mysterious atmosphere that fascinated yet repelled us. Horrible demons grinned from the walls, and equally terrifying masks hung from the ceiling beams. The lama form of Buddhism has been described as a religion of juggling, idolatry and mechanics, and this shrine exemplified very well these elements. Prayer flags and wheels decorated every building, and our ecclesiastic guide, spinning each of the latter as he passed, allowed us to give them a slap to our own credit. While we were not having a particularly hard time of it, a word to the fates from Buddha would not do any harm.

We were led into a great hall, whence came the babble of many voices, and found there, seated on long rows of benches, the entire population of the monastery—over two hundred—chanting passages from their sacred books. The "books" consisted of great stacks of printed card-boards, one by two feet, each one of which was placed beneath the stack as it was read through. Such a bedlam of voices one never heard, though it all stopped instantly the moment we walked in. The students, ranging from half-grown boys to old graybeards, stared at us as we stared back at them, and I do not know which side was the more awestruck.

We were escorted to the monastery trail on the back side of the cliff, and managed to toboggan down it to the floor of the canyon, where the path to Leh, met once more, continued to lead us through more painted gorges, more teriffic heat, over higher passes and across more arid deserts.

We were now in the heart of Ladakh, and indeed it was like nothing else on earth. The entire country seemed to be falling to pieces. The mountains, higher than ever, were cracked into fragments and in the form of shale were slipping into the Indus River which raged beside us like a Niagara. Pinnacled on the cliffs about were the skeletons of ancient citadels and crag-topping castles, indicating that four centuries ago, before the feudal lords had been displaced by Lhasa, Ladakh was a far more populous and powerful state. These once haughty fortresses are in utter ruin to-day and do their share in giving the whole landscape the illusion of falling to pieces.

The rarity of the atmosphere is to blame for another of Ladakh's mad characteristics—its phenomenal climate. The film of moistureless air is so thin that it has neither resistance to the tropical desert sun nor the ability to retain heat after the sun is gone. In consequence this region suffers from abnormally cold weather along with abnormally hot. In summer, the season of our expedition, the thermometer climbs to one hundred twenty degrees in the sun and then drops at night to forty. The shadow of a cloud brought a chill, where the moment before we had been miserable from the scorching heat. In winter, though there is almost no snow, zero is not uncommon after sundown of the very day when it had been eighty-five. Consequently David and I spent a good part of our time putting on and taking off and putting on and taking off clothes in an effort to meet the demands of this temperamental climate.

One afternoon, sixteen days after our departure from Srinagar, we turned an unexpected corner and bumped abruptly into Leh—or at least it seemed so. But it was an illusion, since the vast and dominating castle of the rajah, enthroned on the ridge above the city, was ten miles distant. Not until we had trudged four hours more through ankle-deep sand did we reach the entrance gate, assist our pack ponies over the two-foot threshold, and find ourselves the cynosure of all eyes in one of the world's most curious capitals.

## ⚬ XX. ⚬

# The Strange Story
# of Leh

THE highest inhabited region in the world—that is what
Ladakh, with the neighboring portions of Tibet, claims
to be. In our camp on the outskirts of the town, we
were well over two miles above the sea, yet on one of the very
lowest plateaus, most of the population living from three to
five thousand feet higher. It seems incredible that people can
not only exist year after year at such a height, but can rear their
children and their cattle and their crops of barley and rice at
the same lofty altitude. When the inhabitants of such eyrie lev-
els descend to eleven thousand-foot Leh, they can not tarry
long, for they suffer no doubt from the density of the atmosphere and hasten to climb home where the air is normal.

In keeping with the rest of the country, Leh, with its ten
thousand people, is a fantastic and picturesque little city, composed of a tumble-down cluster of ancient stone huts leaning
at all angles and in all stages of disrepair. It boasts, however, of
its Main Street, a broad straight avenue lined with poplar trees
and swarming with a heterogeneous crowd from a hundred

different races and sects. The city is not far from where India, Russia and China unite, and one finds evidence of this proximity in the features and costumes seen about the bazaars.

In Leh we had the opportunity to observe at close range the lives of the average Ladakhi, and found that they were very contented lives despite the abnormalities of their country. Though there is no real poverty in this rainless state, the land area that can be irrigated is unalterably limited which limits the food supply and that, in turn, the population. In the thirty-five thousand square miles of territory there are only thirty-five thousand people, who while they have a square mile each to provide for them, have a continual struggle to live. As a means of checking the birth-rate it became customary centuries ago to practise polyandry, and this unique custom is now a firmly established institution. A woman of Ladakh should look twice before she leaps into matrimony, for she does not marry the choice of her parents' heart alone but all his brothers as well. While the women have become accustomed to managing three or four husbands through generations of experience, when there are six brothers or more it must become difficult to honor and obey so many all at once. There are circumstances, however, which relieve such a multiplicity of household heads, the eldest brother being really supreme, and his word law. He is the legal parent of all the children, and held responsible for their proper place in the community. The wife, in spite of her many mates, is often left entirely alone as Ladakhi men are usually engaged away from home. When a husband returns he leaves his shoes on the door-step as a warning for rival husbands to keep away, and only the eldest brother, whose shoes are inviolate, dares disturb them. No wonder one sees so few children. But perhaps it is best, for it's a wise child that knows his own father—in Ladakh.

Naturally David and I had a great desire to gain entrée into one of these polyandrous households. The Moravian missionary stationed there could not help us, as the only families he was friendly with were those converted to the uninteresting and common-place Christian doctrine of monogamy. It took one of the local shopkeepers to solve our problem. Having a few rupees' worth of supplies to buy, David and I took Holy Moses on a tour of the market and by means of our interpreter inquired of the salesman, before we made our purchases, if he were one of multiple husbands. When the reply was affirmative, we offered to trade with him in return for the privilege of visiting his family. In this way we soon encountered an accommodating shop-owner who was not only one of several husbands, but lord of the manor as well. He led us some distance out from the city, into the most palatial rock-house we had seen, and, thinking it an extremely amusing experience, presented us (not without a touch of native grace) to his wife, three other brother-husbands, and two common sons. The woman and children stared at us blankly; the men welcomed us with smiling faces.

As we entered just before the serving of a meal, Holy Moses, reading our thoughts, suggested to our host that he invite us to take places at the family board. Although I am sure we were the first white guests this family had ever had, from occasional association with foreigners in the capacity of muleteers, etc., they had come to look upon them as a superior order of being, so that though they served us bountifully with rice and unleavened bread, no amount of persuasion could induce them to partake of their own food at the same time.

The wife, judging from the superabundance of her jewelry, commanded more than average wealth. She was a vision of gaudy glory. Added to the yards of beads and usual burden of barbaric rings and bracelets, she wore the most elaborate turquoise head-dress we had seen. This indispensable and inseparable ornament is the most important part of any Ladaki woman's costume. Even the poorest man's daughter and wife, though they be in rags, maintain this bit of finery. It consists of a strip of leather in the shape of a very much elongated diamond, some five inches wide, coming to a point over the forehead and tapering down the back to another point at the waist. It is studded with graduated rows of turquoises, sometimes two hundred in number, which represent not only the entire wealth of the owner, but of generations of previous ancestral owners. While the stones on these unusual and elaborate adornments would not create a sensation on the Rue de la Paix, they are of a beautiful color and possess considerable value. Attached to the leather are large ear-flaps made of black wool, which, protruding at each side of the face, have a strong resemblance to horse blinkers.

This woman, with all her turquoises, was if possible even less familiar with soap than the men. Her peacock head-dress covered braids of unspeakably grimy hair, and the ear-flaps at the side half concealed a face which might have been fairly pretty had it not been hidden under a covering of dirt. The Ladakhi have an excuse for not bathing in winter—it's too cold; and then in the summer they are out of the habit. In consequence they never remove their clothes until they rot and fall off, which, judging from appearances, happens only once in a decade.

Curious to know if my hostess' treasures could be bought, I offered her five hundred theoretical rupees in exchange for her collection. She refused. I raised my offer to a thousand, and then, much to the amusement of her husbands, to a million. Still she steadfastly resisted my tempting (if imaginary) gold, insisting she would not sell for any price as the spirit of her ancestors would destroy her for parting with the family relics.

Never have I so regretted the world's confusion of tongues. There were a hundred questions I would have asked the members of this extraordinary family, had not Holy Moses' scanty comprehension of English and his even more limited knowledge of Ladakhi prevented. With his feeble assistance we did learn that the three younger brothers, who were usually engaged away from Leh, had all returned home because of a religious festival then taking place. A fifth brother had bolted from the flock and attached himself to a wife of his own choice. There had been six children born to the four husbands; only two survived, one, judging from marked resemblances, the son of the eldest brother, the second, of another. In response to our urgent request, despite the loudly expressed disapproval of the wife who feared the devils in our strange black boxes, they collected in the courtyard to be photographed, and the picture of the four fathers, the mother, and the two children, that we took, is as far as I can ascertain, the only one of its kind extant.

From the missionary I later learned that the action of the radical brother who had reverted to monogamy, was rapidly becoming the rule, rather than the exception, for the economic and moral problems of polyandry were making it more and more unpopular with the present generation. Family ties were being dangerously loosened by the habitual infidelity of younger husbands, while the large number of unmarried mothers and unsupported children was becoming a serious detriment to social order. Each year sees fewer polyandrous families, so that the day no doubt is not far distant when this abnormal custom will be relegated to the past, and every woman in Ladakh may have a husband.

Even before we reached Leh it was evident that the ruling passion of the country was religion. Being essentially a part of Tibet, Ladakh clings tenaciously to the Lama form of the

Buddhist faith professed by the mother country, and there are few districts in Tibet where the population is as priest-ridden and as monastery-dominated as in this its western end. Almost every village has its lamasery to support, with its swarms of red-robed monks who live in a realm of holiness far above the people. These buildings, erected three or four centuries ago when the power of Lhasa was at its height, are pinnacled dramatically on the points of crags so difficult to scale that in extreme cases they can be reached only by basket elevators. One is led to believe that the religion of that era enjoyed desolate surroundings, and sought to isolate itself among the wildest peaks.

With one son from every family in some religious order there are far too many priests who are of no practical value, and in consequence a great majority of them are left free to meditate, an occupation into which they plunge with vigor, taking a recess only long enough to instruct the boy lamas in the art so that when they are grown they may be able to meditate as well as their instructors.

The lamas ascribe to themselves supernatural powers, and control over the elements. The missionary at Leh told me with despair in his voice of a local lama who, during a recent water famine, promised rain if he were paid well enough. He *was* paid handsomely, whereupon one of the heaviest rains ever recorded fell from the clouds and revived the perishing crops, thus bringing renewed faith in the power of the priests and disaster to the mission. The lamas are extortionate moneylenders, and by this means have little difficulty in keeping possession of the tillable land. Indeed between the dread of earthly spoliation and threats of spiritual disaster the layman of Ladakh is kept in eternal subjection.

The rank and file of the people take their religion seriously. Since their prayers and exhortations can be offered, so they believe, much oftener by mechanics than by thought, they take advantage of this dispensation made to them by Buddha and spin and roll and waft prayers to Heaven in a hundred different ways that demand no effort or attention on their part. It is not the man who follows their moral code with the most diligence who soonest attains Nirvana, but the man who manufactures the most prayers. There are several which, if offered a sufficient number of times, no matter how automatically, are sure to win salvation. The most popular is: "*Om mani padmi hum, om mani padmi hum*," meaning, "Oh, thou jewel in the heart of the lotus flower." The single drop of water that is always found in the lotus is the purest and most immaculate thing the Buddhist can think of to call Buddha, and the endless repetition of this complimentary phrase is supposed to flatter the divinity into a compassionate and forgiving mood. From every housetop float cloth flags covered with "*om mani padmis*," which catch the breeze and waft to heaven the invocations of the owner.

Many people have prayer-wheels, made of brass cylinders, which they twirl by hand as they sit idly or walk behind their pack-ponies. These cylinders are filled with thousands of printed "*om manis*" and every spin adds countless prayers to their credit. Most ingenious of all is the water-wheel, which, filled as it often is with a hundred pounds of prayer cloth, makes the other contrivances seem a waste of time.

As grace is sought by these mechanics, so is evil discouraged. At every entrance to the village there is an odd piece of masonry called a "*mani*," consisting of a stone wall six feet high, six broad, and ten feet to a mile in length. It is completely roofed with small flat stones inscribed with "*om manis*" and, while very beneficial to those who walk along it, it is even more potent in discouraging evil spirits from entering the village. Evil spirits, like men, *must* travel only along the trail, and with that protected the community is safe from invasion. Also the devils, if they dare pass the *manis*, must pass on the right side, making it necessary for all Ladakhis to take scrupulous pains to pass always on the left side least they bump into a demon, an encounter that is to be avoided at all cost.

Near Leh there is one *mani* a mile long and thirty feet broad, with an estimated half-million prayer stones on top. There is little doubt, when the unproductivity of the country is considered, that the wall took three generations to build.

The most conspicuous form of religious monument, next to the *mani* is the *chorten*, a hollow pile of stones shaped like an inverted turnip, five to twenty feet high and built in scores near every village. The larger *chortens* are frequently used as vaults for departed priests, whose bones, after being cremated are ground to powder, mixed with clay, molded into the shape of miniature *chortens* and stacked in neat piles inside their big prototypes. I could not resist desecrating one of these vaults and procuring a potted lama, as a curiosity which I intended to bring home; but on the return trip the pack-pony carrying my treasure walked off the trail into the Indus, and the poor lama was lost.

As well as being the commercial center, Leh is also the religious center of the country, and the home of the "Skushok" who, being the living incarnation of Bakola (a saintly contemporary of Buddha) is the holiest and highest lama in the district. He has died about thirty times since he first became lord of the Leh monastic area, only to be reborn of noble parentage in the neighborhood of his demise. Finding a child fulfilling all their requirements of wealth and born at the proper interval after the death of Skushok, the monastery elders choose him as the incarnation of their departed master; and to prove to the people's satisfaction that he is the true saint they place personal possessions of the former lama before him, along with unfamiliar articles. The child never fails to recognize his property, it is said; probably because the elders tutor him thoroughly.

It was our good fortune to be in Leh in time to attend the inauguration of the child Skushok at the local lamasery. There was a festival connected with it, in his honor, such as occurs only once in a lifetime, and which, lasting three days, had drawn the population (including the brothers of my shop-keeper host) from long distances.

On this momentous day, previous to being carried out for public observation, the boy was placed in state within the inner temple, where the leading monks from all the subsidiary *gompas* came to prostrate themselves, and in return receive a strip of colored cloth from him as his blessing. Through a secluded lattice I watched the entire ceremony. It was indeed a solemn occasion, rendered doubly so by the "dim religious light." The gold images and brass jars of oil shone dully, garish Chinese portraits of demons and frescoes depicting the horrors of hell covered the walls, while from the ceiling hung scores of the same grotesque devil-masks we had seen at Lamayuru. The only fresh and beautiful thing in this room filled with depressing ornaments and evil-looking priests was the silk-robed child, whose sweet face and guileless eyes gave him the expression of an infant seraph. He was not more than four years old, and, while obviously bored with this unnatural life, seemed to have resigned himself to it and to be enduring it manfully.

When he was carried out to his throne on the covered stage in the courtyard, from which he was to observe the entertainment, the hundreds of expectant people greeted him with enthusiasm and gave way to festivity. In the center of the open space stood enormous urns of native barley-wine around which the dancers, both men and women, shuffled and turned.

The male members of the assembly, spinning their prayer-wheels, sat in rows about the ring, while the women, wearing their best turquoises, stood in crowds at the edges. The wine was served to everyone with such a lavish hand that before sundown the entire population of Leh was decidedly inebriated, and while they were by no means boisterous (a Ladakhi is never that) they became very merry and enthusiastic about the new Skushok. To the sound of drums and pipes the dancers walked solemnly about the circle, with an occasional side-step or turn of the wrist. As their cups were always filled first they soon became so dizzy that the dancing degenerated into blind staggers—a fact not appreciated by the spectators, who were too dazed themselves to know the difference.

Meanwhile the baby on the throne had gone sound asleep. As his guardian lifted him from his pile of cushions and carried him back to the terrifying, devil-infested "playroom," the child threw his arms about the old priest's neck and dropped his head on the convenient shoulder. No divinity this, no superhuman saint; only a very natural and very homesick baby boy, who, after such a strenuous day, was more interested in his crib and his porridge than in the spiritual welfare of his fold.

I could not resist an urge to follow the child into the monastery, nor did any one seem to disapprove. In the lurid throne-room, with no one present but myself, I asked the devoted guardian permission to take the cherub's picture, and he consented with graciousness, posing him arrayed in all his royal robes, in a sun-illumined spot. This god-child, serene and unafraid, stood motionless, and Buddha smiled upon my undertaking, for the developed negative recorded in perfect detail the sweet and spiritual face of this favored child of Heaven. Later I sent an enlarged print back to the monastery, and no doubt it is to be found to-day hanging on the wall among the demon masks.

It was almost sundown, that memorable afternoon, when the infant abbot, the priest and I returned to the seclusion of the dormitory. Seeing how attracted I was to the baby, the old man allowed me to assist in bed-time preparations. Holding the sleepy child on my lap I removed his yellow robes of state, and wrapped him in a voluminous woolen shawl. A bowl of warm barley porridge was brought to us, and with a big wooden spoon I fed my little charge his frugal supper. Near by stood the ancient blackened cradle that had nestled previous incarnations. Into it I lifted the heavy-eyed cherub, gave him his wooden doll and covered them both with a shaggy sheep skin. Then as the wild fantastic music and the babble of the multitude came faintly from the outside world, I was allowed to stand beside his little Holiness, and with the last ray of sunlight slanting in through the latticed window from the western Himalayas, softly rock this baby god to sleep.

## ᴄᴊ **XXI.** ᴄ

# Back to Earth

THE record of our journey back to Srinagar over the same route by which we had come is anything but a merry one. It had taken us sixteen days to accomplish the outward trip, and now as a plan of economy, we decided to make it in ten, or just about half the time normally required by travelers. I am sure our flight to Srinagar constitutes a record, for it would have been physically impossible to travel faster. We were off at sun-up, rushing on through rock and river, taking no time for a noon-day meal other than dried apricots munched as we tramped along. Night-travel was extremely hazardous, for the narrow trails, devoid of any railing and winding along the face of canyon walls, were unsafe enough by day; yet in our stern determination to follow the vigorous schedule we had set ourselves, we never halted short of our destination, no matter how late the hour.

As it was necessary throughout the entire journey to change ponies every two or three days, we soon abandoned hope of remembering their many names, and reduced all equine nomenclature to "Whinny" and "Ninny." One morning about half-way home, Holy Moses started ahead with Whinny, leaving a lackadaisical Ninny behind with us. It was rarely necessary to give the pack-ponies any thought on the trail, for they were sure-footed little beasts, disdaining guidance. Ninny proved a notable exception. Taking advantage of our inattention he plodded on ahead half asleep, went too near the edge and, with our utensils, food and potted lama lashed to his back, slipped off, tumbling head over heels down a twenty-foot bank into that mad Indus River. Struggling desperately with the terrific current to retain the bank, he needed, we thought, only a little assistance to succeed. Thoughtless of consequences, we ran ahead, slid down the steep slope into the rapids, and plunging in up to our waists, seized the mane of the half-drowned animal as he floundered past. A heroic tug of war ensued, the swirling torrent doing its utmost to wrench the pony away, David and I straining and struggling against it to hold on to him. But we were no match for the powerful drag of the river. Outraged at our seizure of its prey the Indus snatched at us too and had we not let go would have swept us, as it was now sweeping the poor frantic pony, into its boiling cauldron. Clinging to the bank we saw the helpless little animal dashed against a protruding boulder, rushed onward by the flood, and disappear.

For half an hour we were too exhausted from the struggle and too weak from fright to climb the steep bank. We got out of our icy clothes and let them dry in the hot sun, so that by the time we were back to normal our dramatically laundered khaki shirts and shorts were ready for service again. What half-wits we had been to rush thus at disaster just to save the dust of a desecrated lama, half a sheep carcass, and a frying-pan! What if the entire pack were lost? With the pony included it was worth perhaps twenty-five dollars, and any respectable funeral costs more than that.

We went hungry that night, and perhaps would have for several nights had we not met relief in the form of an elaborate cavalcade belonging to Major Wingate, the British Commissioner for Ladakh, on its way to Leh. We had known the major very pleasantly in Srinagar, and now, especially under the circumstances, our delight in seeing him again was profound. Despite a month's growth of beard on our faces, we were invited to attend the state banquet being given in his honor by the local chiefs of a neighboring village. If we consumed more than a genteel sufficiency I am sure Major Wingate overlooked it, since he no doubt knew this was our first real meal in a long, long time.

Sonamarg, our next stop, was thirty miles away and beyond the Zogi Pass. Here, in camp, we hoped to find a number of our Kashmir acquaintances, so leaving Holy Moses behind with the single pony, we struck out guideless and provisionless, counting on chance to take care of us at the other end. The pass was a sea of slush and swollen streams. Cold rain drenched us and wind flapped our soaked clothes. It was two bedraggled, creeping, frozen, starved vagabonds that sought and found their friends. They gave us warm clothes, a hot supper and soft beds, and sent us next day on our way loaded down with a great chocolate cake.

Because of delays it was the night of the tenth day before we reached the "Srinagar-25-miles" post. It seemed as if we must fail to achieve our ten-day program. David, however, was determined to save us from the total defeat. The moon was bright that evening, so after supper, leaving me to follow next day, he forged ahead, walking all night, and at dawn reached the agency after a forty-two-mile tramp.

United once more in Srinagar, it was a question which of us was the more happy to be "home." After such an unusual trip, we enjoyed something of that smug, superior feeling explorers must have, who, though they discover nothing but wastes of ice, have the thrill of knowing they were the first to tread there. Thousands of Americans have been to India, many to Kashmir, but we were two of the merest handful ever to have called upon this strange orphan of the nations, this topsy-turvy, half-lost plateau of Ladakh far up in the heart of the Himalayas.

Six weeks' absence seemed only to have impressed Srinagar's charm the keener upon us, and once more in its grasp we set ourselves to invent some excuse for remaining. I felt my own excuse would be my empty pockets, but the empty-pocket argument proved fallacious. Not only was our bill from the agency much less than we expected (*mirabile dictu!*) but we sold our equipment and got back two-thirds as much as we had paid for it. So I found that instead of being short of funds I had fifty-six rupees, or eighteen dollars left after all was said and done.

Thus rolling in wealth once more, we lost no time in applying for a houseboat. Ever since our visit on the *Lucky*, house-boating in Srinagar had been our idea of Elysian existence. There were a number of idle craft available and by making their owners bid against each other for our patronage, we secured a completely furnished boat with two bedrooms, two baths, dining-room, living-room, roof garden, kitchen "me too," five servants, a gondola and meals to order—all for one dollar a day each!

For the first four days David and I scarcely stirred from our beds of asphodel, not even to inform friends of our return from the wilds. As twilight came we filled our gondola high with pillows, and had ourselves rowed like Egyptian kings out on Dal Lake, where we could watch the sun set below the mountain-rim, then on to Shalimar that we had learned six weeks before to love so well, then softly home in the darkness, to sleep till noon next day with the willows weeping overhead and great beds of iris growing on the bank beside our window. It was a life of unmitigated, conscientious Epicureanism. We dined and we drifted and we dreamed, for to-morrow we would be penniless. Ten idyllic days passed, days without a care of responsibility, almost without motion. Only one thing saved us from complete ossification—each of us was inspired to write an account of our expedition to Leh. Had we known at that time that *Travel Magazine* was to accept David's manuscript, and *National Geographic* mine, I doubt if, in our exhausted condition, we would have survived the shock.

When my capital had shrunk to four dollars I felt the danger-point had been reached, and insisted to a reluctant David that I must get back to India before the last *pice* was gone. He agreed to accompany me, so, shouldering our knapsacks, we bade farewell to the poppy-city, and took to the road again. With our usual good luck we were picked up by an army officer in a motor-car before we had tramped one mile of the two hundred, and deposited back in Rawalpindi, whence we had departed the previous May.

Four dollars!—and sixteen hundred miles from Calcutta!

## ᴄ XXII. ᴄ

# Through the Khyber Pass

HYBER Pass!—one of the goals, along with the Taj and Kashmir, that had lured me East, when in Egypt I was debating which course to follow. In all Asia what better goal could there be? There is perhaps no other mountain passway in the world so historic as this, so filled with the ghosts of armies, so thoroughly soaked with romance and battle and blood. Since time immemorial it has been the key to India. Alexander and his Greeks, the Moguls and their conquering armies, the Afghans, the Persians, the English, have advanced and retreated through this rift in the desolate hills. For thirty centuries the Khyber Pass has been the portal to vast international commerce. By means of it conquests, empires, even civilizations, have made their exits and their entrances.

There is scarcely a page of Indian history but contains the name of Khyber, and as I write with a debacle threatening in the East, with the Islam Levant reaching toward India for sympathy and support, and with a potential Russia waiting for the psychological moment to pour her soldiers through the funnel, it seems probable that the Khyber's day of service for and against the order of things has only reached its noon.

Having learned from bitter experience, no one realizes this better than England, and to fortify her grip upon the Achilles heel of her eastern empire, she has made of it an armed camp from end to end, has strewn it with military highways, and is pushing with furious energy a railroad through this desolate gulch that for three thousand years has seen no other burden-bearers than the tinkling caravans of mule and camel.

For a century England has been at war spasmodically with the Afghan tribes, who, whenever they felt their chances of success were reasonably good, made a dash through the Pass, plundered and pillaged as far inland as they dared, and escaped home again, posting their snipers on commanding positions in the Khyber to threaten pursuers with ambush and disaster. These tribes have always had a holy hatred for England and believed that the best way to repel her invasion was to make it impossible for the individual Britisher to get across the border. Their policy has succeeded beautifully in keeping Afghanistan independent. So many "visitors" have been murdered and robbed in the Pass that all white men, unless guarded by a military escort, give it a wide berth. At present there is a treaty in force by which the Afghans have pledged their word neither to snipe nor rob on Tuesdays and Fridays. These are called convoy days, and it is only then that traffic from both ends swarms through in safety.

After a night's ride (stolen as usual) from Rawalpindi, farther on into the northwest, David and I arrived at Peshawar, the Indian outpost to the Pass, on a Thursday, and established ourselves, without daring to ask the price of things, at the government dak-bungalow. In fact with my twelve rupees now reduced to nine we decided to postpone any discussion of tariff until our Khyber expedition had been accomplished.

With the proper passports in hand, we set ourselves to solve the problem of transportation into the Khyber. As it was already Thursday night, and Friday a convoy day, we had no time to lose. Walking could not be considered, since the Afghanistan border which we hoped to cross lay thirty-five miles away, and the late-July heat would have murdered us before we were well started. Though bitterly cold in winter, "in summer," reports a contributor to the *National Geographic Magazine*, "this gash in the sunshot hills is a fiery furnace and a living hell. The atmosphere shimmers in heat waves like the surface of a boiling cauldron." The author of those phrases had proper appreciation of the heat. I shall not say personally what I suspect the temperature was during our passage since no one would believe me.

By good fortune we learned that the mail-motor passed our bungalow at six A. M. Here was our chance. Unable to pay for the ride, we stood in the middle of the road waving our arms at the oncoming car, and, when the driver stopped to ask petulantly what we wanted, climbed in. I had seized three bananas from our breakfast table, hoping they would be accepted as bribes by the chauffeur. They were.

Although we entered the Pass before seven o'clock, even then we had missed all but the last straggling caravans, for in an effort to avoid the terrific heat the others had passed during the night and early morning hours. Army motor-trucks, not so sensitive to temperature, roared up-hill along with us or slid down-hill with grinding brakes in an enveloping cloud of dust.

Every mile or two we came upon parade-grounds where Indian soldiers were being drilled by English officers. At seven-thirty the sun rose above the gulch walls, and all activity stopped instantly. What a dreary place it was—rock and dust and desolation. Of all the places for a soldier to be stationed this is the last choice on earth.

Our mail-car ended its journey at the summit of the defile before a big walled camp called Lundi Kotal, and not even whole bunches of bananas could have persuaded the chauffeur to take us farther. After all, our passports had distinctly stated. that we were to go no farther. Feeling it was a waste of time, however, to reach a point only four miles from Afghanistan and then not cross the border, we deliberately set about finding some way to circumvent our restrictions.

This was not hard to find. The commanding officer of the guards at this gate to India happened to be in a most melodious mood, as we rather hesitatingly entered his office to present first our respects and then our requests for border permission. He was singing as if it were not one hundred and ten degrees in the sun outside, and a barren cruel inferno. Our timidity departed on finding his colonelship so care-free, for all other British colonels we had met in India had been decidedly hard-hearted and hard-bitten. Not this soldier—he sang.

"Good morning, young gentlemen, for what reason am I granted the honor of your visit?"

We showed him our passports, and, assuming our most jovial air for fear of discording his musical humor and making an officious colonel out of a human being, we asked him to please visé them for Kabul.

That was such a preposterous request he laughed out loud. Engaging him in informal conversation we learned that he was going home to England in a week to marry. This was why the birds were singing in a place where only a buzzard could exist.

The results of our call were many. He showed us his fiancée's picture and his seven tooth-brushes, one for each day, invited us to breakfast (while we had breakfasted once already, twice wouldn't hurt), supplied us with two of his own saddle-horses, ordered an escort of Sikh cavalry to accompany us, telephoned to the smaller camp on the border to have drinks prepared, and topped everything by apologizing for not being able to act as guide and chaperon himself. His parting words as we clattered off were not to hurry back, as lunch would wait and a motor-truck transport us home whenever we chose to go.

David and I were in a daze. We had never felt quite so important in our lives—riding at the head of our spectacular cavalcade, in which each guard was a dashing figure carrying a long lance with fluttering colored pennants streaming from its tip in the scorching wind.

We were content to walk our horses, as it was too unendurably hot to exert them. For an hour we moved along the writhing white road, between glowering rock walls that rose for a thousand feet on either side, from which the heat waves danced and shimmered. Turning a corner we suddenly beheld the border camp at our feet and the barren plains of Afghanistan stretching off to the distant blue hills that looked upon Kabul. The "lime squashes" ordered by the colonel were brought out to us as we threaded our way through the tangles of barbed-wire that surrounded the post, and, thus refreshed, we rode on past the "Halt—Afghanistan Territory" sign, and penetrated several hundred yards into forbidden territory.

Back at Lundi Kotal, we were very ready to get out of the midday sun, which had blistered anew our bare knees and given David reason to complain of a severe headache. True to his word the colonel invited us to a well-served tiffin in his cool dining-room, and then, having ordered out a truck and instructed the driver to deposit us wherever we desired, received the sincere thanks of two very grateful vagabonds.

If his disposition continued after his marriage to be as affable and courteous as it was shortly before, his wife is the luckiest woman in the world—that is, unless he brings her back to live in Lundi Kotal.

After dinner that night in the dak-bungalow, David and I had a finance conference. Our train back to the plains left at seven next morning, and by that time our bungalow bill would be eight rupees each.

With just nine to my name it was a serious problem what to do. Calculating what our upkeep had cost the native manager, we decided it was about three rupees each, so we agreed that this amount plus one rupee for service was all we could pay and at the same time keep on friendly terms with our conscience and our sense of honor.

Before going to bed I wrote a note to the manager saying that we were two financially embarrassed students who, unable to pay the bungalow bill in full, were enclosing four rupees each which would meet all the expenses he had incurred on account of us. As a proof of our good intentions I left as further reimbursement a camel's-hair sweater which had been given to me in Kashmir, and which though somewhat delapidated had proved very useful in the Himalayas. In the Punjab, with the mercury wrecking thermometers every day, a woolly sweater was not listed among my most indispensable possessions. However I felt sure the manager would be more clever at finding a use for the garment than I.

After packing our sacks we slept till four o'clock, then, feeling utterly despicable—especially since our crime was for so paltry a sum—we slipped out on the side door, carrying our shoes, and tramped through the coming dawn to the station.

In crime as in other things, only practise makes perfect; and neither David nor I, despite the liberties we had taken with the Indian railroads, had had much practise. This was very obvious when, on leaving our apartment, I forgot to close the door leading from the bathroom into the bedroom, so that not an hour after we left, the water boy coming with his buckets to fill our tubs, perceived and reported that the bedroom was empty. Straightway the manager, whom we carefully instructed not to disturb us till nine o'clock—or two hours after our train had gone—came to investigate this alarming report.

Wild-eyed, dripping with perspiration, with a crowd of hoodlums at his heels, he found us sitting calmly on the station platform, and for a moment raved so excitedly he was incomprehensible. An English plain-clothes policeman approached and told us very politely that the bungalow manager accused us of leaving his establishment without paying our bill. Would we please explain?

We told him the whole story in the frankest possible way, quoting the letter we had written and emphasizing the sweater. Then the manager made a disastrous gesture. Calling on Allah to be his witness he swore there was no letter and no money left as we said, but that we were inventing the story. Our train left in ten minutes, which would give us no time to return to the bungalow, and even if we did return, the letter naturally would not be there. Fortunately the manager showed as little subtlety in lying as we did in "beating" our bill. Unconsciously he put his hand inside his coat pocket and I almost *knew* it was to fortify his wavering false position with the assurance that our money was *not* on the table.

Watching my chance, I thrust my fingers into the suspicious pocket and snatched out the letter, torn open but with the eight rupees still there. For two *pice* he would have murdered me and gone happy to the scaffold, for the embarrassing position he had put us in had become a boomerang. The half-hundred people who had crowded round our altercation roared with laughter, and the manager, having received his rupees again, slunk away, the most vindictive man in the Punjab.

Eager to get rid of our troublesome presence, the station officials were more than willing to transport us free of charge as far away from them as we would go.

During the long blistering ride toward Delhi, David's headache, having steadily grown worse since our ride through the Khyber furnace on the day before, became painful beyond endurance, and on reaching Lahore (the place where we had enjoyed the cholera cure ten weeks before) we felt it impossible to continue farther. In this crisis, casting off our rôles of self-supported vagabonds, we sought the best hotel and the best medical aid in the city, ready if necessary to cable our families in America for assistance. A physician came none too soon. David had become delirious.

## ~ XXIII. ~

# Princess Padmini

VEN though thirty hours had elapsed since exposure in the Khyber, the physician diagnosed the case as sunstroke. For four days my companion lay prostrate with a raging fever; on the fifth the fever decreased; on the sixth disappeared.

Meanwhile our hotel proprietor had been won over to the proper state of benevolence. Hearing the story of our vagabondage and realizing that David was desperately ill, he gave us room and meals in his hotel free of charge. Realizing that we had become a burden to our obliging host, the moment David was out of danger, I left for Delhi, with five rupees in my pocket, planning to meet my comrade there as soon as he had recuperated. A strong urge had come to me to visit, before leaving India, the cities of Jaipur, Chitor and Udaipur, four hundred miles south of the capital in Rajputana, simply because I had learned that they were romantic and beautiful.

As in the Pyrenees, as at Gibraltar, as in Ladakh, Discretion tiraded against such a foolhardy expedition. It would take me four hundred miles farther away from Calcutta just at a time when, considering the decrepit condition of my pocketbook, I should have been hurrying with all possible speed to that city where in three months' accumulation of mail perhaps new funds awaited.

But Curiosity and Adventure taunted me. Had I become a soft tourist that I must have *money* to travel? Was my vagabond stamina, ridiculed by my friends in America before departure, really as feeble as they prophesied it would be?

Indignant at these self-accusations I jumped on the Delhi night express, defying all the conductors in India to collect a ticket; reached the capital in safety and, realizing that if I were to visit Jaipur, Chitor and Udaipur on five rupees I must, in anticipation of a fierce struggle, strip myself of every possible impediment, checked at the station everything I owned except the faithful camera, pocket knife and tooth-brush.

Second-class to Jaipur alone cost fourteen rupees. That being the case I went first-class.

All day long it was necessary to fight off collectors, as the news of my default spread by telegram up and down the line. Not only conductors were on hand to hound me, but inspectors, police and station-masters. I was diving out of windows, changing compartments and haggling from morning till night. One particularly obnoxious collector would have pushed me bodily off the train had I not pushed him off first.

The last station before my destination the train guard came to me with bad news:

"You will be met at Jaipur by the police. I have telephoned to them. Good afternoon."

Indian jails did not appeal to me at all, and I realized that any further defiance of the law would *mean* jail, so I jumped off the train and let it greet the Jaipur officials without me.

I had no idea how far it was to the city, nor, in the coolness of the twilight, did I care much. The rains had begun two weeks before in Rajputana, and the weather was truly delightful. I could not have believed the northern plains could be so fresh and green as I found them here. Pools of water stood in the road, and blossoms of a hundred kinds lent color to the landscape. Peacocks, which swarm unmolested by the thousand throughout this part of India, strutted and screeched and animated every field and grove. There was a soft caress in the breeze where a month before the air had parched one's skin. I had found India seared and ugly and drab; I was soon to leave her clothed in emerald and transformed by the rain-drops into a luxuriant garden. Never have I enjoyed a tramp so much as this. Escaped from the railroad annoyances, unencumbered by luggage, free as a lark, I walked on through the gathering darkness. Yes, Blake was right: Discretion was nothing but a "rich, ugly old maid wooed by incapacity." How much more entertaining it was to woo Folly.

I reached Jaipur station about ten that night, and though I had gone the entire day without food, had no difficulty in sleeping soundly on one of the iron benches in the waiting-room. Next morning the station-master looked rather scrutinizingly at me, since I fitted exactly the description telephoned to him of the adventurer he was to arrest, but as evidence of my guilt was only circumstantial he hesitated to disturb me.

By breakfast-time I had lost all interest in economy by starvation, and extracting one of my five rupees asked the manager of the station restaurant to give me all the food he could for the coin. With more generosity than prudence he placed a fresh loaf of bread and a jar of jam before me. Both met with obliteration in such an astonishingly short time the waiter hesitated to serve the eggs he had prepared lest the restaurant lose money on so hungry a customer.

I need not relate the details of the stolen ride during the all-night journey on south to Chitor. It was eventless. Arriving there with only four rupees, I felt I could ill-afford to spend one of them on breakfast at the dak-bungalow; and yet breakfast I had to have, as it would be my only chance for food all day. So I ordered and ate it. Then the question was how to pay for it. My sweater was left in Peshawar; I could not part with my shirt; shorts I had to have; it was dangerous to go without a topee. I finally decided that the belt was the only article of my scanty apparel I could do without. The manager was loath to accept a belt in payment, as he wore neither shorts nor trousers. However it was that or nothing, so he took it.

Chitor is one of the most renowned cities in the Orient, and justly so. Once the capital and principal fortress of an empire, its noble ruins still crown the top of a great rock-island that rises five hundred feet above the plain. The story of its struggle with the Mohammedan invaders and its final fall is written in blood; its history is a history of violence and heroism and great tragedies. Always the victims of lust and greed on the part of the Moslem invaders, the men of Rajputana fought not only for the integrity of their country but also for the protection of their fair women, whose enslavement was the avowed purpose of more than one conquest.

In 1290 Ala-ud-din, a Mohammedan invader hearing of the extraordinary beauty of the Rajput king's young daughter, Princess Padmini, commanded her father to deliver her to him or else submit to forcible seizure.

The king sent back a mocking reply.

In a rage Ala-ud-din hurled his armies against Chitor—without avail, for the Rajputs were entrenched behind their walls that lined the rim of the rock island. But even the bravest men must be nourished, and as the siege lasted month after month, this became increasingly difficult. At last Princess Padmini, watching from her castle tower, saw her father's armies, inflexible at first, begin to weaken as famine and pestilence decimated their ranks.

Fired by the Rajput's failing resistance, Ala-uddin intensified the onslaught. A breach was made in the walls at last. Triumphant, irresistible, the invaders poured in upon the starving city.

And all this death and bloodshed was in vain. The one lovely prize escaped the harem of the conqueror. Accompanied by the young noblewomen of the doomed city, each carrying a fagot and a torch, she descended into the subterranean passages beneath the royal palace, and marshaling them before her, barred the door.

Followed by his victory-maddened soldiers, the Mohammedan leader had already slashed his way to the palace. At last this fabulously beautiful girl, this Padmini, for whom he had destroyed a city, was his. Anticipating the seizure of the coveted princess he rushed into her apartment. She was not there. In the reckless search that followed, the barred crypt door was found and hurled aside. A cloud of smoke and flame enveloped him. Padmini had been faithful to the First Commandment of all Rajput women: "Death always, before dishonor!"

To-day this same revered doorway, deep down in the foundation of the roofless palace, is still to be seen. It is sealed, but one who knows the history of the tragic princess feels awed and deeply moved even to stand before the scene of martyrdom, neglected now and silent except for the mournful screech of countless peacocks that inhabit these storied ruins.

As Chitor, the ancient capital of Rajputana, is one of India's most romantic cities, so is Udaipur, the modern capital seventy miles to the west, one of the most entrancing. All during this economical expedition, Jaipur and Chitor were only stopovers—Udaipur, the marble fairy-castled "City of Sunrise" was really the goal. Why Udaipur is so called, I do not know, unless it is for the splendor of its coloring. Drab and burned in the dry months, in August with the surrounding hills clothed in fresh verdure, the trees refoliaged in feathery green gossamer, and the blue lakes filled to the brim by the rains and bound by ornate marble dams reflecting the multicolored palaces on the shore, Udaipur was to me an enchanted spot.

As the residence of the rajah of all the rajahs, the city has been made into a royal abode that is in keeping with his exalted position. His dream palaces are built close to the shore of the most picturesque of all the lakes, and in a country where extraordinary buildings are common, these attract unusual interest and unusual praise. Of marble and tinted plaster they raise their graceful towers and their battlements "bosomed high in tufted trees" above the city on one side, while on the other their "magic casements opening on the foam of perilous seas, in faerylands..." might have suggested to Keats those very lines. I climbed to the castle roof, and looked down upon islands covered with the marble summer apartments of the king. About them the blue lake shimmered, and beyond, from the distant shore, blue hills rose high into the blue sky. Swans and bright-sailed craft moved upon the mirror. Flowering trees bent over snowy lake-side shrines, to trail their branches into the cool ripples. For an hour I sat a hundred feet above this union of Oriental artifice and natural romantic beauty, and for the moment I forgot that the Taj Mahal was the most beautiful thing in the world.

Wishing to get the view from the lake back toward the rich buildings piled on the water's edge, I descended from my perch and went in search of a row boat. With little difficulty I found one, and on payment of half a rupee the craft was mine for the afternoon. The boatman at first could not understand that I wanted to row myself, and did not desire his services or his company. But as I prepared to start, it did seem a rather lonesome excursion, and I began to look over the circle of staring Rajputs that had gathered round (a white *sahib* is a curiosity at Udaipur in summer) in an effort to find an interesting companion. It was a simple matter—I being a man—to find one, for standing in the crowd of natives was as lovely a little maiden as I had seen in India. While I could not be sure of finding her an intelligent comrade, I was sure of a pretty one, and of the two female virtues is not the latter the more important?

She was not over sixteen, unusually pale in coloring, barefooted, bareheaded, weighed down with silver jewelry and draped in a combination of colors that suggested the rainbow. She would have caught the eye of any man, anywhere, much less of a lonely vagabond in search of a companion to go boating with him on this romantic lake. Right before the surprised onlookers I asked her in jumbled English and Hindustani (four months in India had taught me a few phrases) to get in my boat. She hung her pretty head in abashment at being addressed in public by a *sahib*, and would no doubt have run away, had not the crowd, thinking my idea a huge joke, urged her with much laughter and great merriment to do as I requested.

I had often been told by some of my sophisticated friends that women would rather be bullied than argued with, and that the rôle of cave-man was a very effective rôle to play at times. Perhaps, I thought, that same philosophy was as true in India as in Princeton. I decided to risk it anyway, so I seized her wrist and pulled her, half resisting, half responding, to the forward seat. The crowd roared with delight, and the girl, not without a sense of humor, finally saw the funny side and laughed as heartily as the rest. It was the most hilarious kidnapping that ever took place in Udaipur—and the most public.

As the lake in mid-afternoon was dotted with boats, my fair companion had no reason to feel unsafe. But though she may have been perfectly at ease our conversation was anything but brilliant. I ran through the two dozen disconnected Hindustani expressions I knew, counted from one to ten and was generally as garrulous as possible, all of which amused her hugely. She chattered back at a great rate, and, never before having conversed with a white man, thought I was deaf because I could not understand and shouted.

I was so amused by my naive companion I quite forgot to notice the panorama of palaces back on the shore—the very thing I had gone boating to see. What I did notice was that the sky had suddenly become overcast, indicating that the daily three o'clock rainstorm was fast approaching. Feeling very indignant at the weather, I turned our boat about and raced for the nearest shelter. But I had waited too long. When we were still a thousand feet from shore the sky opened, rain fell in torrents, and in two minutes each of us was a dripping bedraggled figure. The red of my passenger's veil ran in streams over the purple scarf; the red veil and purple scarf over the green bodice; the green bodice and red veil and purple scarf faded in great streaks and splotches upon the yellow skirt; the yellow skirt and the red veil and the purple scarf and the green bodice ran all over the boat. Oh, inconstant dyes! Oh, fragile cheesecloth!—and all I could do to comfort the distressed child was to row harder than ever into the teeth of the rainstorm.

When at last we reached the stone ghat from which we had embarked so merrily an hour before, we found that the crowd had scattered, leaving no one behind to witness our humiliating return. I assisted the poor girl ashore, tried to express my distress for her sad plight and to apologize for the weather. But she was too cold, too drenched, too miserable, to notice me. There were tears streaming down her face along with the raindrops...her gay veil...her faded dress.

"Good-by, Padmini," I said as she turned with a most pathetic expression to seek her home and refuge.

She stopped abruptly. Padmini? Padmini? Had I called her that? Did I really think her, half-drowned though she was, still exquisite and desirable and heroic—like the fabled princess? The light suddenly came back into her dark eyes. She turned her pretty face up to mine, and smiled—radiantly.

Then, like a frightened deer, the dripping little flower darted away down the marble ghat, and half running, half dancing, reached a grove of trees. One laughing backward glance, one flourish of her jeweled arm, one flash of color— and my Princess Padmini was gone.

## ఌ XXIV. ౭

# Renaissance

*I*T seems incredible that anything more could have been crowded into this eventful day, yet more there was. With my last rupee I bought a third-class ticket back to Chitor, and as before was granted a compartment bench to myself. The passenger traffic that evening was so heavy that native passengers, unable to find seats elsewhere, began to push into mine. Immediately there was war. I informed the insolent train guard that unless he gave me privacy and protection I would ride first-class. He retorted that I had no right to isolation, and that having bought third-class accommodations I would have to ride as the others rode.

With an expression that sounded very much like "I'll be damned if I will" I moved forthwith into the first-class coach. The guard was furious. He had found me, a hated arrogant white, in an embarrassing position, and he took fiendish delight in tightening the screws, planning to gloat over the humiliation that would come to me from being made by a native to sit and suffer among other natives. It threw him into a rage to see me scorning his authority. He came to the door at the end of the dinky coach and yelled at me in a frenzy of rage; "You buy third-class—you *go* third-class. You not sit with Indians—why come to India? You go to jail—jail…."

I slammed the door and locked it. As the train was at a station he ran around to the window and leaned through to howl anew. He might have seen that I was about to close the window, but he was too excited and left his flushed face in the most desirable position to have all the skin raked off his nose as I jammed the window down. One could have heard his shriek in Delhi. After that I was left in peace;—that is, until we reached Chitor, where the maddened guard, unable to wait for the train to halt, jumped off and ran ahead to fetch the station master. When, as calmly as possible, I ignored all their threats and imperatives, the train guard became so abusive the last leash on my temper gave way and I struck him as hard as I could. And that was the end of that.

It was not difficult to imagine the belligerent state of mind I was in while waiting for my train back to Delhi, where David was now awaiting me. It came about midnight, and as Chitor is the place on the Bombay-Delhi line where the expresses pass each other there was enough confusion to permit me to enter a first-class compartment unobserved.

You can never tell in India what you will find in the compartments if you break into them at random with the lights out. The windows of all the compartments were closed, so I could not peer inside and look before I leaped. Praying that if it were ladies I was intruding on, they would not scream and betray me, I opened the nearest door and crept noiselessly inside into utter blackness. While there was no challenge, the sudden nasal snort that greeted me could not have startled me less. It was the most vigorous snore I have ever heard, but Beethoven at his best was never sweeter music to my ears, because I knew that such stentorian sounds could never have come from a lady.

As the train moved away we passed a signal light, and by its rays I made out a great mountain of bloated Hindu flesh rising and falling like the restless ocean. How he slept through all the noise I can not tell—certainly I couldn't, all the way back to Agmere where I changed cars for Delhi.

The Agmere station agent was a white man, and after listening to my tale instructed the train guard to let me ride as a "blind" to the capital.

Delhi found me approaching the lowest ebb of my vagabond career, physically, financially, gastronomically, sartorially; and I was glad the darkness hid me as I walked from the station to the old hotel.

Next day—our last together—David "entertained" me. If I ate over well of the three meals he provided I should be pardoned, for I did not know how long they would have to last.

It was hard to believe that David and I were actually parting for good. We had been through such exaltations and degradations together; yet part we must, for he was going west and I east. We had met, tarried, and now must pass on, he to Bombay, I to Calcutta.

Despite the fact that I had been well laundered during my day in Delhi, my equipment, minus a coat, belt and tie, was still far from prepossessing. I fully realized this when three fledgling station guards, seeing me wandering aimlessly about the platform as I waited for the midnight Calcutta express, eyed me suspiciously and finally challenged my right to be out of jail. I retorted over sharply, considering my ticketless condition, and while it relieved me immediately of their insolent inquisitiveness it made for me three good enemies who vowed that if I *were* up to any crimes they would see to it that I got jolly well caught.

At twelve the heavy *train de luxe* roared in and stopped on the other side of a string of dead coaches. For ten minutes the guard watching me did not give me a chance to move. Then, just as the whistle blew, I dived through the string of intervening cars, down into the black ravine between the two trains, through the window of the first compartment that presented itself, and into the washroom, until times were safer. Before the guard could raise an alarm the express rolled away, and soon left Delhi and mine enemies far behind.

By good luck and fast dodging I clung to my train as far as Mogul Serai, reached in the afternoon. Here a tyrannical conductor—one who had ejected David and me twice before for riding ticketless—swooped down with a roar:

"If you get on my train again without a ticket, I'll stop it and put you off if we're in the middle of the Ganges River. The Indian railroads have arrest warrants in store for you all the way from Calcutta to the Khyber."

What was I to do? I had not an anna in my pocket. I had not eaten all day. I *must* get to Calcutta!

As I stood on the platform, utterly despondent and weary of the struggle, I saw the old locomotive detach itself and move off, a new one taking its place. The new engineer was *white* beneath his coal dust.

I climbed up into the cab, and in the fewest possible words pleaded for the assistance of one white man for another. I explained my desperate situation and asked him to take me in his engine to Calcutta.

"Can't, brother, much as I'd like to. I'd be fired."

"I promise to keep under cover in the coal. No one will see me."

After all in India Anglo-Saxons must hang together, or, as Franklin said, "hang separately." Reluctantly he let me stay.

On through the afternoon, on through the night, I stuck to

my promise and remained hidden in the coal tender. Rain (the monsoon had been drowning everything for three weeks) fell in torrents. The coal dust was washed in black streams over me; the engine-smoke poured in black clouds into my face. Hungry, drenched, foul with dirt, I clung to the swaying tender and cursed myself for this madness.

For those fifteen grueling hours all romance and all joy vanished from my *wanderjahr*. I abhorred this ignoble predicament—riding on a cloud of engine-smoke in the endless downpour in order to escape just punishment for having defrauded the railroads. I became desperately homesick, self-contemptuous, miserable—and oh, so hungry. Between clenched teeth I vowed that if I ever got to Calcutta I would cable home to my despairing family and put a stop to this career of suicidal self-denial.

We thundered into the station about seven in the morning. I was so exhausted and stiff I could scarcely descend from the cab. Thankful that few white people were abroad at this early dripping hour to witness my ignominy, I tottered across Howrah bridge, hatless (my topee had been lost from the tender), coatless, beltless, torn, grimy, haggard, shivering from fifteen hours of wet clothes, and dragged myself up to the steps of the American Express Company which was taking care of my mail.

The doors were not yet open. I sat on the stoop, listlessly letting the monsoon wash my blackened face. Presently the porter came to open the office, and started back when I walked in. A passport proved my identity, and that I was the proper claimant of the fat packets of letters that had been accumulating for weeks.

Forgetful of the puddles of sooty water I was leaving behind me, I dropped on to a bench and read and read and read.

There was one registered letter. I opened it curiously. Within I found—a *check*—a check for one hundred and seventy-five dollars!!! I was too stunned to get up and dance the can-can, so just sat and stared at the unexpected, psychologically-timed piece of paper. Perhaps I'd become cross-eyed from coal dust, perhaps my meal-less days had begun to cause hallucinations. No, "Pay to the order of Richard Halliburton" was too indelible for that. The reason why did not concern me. Had it been from Mephistopheles in payment for the sale of my soul I would not have cared two snaps—in fact he could have had Marguerite in the bargain.

As a matter of fact, the check did not come from the Devil but from the editor of the *Commercial Appeal*, the morning paper of Memphis. He had printed seven of my articles on foreign affairs, which resulted in this Spencerian masterpiece. As acceptable as the check, was his request for "as many more articles as I would send."

It was still raining in torrents outside, but as I splashed my way to the Y.M.C.A. I was far above the clouds where the sun was shining, the larks singing, and all was right with the world.

## ❦ XXV. ❧

# Byroads to Bangkok

ITH the prospect of a steady if small income, my inclination toward America vanished like mist before the sun. Not only would the one hundred and seventy-five dollars, economically spent, last another two months, but six more articles sent from Kashmir had no doubt been published since the date of the check, meaning that if the editor continued to be a good sport I would have one hundred and fifty dollars more waiting when I had flung away the present funds.

For five days I reveled in soap and respectability. A native valet helped me bury my khaki shirt and shorts, shined my new boots, pressed my new white cotton clothes, served me my meals at the "Y," and stood waiting with new topee and cane whenever I chose to stir abroad. Accompanied by a very aloof and exclusive hauteur I paid off the social obligations incurred during the two previous visits to Calcutta, and in an effort to counterbalance the savage life led during the past four months, broke all records for tea-drinking during the five days I competed.

When my new capital had shrunk to one hundred and twenty dollars, I awoke to the realization that I was getting nowhere wafting teacups at my friends, and, abruptly terminating the "cookie-pushing," turned my attention to maps, upon which I saw that in my aimless peregrinations I had wandered half-way round the world. It was now as near home eastward as westward so I resolved to return to America via Japan, despite the fact that this move would make me eligible for the dreadful epithet "globe-trotter."

The routes that presented themselves were few indeed, and each one of them worn threadbare by thousands of scrupulously chaperoned tourists. The commonplace, stereotyped highway to Rangoon, Singapore, Batavia and Hongkong must be avoided at any cost. Only one route interested me—by boat up the Irrawaddy, through Burma to Mandalay and Bhamo, thence overland through the Chinese province of Yun-Nan, with a jade caravan to the city of Yun-Nan, and south again to Hanoi by the French railroad into Indo-China. This seemed the most original solution of the problem, and I set about at once making plans for the expedition.

It was first necessary to get to Rangoon. There being no other boats sailing to Burma than the P. and O. passenger liners, I had to reconcile myself to a deck passage, since anything more luxurious seriously menaced my funds.

White clothes and walking-sticks were, to say the least, non-essential for a deck passage, much less for a caravan journey through the wilds of southern China. I exchanged the cotton suit for a sturdy combination of familiar khaki shirt and shorts, and adding a new knapsack to my toothbrush and camera went aboard the steamship *Ellora*.

A tip to the steward assured me three meals a day in the second-class dining-room. Sleeping-quarters, all that was lacking, did not lack long.

Shortly before the ship cast off, a portly Hebrew seized my arm and with enormous cordiality asked if I was going to Rangoon. I admitted that I was. Then followed a series of ingratiating questions in regard to my health, my age, my nationality, that rather puzzled me. Everything was clarified when he led me to a great hamper of Kashmir apples, and asked if I would allow the basket to go as my personal baggage and be delivered to his "vife" in Rangoon, since the prohibitive cost of shipping was nearly fifty cents.

I was loath to assume the new burden, already having sacrificed all but a last claim to decency in an effort to keep clear of baggage entanglements. But just in time my guardian devil whispered evil counsel in my ear: "Take the apples," he hissed. "Apples in India are powerful arguments when one needs a stateroom." I listened to temptation and was lost.

On the second-class deck, where the steward had allowed me to sit, I found a British soldier going back to Mandalay with his wife and two half-grown children. Since he had two cabins I asked if I might put my apples in one of them for safe-keeping. He readily assented. This was followed by an opening of the basket and a generous dispensing of the choice fruit to the son and daughter, and *that* was followed by an invitation to make use of one of the empty bunks in the soldier's stateroom. Thus Adam and Eve and I all betrayed an apple trust. In consequence of our respective crimes, they were dispossessed of their cabin—I was presented with one.

Rangoon is a rather stupid place. For some reason, before landing there I was determined not to like it. Everybody that visits the city always rushes with bated breath and beating heart out to see the famous elephants piling teak. That's because Cook's guide says do it. One may as well, however, as there's nothing else to do in Rangoon except watch Burmese women smoking "whackin' big cheroots," and even that begins to lose its thrill after three or four hours.

No one in Rangoon had ever heard of Yun-Nan. The American consul told me that Mandalay, being nearer the field, would be a better place to investigate. The night train had the same noble system of non-disturbance for first-class passengers found in India, so I rode free. Friends directed me to a missionary who had spent his life in Bhamo, the terminal for the overland route to Hanoi, and this gentleman straightway proceeded to wreck all my hopes:

"It's an extraordinary trip, but you can't go now. Nobody can, during the rains. There are no bridges, of course, and the rivers are too swollen to cross. I doubt if a caravan could start for six weeks."

Not caring to wait that long, I returned dejectedly to Rangoon.

Now what? It seemed that the monsoon season, which was flooding every trail and making impassable every river, would force upon me that dismal fate of becoming a tourist and moving eastward with the herd to Singapore and Hongkong.

In despair I rushed hither and thither, trying to escape. The direct overland route to Bangkok lured me, until I heard that another American had just come across it and was dying in the local hospital as a result. Hearing me say that I would like to reach Bangkok without going all the way round the Malay Peninsula, the manager of the Rangoon Standard Oil office suggested that I might get across the Siamese isthmus, even at this season, by elephant. He had heard of a man several years ago who had gone to Victoria Point, the extreme southern tip of the Burma coast line, (see map inside back cover) had sailed some miles up a river, then crossed over to the railroad on the east shore and by rail reached civilization. This was at the very narrowest place of all, it being not over forty miles from the river-head to the Gulf of Siam. On further investigation I found that this trail did exist, and was occasionally used by natives in the dry season, so, though no season could have been wetter than this, I seized at the straw, ready to try forty miles of anything if it would assure me a more novel adventure than sailing to Singapore on a passenger ship.

I was not in the least unwilling to explore Malay, now that Yun-Nan had been eliminated. After all, if half the stories heard about the peninsula were true, where better could one go in search of what I sought? On a map of Asia, look at the eccentric strip of topography extending snakelike hundreds of miles south of Siam and tipped at the very end with the city of Singapore. Its very shape is intriguing. No wider in places than the Isthmus of Panama, it presents a barrier to navigation similar to the isthmus in pre-canal days, for to get from Bangkok to the opposite side of the peninsula—a distance of only one hundred and fifty miles—one must travel two thousand two hundred miles around the southern end, and if one is on a freight boat take two weeks in doing it.

While the peninsula is only fifty miles wide in one place, along this fifty miles the climax of jungle impenetrability is reached. With one exception this land receives the heaviest rainfall in the world. The rain seems never to stop, the tropical steaming heat never to subside, and in consequence the vegetation reaches a tangle of profusion inconceivable to one who knows only the forests of milder climates. Naturally these jungles make an ideal residence for wild animals. The tigers, the elephants, the great pythons, the crocodiles, the rhinos, the venomous king cobras, the leopards and huge monkeys, that populate our zoos in America and awe the circus crowds, in a great many cases once claimed Malay as their home.

The steamship company at Rangoon informed me that though there was no direct transportation to Victoria Point they ran a boat to the little port of Mergui, which, while not what I wanted, was only two hundred miles away. The agent had an idea it might be possible to cover the intervening distance—just how he was not sure. Being of a trusting and optimistic nature, I bought a deck passage as far as possible.

My ship, the *Adamson*, while not an *Olympic*, did have a nice clean deck, and having found some one's ill-hidden canvas cot, I stretched myself comfortably there. Perhaps it was because Fate already repented the slings and arrows that she had in store for me on the peninsula, that she was so ingratiatingly kind en route. Perhaps it was caprice. Anyway, things were beautifully arranged for me on the *Adamson*. The chief engineer was a soft-hearted, hard-bitten old Scotchman who felt it to be his patriotic duty to keep all the home distilleries producing day and night. He had been working overtime when he looked out of the port-hole of his cabin, and, seeing me reclining on his private cot, made somewhat profane inquiries as to who and what I was. When he learned that I was traveling "*sur le pont,*" and thought Scotland the noblest country on earth, he literally dragged me into his cabin, ordered whisky-sodas for two, and informed me in thick and thundering tones that I was to be his guest on the trip. Who would have declined? The meals and bunk were excellent, but his roaring voice and tyrannical manner were hard to bear, or rather would have been had he not kept me semi-intoxicated myself with his steady streams of whisky-sodas. His chief vice when drunk (which was the only way I ever saw him) was poetry. He quoted Burns *ad nauseam*, and then demanded in bloodthirsty tones if I did not like it. I recklessly and brazenly told him no, whereupon he retorted that I was a doddering idiot. One favorite verse of his—not Burns'—is memorable, not so much because he shouted it at me a hundred times a day, as because its philosophy was burned into my memory on the occasion of a miraculous escape from death I had a few days after leaving the ship:

> For good undone and gifts misspent and resolutions
> vain,
> 'Tis somewhat late to trouble, this I know.
> But I would lead the same life over, if I had to live
> again,
> Though the chances are I'd go where most men go.

Mergui is an ideal place to live—for about three days. It is as beautiful a little town as one can find on a tropical coast, but, oh, so lonely! When the tin and rubber booms were on, it became a place of comparative commercial importance, tin ore being found in great quantities near by and rubber planting being very successful. At the time of my visit, it was the picture of commercial despair. There were scarcely a dozen white men left in the place, and they would have deserted too had not inertia and domestic complications held them back.

These complications, in the form of native wives and half-caste offspring, present one of the gravest problems the white man is having to face in the East. Removed, as he is in Mergui, endless miles from civilization, living in a primeval jungle village where life is cheap and impulses unrestrained by any Ten Commandments, he usually takes the course of least resistance, and, according to our civilized standards, makes a wreck of his life.

This unhappy situation was disclosed to me in a rather unconventional way before I'd been in town two hours. A middle-aged Burmese woman called at my headquarters to pay her respects, and, with the aid of a native interpreter, to make what I thought rather personal inquiries. First she wanted to know if

I had come to live in Mergui, and just to find what motivated her visit I replied, "Perhaps."

"You bring wife?" asked the interpreter.

"What difference does that make?"

"You not bring wife, her daughter make good wife. Can cook. She not cost much to keep."

When I declined and explained that I was only a transient visitor, she requested that in case I *should* stay would I please not forget that she had come to me *first*, and that in consequence I should pass on her daughter before entangling myself with other daughters. This ambitious mother felt it a great honor to have her child mated to a rare and comparatively rich *sahib*, and since I was a white man and therefore going to attach some one's daughter, why not hers?

That same day on passing a makeshift dwelling, a European hallooed from the doorway and invited me to come in and meet one fourth of the white population at one fell swoop. The three men were lounging inside, each the possessor of a brown wife or two and several tan children, all wallowing in what was, for the fathers, a miserable and debased existence. These Merguians were among the great number of foreigners who have attached some one "just to cook and keep house," and now here they were with children—their children, and at the same time unmistakably Burmese children, who could not be taken home to color-intolerant England or America, yet if left in Asia would grow up aloof from their mother's race, despised and ostracized by their father's.

The owner of the house, with arguments that were false and incomplete, tried to defend this beachcomber existence, condemning the futility of ambition, and insisting that he was happy in these surroundings. As he philosophized rather mockingly about duty to self and race, he lay, barefooted and unshaved, stretched out on a wicker deck-chair in the dirty and disheveled living-room. A naked baby or two trotted about the place; two rather pretty, scantily-dressed Burmese girls were in and out. This was home—a home that a once fine and useful Londoner had convinced himself was Utopia.

In a few days a tug-boat, the *Daracotta*, took me on down the coast to Victoria Point. Being the only white passenger aboard, the captain scorned my idea of traveling on deck, especially as there wasn't any deck. He listed me as a guest of the ship and for three days almost free of charge, I traveled as luxuriously as one could travel on the *Daracotta*. I was glad to leave Mergui. The wrecks in its foreign colony haunted me, and upset the equilibrium of my social philosophy. An even worse shock was in store however at Victoria Point, for where the white men at Mergui had wandered from the flock with two native women, those at the next stop were found wandering with four.

As our boat anchored at my port of disembarkation the three white citizens came aboard. One was the police force, one the "Uncrowned King of Lower Burma," so-called because he had a harem rather than because he had any royal attributes, and the third a young Englishman of unexpected culture who, having seen no other white non-official visitor for a year, welcomed me to his private island, where I could reside until plans for the journey on to Bangkok could be completed.

His little empire was well adapted for absolute autocratic government. Four miles long it measured, and two across, from the white sandy beach before his bungalow to the lagoon on the opposite side. He had bought it outright for the wonderful timber that covered it, and had erected a crude sawmill from which he shipped teak and camphor planks to Singapore.

No ancient maharajah was ever more all-powerful than this man. He ruled his natives, about one hundred, with a hand of iron. They were his property to dispose of as he chose, and while he had punished several for leaving the island without his permission he had not decapitated any one to date. He rarely left his bungalow castle. Fruits and coconuts fell into his lap; lemons and limes, pineapples and bananas, grew for the asking. Fish was brought to him daily by the Marine Food Minister, and the Meat Administration supplied him with wild fowl and pig. His only disparity from the life Crusoe led was that he had hot and cold running water in his bathroom, dressed in flannels for dinner, and had a speed launch for trips to the mainland.

Needless to say my visit was so prolonged I began to lose interest in the isthmus expedition, for indeed this was the perfect life. The smooth clean beach was irresistible, and we swam by the hour, sometimes in sunlight, sometimes in moonlight, often in the rain, along the whiteness of the sand before the palace—until one morning we found about six crocodiles sleeping on our favorite bank where they had made their way from the near-by mouth of a river. After that we abandoned the sport, and ignoring the intermittent downpour took to tramping through the jungles, using the swollen streams for paths.

The entire island was a paradise of flowers and vegetation. Enormous teak trees, festooned with lavender-blossoming vines, tangled with rattan creepers, and inhabited by screeching parrots, towered above the semi-solid mass of bamboo, palms, ferns, writhing roots, and the not infrequent snakes the roots resembled.

There were cobras and pythons to be had on the island, if any one wished them. Personally I could do well without, especially after what I saw happen to the half-grown fox-terrier, the island king's only companion other than the dozen Chinese slaves. During my visit, the dog found a cobra creeping into its hole in the roots of a tree not far from our castle. In a flash he had the tail of the snake in his teeth, and pulled it bodily from its retreat. Though the enraged cobra lost no time in giving the poor pup a good biting, nevertheless he came running back to us barking merrily and apparently none the worse from his encounter. In a few minutes he became strangely quiet, and in a quarter of an hour—he was dead.

Except for grief over the loss of his pet, the swiftness of this poison tragedy seemed to have no effect on my host. He was accustomed to the "tooth and claw" of the jungle. On me it made an impression that was deep and disconcerting. In view of future events it seemed that destiny planned it and that this incident was a prologue to the drama on which the curtain was now about to rise.

## ꭗ XXVI. ꭘ

# Great Snakes!

AIN! rain! rain! During two days and nights the monsoon had not let up for as many hours. Yet it was in this flood of water that I had planned to cross the peninsula through practically virgin jungles, without map, compass or interpreter. My plan seemed suicidal; the three white citizens of Victoria Point insisted that it would prove so. To combat their arguments I took advantage of every momentary respite from the downpour to draw their attention to the fact that at last the rain had stopped. Then just as I had screwed my courage to the sticking point, the heavens would open up for a greater bombardment than ever and drown out my resolutions. However, I had come too far now to go back. The railroad to Bangkok was only eighty miles away—Rangoon, six hundred. And so, soundly damning my predicament the while, I declared war on the elements.

The Standard Oil manager had not misinformed me. My host at Victoria Point not only knew of the trans-peninsula trail but also how to reach it. We were at the mouth of the

Pukchan River which, dividing Burma from Siam, runs north-east so that the longer it is followed the closer one gets to the east coast and the shorter is the tramp across. With the island king's assistance I procured two boatmen and a sampan, which in Malasia is nothing more than a big dugout decked with boards, roofed with a low arched mat of palm leaves and propelled by the wind. Provisioned with a dozen bananas, I pushed off in an especially furious rainstorm, followed by the good wishes of the entire white community, and with the aid of sail, oars and tide, in twenty-four hours reached the headwaters of the river at a place called Taplee, on the Siamese side, forty miles from Victoria Point and forty miles from Chumpon, the railroad station on the eastern shore.

The Pukchan River is just what one expects an equatorial watercourse to be, lined with overhanging masses of branches and clogged in the shallow places with forests of prickly palmtrees. Cranes and herons flew overhead or stood knee-deep in the river, waiting philosophically for an indiscreet fish to approach, while at low tide crocodiles could be seen on the mud-banks, as much a part of the landscape as the old drift logs they passed for. Had I possessed a rifle it would have been rare sport, for I was in range during the day of fully a score of the beasts.

My boatmen, having deposited me in this dripping wilderness, sailed home, and I was left in the heart of the peninsula. I found the village chief, and after a long struggle conveyed to him the fact that I wanted to cross to Chumpon.

"It is not safe," he replied, by indicating water up to his neck. Then I pantomimed an elephant. He laughed in derision and shook his head, in turn pantomiming the elephant sinking in mud up to its hubs. Even so, there could be no turning back now, and I determined to go on if it was the last thing I did on earth. After two days of failure, I procured the village idiot as guide for three dollars (about three weeks' wages) who was willing to risk his neck for such a fortune. During the delay I had to spend two nights in the chief's mat-strewn attic, with lizards playing tag over me and the ceaseless monsoon dripping through the straw roof. On the third morning, in the hardest rain that had yet fallen, we set out along a path that made a travesty of the name.

While a century ago there had been a cart-road along the route, several decades past it had been smothered by the jungle and all but obliterated by floods. Elephants made the trip across when the rains relaxed (which I am sure they never do). Indeed it was obvious that several pachyderms had gone over all too recently, for they had left their tracks in the earth—deep, broad, water-filled holes into which we plunged every few yards. I was wearing brogues—but only about half the time, for the mud kept sucking them off, necessitating a short plowing process to recover them. To combat this annoyance, I did not hesitate to tear strips from my one dripping shirt, and bind the shoes to my ankles—a move that accelerated our progress to the rate of almost one mile an hour. From six in the morning till six in the afternoon, my guide and I fought our way yard by yard through that clutching jungle. The rain poured in sheets without ceasing; every gully had become a torrent and every stream a river. We were in mud and water up to our knees at every step, stumbling over roots, tripped by creepers, thrusting aside bamboo, falling, slipping, half-drowned. Most of the rivers we could ford, my guide holding aloft the can of salmon and tin of soda crackers, while I, being the taller, took care of camera and knapsack. Two or three times, however, the water was over our heads, and we had to swim for it, landing on the other side a hundred feet or so below our starting-point and perhaps taking a quarter of an hour to fight our way through and around the bamboo back to the so-called trail. One would have thought we were enduring enough; but no, the leeches crawled upon our half naked bodies from every twig and leaf, sank their insidious painless scissors into our flesh and feasted there unnoticed until a stream of blood indicated their presence. Except for the rain and swims we would have been gory sights indeed.

Enough unpleasant details: Almost unendurable at times as the ordeal was, when I looked beyond these temporary trials, I took a sort of fierce joy in the entire adventure. After all the blinding rain did not hurt me, the immersion of mud would wash off, my cuts and bruises would heal. They were small punishment for the experience I was having.

The Siamese guide fortunately knew the trail, both where it existed and where it did not exist. Realizing this, I followed him with entire faith, and asked no questions as darkness came and he continued to lead me, plunging and sinking, on and on without rest. He knew what he was doing, for just at dark we came upon a small group of jungle dwellings in a clearing. About two dozen natives inhabited these wretched shacks, and all came out to gaze in astonishment at the two bedraggled apparitions that had dropped with the rain from the clouds. Few indeed were the people who passed their doors at this season. Wigwagging with fingers, and by marks on the ground, I learned that we had come twelve miles—twelve miles in twelve hours—and had twenty-eight to do. No doubt I was as strange a sight to them as they were to me, though with my shirt missing and khaki shorts in shreds there was little to choose between us either in attire or, thanks to the mud, in color. The native adults, both men and women, were naked to the waist, with a cloth that bagged to their knees wrapped about their loins. Of course they were barefoot. The women of this group, as is the custom in Siam, had cut their hair to the same length as the men's, and as every one chewed betelnut, which blackened their teeth and befouled their mouths, to look at their heads one could scarcely tell which was man and which woman. The half-dozen children were artistically arrayed in a brass anklet each, with a string of beads modestly added for the girls.

I slept that night on a mat at the head of a long row of these savages. Next to me was the community chief, followed by his favorite wife, secondary wife, brother, brother's wife, grandparents, ordinary citizens, grown children, middle-size-children, tapering on down to the small, smaller and smallest child. Our common bed was an elevated platform two feet above the floor, which in turn was six feet above the flooded and snake-infested ground. Despite the grass mat this bed was very, very hard, but had it been granite I should have slept.

Next morning curry was added to our rice, and not knowing it was almost pure red pepper, I helped myself bountifully. One "chip full" so blistered my mouth I was unable to eat anything else, and in consequence set out for the second day with fuel very low.

The rain had not ceased all night, and at daybreak fell with renewed violence. All morning the wind rose higher and higher, until by noon it was blowing with hurricane force and driving a veritable cloud burst against us. A storm in the mountains, an awesome sight to be sure, is no more spectacular than a storm in the jungle. The roar of the wind rushing through the walls of vegetation was deafening. It was a mighty conflict between the storm and the forest—the wind attacking, the jungle resisting—all in vain, for the storm tore into it, gnashing, raging, lashing the branches against one another, ripping up the underbrush and leaving chaos and havoc in its wake as a warning to other jungles that might defy *its* passage. The army of close-packed bamboo-thickets, held back in reserve, met the onslaught of the storm. Down they went with a piercing crash that made terrible the noise of battle. These great cane trees resounded even above the scream of the wind, as they crashed and split before it with staccato reports that might have been mistaken for the escape of all the wild lightning in the firmament.

The storm, thank heaven, was only a passing one, and by two o'clock had rumbled on east to imperil ships on the China Sea. With it went the rain, to the great joy of us both, for during seventy-two hours it had not ceased as many minutes. While the trail was a worse morass than ever, who cares when there is an occasional promise of sunshine?

Meantime, what about the many animals that I forecast at the outset of this journey? Up to the end of the storm I had not seen or heard any sign of life, not even the smallest lizard or toad, much less tigers and wild elephants. The rain had been so violent nothing had cared to stir about in it. Now, with the first flicker of sunshine there was a resurrection of the jungle. A pair of large grouse flew up under my very nose. From far and near parrots began to screech their relief, monkeys to jabber it and to scamper through the tree-tops just ahead of us. Several small snakes scurried into the thicket as we passed, and a deer ran across the trail ahead.

There is so much material for psychologists in the association of thought and events. How much does thought influence events? How much does fear of danger encourage it, or ignorance of danger discourage? For a day and a half I was completely unconscious of the fact that this isthmus more than any place in the world was the home of the wildest of wild animals and of the largest, most venomous of snakes—and I had seen nothing. Now the deer, the monkeys, the grouse, reminded me of what a zoological garden I was in. From that moment— since I was completely unarmed—I began to be uncomfortable and to feel myself in the presence of all the beasts for which I knew the peninsula was notorious. The creaking flight of four huge black-and-white herons overhead quite startled me with its unexpectedness. I began to anticipate danger, to *look* for it—and as one always can, I found it.

We were approaching a stretch of bottomless mud flanked on each side by knee-high grass. Having seen how the guide, some distance ahead of me, had floundered in the slough, I chose to go through the grass, and as I did so the most dramatic and terrible moment it would be possible to experience fell upon me—or better, coiled about me, for I stepped squarely on top a cobra's nest. In a flash the outraged occupant had wrapped itself around my unprotected ankle, and with its hood expanded not two inches from my shin, glared with diabolical, lidless, indescribably malignant eyes straight into a very ashen countenance.

A dozen things flashed through my mind almost simultaneously: My hopeless position—hours and miles from assistance—the idiot guide's inability to carry or drag me the remaining distance across the swollen streams and morasses—and the dog on the island—in five minutes he was prostrate, in ten minutes he was unconscious, in fifteen minutes—! And so I too would die and remain in the Siamese jungle, having paid the price of indiscretion. There was no fear of death, but utter despair at leaving all that was life. I had no questioning or anxiety about the future, no repentance, no regrets, no supplication. Memory of the *Adamson*'s swashbuckling Scotch engineer came back to me and his shouted defiance of hell: "The deeds undone, the gifts misspent, the resolutions vain, my sins, my mistakes, my guilt—be damned!" And likewise for the past, whether red, black or white, I was not the least concerned. I would lead the same life over if I were ever allowed to live again, though the chances are I'd go a second time where most men go. And all this passed through my mind in no more than a second, as I stood frozen and aghast, staring into those two murderous eyes.

What I did was done mechanically and without order from a paralyzed brain. Thus nature often rescues us from ourselves. In my hand I carried a cane staff, picked up along the route and employed in an absent-minded way. Not ten minutes before I had leaned upon it too heavily and it had split half in two, leaving a sharp splinter-like end. I was still carrying the upper half from force of habit, though it was too short for service. Not knowing too well what was happening, I clutched the broken end of the cane, and summoning all my strength struck at the tender nether side of the cobra's swollen hood. The blow went true, knocked the reptile from my ankle, and gave me a chance to beat a strategic retreat. Once freed from that poisonous embrace I jumped aside, and neither knowing nor caring what happened to the enemy, hurried forward as fast as my very weak knees could carry me in pursuit of the guide, who, during the entire melodrama, had been plodding farther and farther ahead blissfully ignorant of the mortal combat raging behind him.

I did not get very far. The reaction that always follows petrifying fright suddenly seized me. All strength evaporated; my head swam dizzily; my legs gave way, and I crumpled up in a convenient mud-puddle. But, oh, what nice mud it was, what lovely rich brown mud. It oozed through my fingers; I could feel its warmth and stickiness. The rain had begun to fall again. It trickled in gentle rivulets down my prostrate nose—sweet rain—so clean and cool—and the idiot coolie—he was standing over me with a puzzled expression—what a faithful, amicable old boy! Beautiful jungle—beautiful world—beautiful life.

The third day of this desperate struggle was about to close. Becoming impatient at the elusiveness of our destination, I turned aside from our route, and with what little strength I had left, fought my, way up a hillock, the height of which gave me a commanding view of the east. I hoped to find the ocean, our goal, and had it not been visible I should not have had the courage to move another foot—but there it was, not half a mile ahead, and the railroad running close to the shore. The sight of the undiscovered Pacific, after his struggle across the pathless Isthmus of Panama, never gladdened Balboa's eyes more than the sight of the old, old, China Sea, after my struggle across the submurged Isthmus of Siam, delighted mine, nor was Columbus more thrilled at the cry of "Land!" than I at my own cry of "Ocean!" It is said the great admiral at once fell upon his knees in thanksgiving, and I should have done likewise, but as I had been falling on my knees every few yards for the last three days they were too black and blue and battered up to permit the proper sort of prayer.

As a train bore me northward toward Siam's capital and away from the isthmus, I admitted to myself that my interest in Malasia was a thing of the past. All the dreams I had dreamed about the wild peninsula had been realized, though too many of them had proved nightmares. Indeed as the days pass now and the sharp memory of the isthmus' terrors become blunted, I am beginning to think it a very splendid expedition. But even now I should hesitate to recommend the journey, especially in the monsoon season, to rheumatic invalids or to elderly maiden ladies traveling alone; while as for myself glad as I am to have tried it once, the next time I am in Rangoon I think I'll follow the herd of tourists who take the highroad—not the byroad—to Bangkok.

## ✜ XXVII. ✜

# Interlude

*I*T was rather a noisy railroad trip northward from Chumpon. We passed through Bangatore, Bangatang, Bang Peunom, Bang Bang, and finally into the loudest of the bangs, Bangkok.

The American consul and the secretary to the Legation, were both Princeton graduates, and learning that my Alma Mater was theirs they gave me the key of the city. Through them I made the acquaintance of the American minister and his charming wife, and as the protégé of this hospitable family held an open sesame to official society in the capital.

The secretary, being a rather young man, was greatly embarrassed when I first called on him, dressed in my usual shorts. He prayed inwardly that the minister would not come into the office and find him entertaining a khaki-clad vagabond. Of course that's exactly what happened. But to the great relief of the secretary, instead of being treated coldly by our envoy because of my outrageous costume, I was invited to dine that evening at the legation.

A rented coat, a pair of borrowed trousers, a purchased tie, and a few apologies prepared me for the occasion. A personal interview, along with my story of the peninsula crossing (for which I was paid enough to cover all my expenses in Siam) had already appeared in the local English newspaper, and my cobra experience was the talk of the town. Naturally at dinner I was made to recite the adventure in full, and no end of others that had befallen me since leaving America. I was only too ready to tell my tales to the other guests, as I felt it was the best way to distract their attention from the incongruity and inappropriateness of my attire.

That dinner at the legation proved a sort of social "début" in Bangkok. During the ten days that followed I became acquainted with everybody in town but the king.

It was a struggle to put aside this colorful life and return to vagabondage. Yet return I must lest my vagabond stamina become weakened by too long a relapse from the stern rôle I had played for fourteen months and was determined to play till the bitter end.

And so back to its owner went the borrowed trousers, back to the tailor the rented coat. On went a new khaki shirt, on went the shorts. To drain more draughts of life I climbed aboard a French coastal steamer—once more a vagrant, once more a romanticist in pursuit of new sky-lines. Malay horrors were forgotten, Bangkok's hospitality put away. New and wonderful territory lay before me. I was on the threshold of a spectacle that alone made all I had endured worth while; I was soon to become one of those god-favored mortals who had been granted the privilege, granted so few, of looking upon *Angkor*.

For two days and nights the little ex-yacht that plies between Bangkok and Saigon carried me as a deck passenger (a misnomer, as a French merchant invited me to share his first-class cabin) along the coast of Indo-China.

Saigon is the place all visitors to Angkor embark. A Mekong River steamer takes them three hundred and fifty miles inland, almost back to the Siamese border, and that is the way I would have gone had I not learned from an old resident in Bangkok that by disembarking at Kampot on the southern coast of Cambodia and going overland to Pnom Penh on the Mekong I could cut the length of the journey to Angkor almost in half.

Disembarking at the little port, I spent a night on the beach, and next day covered one hundred and forty miles in a motor-bus over magnificent rock roads, through continual alternations of dense jungles and neat villages. This put me in Pnom Penh just in time to meet a steamer from Saigon sailing up the river to Angkor.

Again, in an effort to counterbalance the motor-bus extravagance, I was a "decker," much to the disapproval of an English mother and her grown daughter, the only other white passengers aboard.

At sunset we entered the Great Lake at the far end of which Angkor lay. The lake is navigable only in the wet season, when it fills to a depth sufficient to float big steamers. During the six dry months it shrinks to nothing, becoming a sea of mud with scarcely enough clearance for a sampan dugout in which for four days and nights the resolute tourist must plow his way up the lake bed. Now in early October the water had reached its highest point and all one could see on every side were the tips of inundated forest-trees, through and over which our ship wound its way. Since early morning the wind had been violent, and here in the open water it howled about us with fresh fury. At three A.M., with the rain pouring in torrents the two English ladies and I were awakened and told "*C'est Angkor, ici.*"

"Where?" the three of us asked in weak voices as we looked out into the raging night, and instead of seeing Angkor saw that we were in the middle of a tossing lake with five or six miles of tree-tops to navigate in a ten-foot sampan.

"Oh, out there," the captain replied, waving his hand into the impenetrable void.

The ladies were almost in tears. They had come all the way from Singapore to visit Angkor, and here at its front door were met with a sampan in which they must run the gauntlet of waves and deluged forests, or go the three hundred and fifty miles back to Saigon, empty-handed.

To bolster up my own faltering spirits I encouraged them to take this last leap into the dark and guaranteed to see them ashore safely, though what was back of the guarantee I should like to have known myself.

With our hearts in our mouths, the three of us clambered down the ladder and into the fragile plunging dugout. Crack! The lightning blazed over our heads. Crash! The storm hurled us against the steamer's hull. Boom! Hiss! The waves, in a flood of cold water, almost swept us out of the tiny boat. The daughter screamed between gasps for breath; the mother clung to her, speechless with fright. A fresh swirl of rain, and our ship had disappeared into the wilderness. We had a boatman, but whether he was black, white or green we could not see. No word came from him. In dead and desperate silence he plied the single stern oar, pushed the tree-tops aside, fought our way yard by yard through the dense masses of floating water-plant, unable to find his hand before his face. Whether we were going north or south we did not know; whether this was Charon taking us across a tempestuous Styx into Hades—we did not know that either. It certainly was dark enough.

For nearly two hours, that seemed as many days, this exhausting struggle through the ink and rain and forest-tops lasted. Before the end we had become somewhat accustomed to the onslaught of waves and weather, and concluding that, despite everything, we were going to live, decided to get acquainted.

How easy and natural getting acquainted is in times of danger such as this, when the peril and the cold and wet and wretchedness are being shared by all alike. My companions no longer despised the deck-passenger; I was no longer contemptuous of their contempt. After the first murderous drenching they were extraordinarily composed during these two hours when the weakest elements in their natures would naturally have manifested themselves. They were brave and British through and through, and set me an example for fortitude, rather than I them.

How our boatman ever found his way to the proper point on land is a mystery.

With thanksgiving for our deliverance from the sampan we splashed ashore, to be met by an archaic Ford—unescapable even in these jungle wilds—with its light showing dimly through the rain.

"How far is the bungalow?" I asked the native French-speaking chauffeur, expecting to be told only, a few steps.

"Twenty-five kilometers"—fifteen miles.

And the tourist bureau in Saigon advertised that their river steamers deposited one at "the very gates of Angkor"!

If possible, this part of the journey was worse than the boat-ride, for the road ran alongside a river which, swollen and rushing from torrential rains, had overflowed its banks. Long stretches at a time our path was completely covered with water, and in consequence we could not tell which was road and which river. The chauffeur crept cautiously forward, foot by foot, greatly handicapped by the antiquated lights which went out whenever the engine went dead—which it did every few yards.

As we crawled in sight of the bungalow about eight, half-dead from exhaustion and strain and cold, I saw a curious gray cloud with blossoming towers disappearing into the mist—no, by heaven it was not a cloud. It was *stone*—it was what I had come to see, "the wonder of wonders, the most colossal and perfect monument ever built, the prodigious temple of Angkor."

# ☙ XXVIII. ❧

# The Magic Stones
# of Angkor

*I*N Cairo I met an Englishman who had seen Angkor. He
spoke of it in awesome tones as if it had been a superhuman experience. Again and again in India I heard
the name linked with superlative adjectives relating to its mon-
strous size and exquisite detail, yet always encompassed in
rumor and obscurity. No one there had seen it—everyone said
it was a miracle. Angkor—the murmur of its name grew as I
moved eastward. *Angkor*—tales of its reputed glories were
rumbling in my ears at Bangkok. ANGKOR—the wind and the
jungle and the vast gray cloud of stone roared at me now as I
hurried from the bungalow toward the mile-distant mystery:
"Here is the superlative of industry, here the crown of human
achievement. Here, here, is Angkor, the first wonder of the
world, and the greatest mystery in history."

Jungle, jungle, for mile after mile on every side it smothered the earth, dense, black, consuming—and from out of it,
unheralded and unbelievable, rose the gigantic, the magical
temple with its tier on tier of gray tapestried stone, acres of

226

carving, hundreds of delicately-wrought windows, miles of galleries, great lace towers—all powerful and beautiful and desolate beyond imagination.

The spectacle was so amazing, stumbled on here in the forest, I would have scarcely credited my eyesight had I not been prepared by the fleeting distant glimpse of it snatched over the tree-tops early that morning. To have blundered upon the Pyramids or St. Peter's suffocating in the jungle depths of this wild corner of Asia and utterly deserted but for bats and lizards would not have astonished me more—indeed not nearly so much, for Angkor, built by gods for a fabulous vanished empire, in the might of its dimensions, in artistry, in purity, in magnificence, and above all in preservation, Angkor surpasses anything Greece or Rome or Egypt has ever seen.

Whence came this superhuman monument and the even more extraordinary dead city that surrounds it, both lost for seven hundred years in the impenetrability of an Indo-China wilderness and but recently uncovered to the amazement and admiration of the world? No one knows exactly. Whither departed the Titans that piled these stones together and deluged them with incredibly lavish carvings? No one knows that either. All trace of their beginning, all records of their destruction, have been utterly lost in these merciless jungles.

For lack of a better name, history calls the mysterious race that once dwelt here the Khymers. Conjecture founds their empire in the fourth century and obliterates it in the twelfth. Except for miles and acres of bas-relief pictures of battles and mythology and common life carved on the stones of the six hundred ruined public buildings found in the space once covered by the Khymer capital, we should not know one single thing about this race, whose ability as artists and architects has rarely been approached.

It seems impossible that this masterpiece could have

escaped for so long the attention it is now beginning to enjoy. However, when one sees the flood of vegetation it is buried under, and realizes in what an isolated part of the world it is hidden, one can understand why it remained unknown and unsung while archeological monuments of a far lesser magnitude were being explored, and in picture and story made familiar to the whole world.

As far back as 1857 a Frenchman, urged on by the fabulous legends of an angel-built temple then within the southeast borders of Siam, fought his way through leagues of jungle to the spot, and on his return to civilization told such unbelievable stories of the size and magnificence of the ruins he had seen, obviously erected by a lost race of superbeings, that people laughed at him and thought his deprivations had weakened his brain.

No one laughs to-day at the first superlatives of praise that came from Angkor. To quote one recent archeological writer, it is: "The most amazing archeological site in the world. It stands, and is perhaps destined to stand, the noblest monument raised by man."

All during the latter half of the nineteenth century Angkor the inaccessible was left as it had been left since 1300, at the mercy of the elements and inhabited by wild beasts. In 1907, France, by a "treaty" with Siam, seized a large slice of the latter's eastern forest wilderness that includes the site of the ancient Khymer capital, with its fifteen square miles of magnificent ruins—ruins of palaces, libraries, gates, walls, and Angkor Vat, the mighty temple. Owing to the fact that it was the latest and most ponderously built, it stands to-day in all its original glory, while the other Khymer structures have fallen prey to the gourmand jungle and the assaults of time.

The Siamese, who are believed to have driven the Khymers from Angkor Vat, insist it was built by divinities, because human beings could not have been powerful enough or inspired enough to do it. You may not be inclined to believe this legend from seeing pictures or reading descriptions of Angkor; you may not believe that it took four generations of constant industry to complete, or that kings commandeered and kept occupied five hundred thousand slaves from their sixteen provinces; but when you at last look upon Angkor in reality, you believe *anything*.

The temple is in the form of a pyramid, with five hollow squares each fitting into and above the other. Each corner of the last two terraces is adorned with an elaborate tower completely covered with carvings of seven-headed cobras, medallions, deities, chains of dancers; and reaching higher and higher with each tier until the great supreme tower of lace soars two hundred feet and looks with majestic defiance over the miles of waving, waiting jungle-tops that stretch unbroken on to China.

Alone—for my companions of the night before were still prostrate from our encounter with sampan and Ford—I approached the entrance, along a twelve-hundred-foot stone viaduct, forty feet wide, that led across what was once a lake. Raised well above the bed, balustraded with seven-headed nagas and deeply rutted by the passage of ancient chariot-wheels, this great bridge is a fitting approach to so great a building.

I moved toward the stone mountain with a feeling half of awe and half of wonder, that I, a product of the materialistic, modern age, a vagabond, a pagan, should be granted a sight of this handiwork of the gods. In solitude I climbed the worn steps that led up to the second gallery, and found myself in the midst of the most magical array of stone tapestry on earth. It is this proximity that lends the greatest enchantment to the gigantic temple. From afar Angkor with its ascending rows of colonnaded galleries, its hundreds of elaborately barred windows, its labyrinth of roofs, steps, cupolas, towers, looks more like a mirage than a reality. Only close at hand can one fully appreciate the inconceivable intricacy and beauty of its details and ornaments. The Egyptians might have raised this vast pile of stones in place, but only the Khymers could ever have executed the carvings. Every inch of the wonderfully-wrought structure is covered with finely-chiseled decorations. The splay of each window, the facing of each door, is a masterpiece with an individual design unapproachable for delicacy and grace. Kings and cobras, smiling deities and dancing figures, riot over wall and tower. There is no mechanical ornamentation, but dash and reality to everything. The fancy of the decorator has been given free play, yet more perfect blending of detail could not be conceived. However, I can not do justice to the stones of Angkor—only a Ruskin or a Chateaubriand could, and either would fill many volumes in the task.

Of the many Angkor wonders, the most wonderful is the bas-relief that stretches unbroken for a half-mile around the second terrace. Protected from the weather by a gallery, it has withstood the ravages of time, and is as vivid and fresh to-day as it was seven hundred years ago. One could spend weeks before this great stone picture and not see it all, since there are fully fifty thousand figures chiseled upon it in such inextricable confusion one's head begins to swim from examining them.

One wall, three hundred and fifty feet long, portrays the battle-scene between a Khymer king and his enemies. There are hundreds of fighters in armor with shield and sword, on foot, on horseback, hundreds more in chariots and on elephants, yet not one figure is passive. It *is* a battle. Each army sweeps against the other, and the clash in the center is terrific. Men are piled on one another, struggling in groups, in pairs, with clenched teeth, in agony, in fury, in despair, in triumph;

arrows and spears fly thick and fast; the officers urge on their followers: the trumpeters sound the charge; the horses and elephants rear and tremble with excitement; the dead and dying are piled on the ground to be trampled by succeeding waves. At the rear deep ranks of reenforcements, cheering and hurrying, are marched forward into the slaughter. There is action, action, and carnage and the roar of battle. One's eyes stare at this realism; one's heart beats faster in sympathy with this mortal combat. Yet all this is in stone—cold, silent, colorless stone. Some day the artistic world will recognize the Khymers as the greatest artists that ever lived—though perhaps they never lived. Perhaps they were angels, as the Siamese insist, descended from Heaven to carve this superhuman work.

Their conception of Heaven and Hell takes up another hundred yards. They were none too prolific in their ideas about the rewards of a virtuous life, Heaven being depicted as a pleasant grove of trees filled with peacocks, where the men sat around eating and the women (off in one corner) played with their children. But ah, Hell!—that was different. The pictured purgatory was a museum of all the physical tortures the devil himself could think of. No vagueness about the punishments of evil. Great horned demons drive in their victims, all reduced to skin and bones, and, by rings in their noses, drag them through endless diabolical torments in comparison with which drawing and quartering would be a springtime frolic.

A flight of steps worn almost to a slide leads from terrace to terrace, and into the galleries, through which one could walk all day and never retrace one's steps. They were once the scene of great activity; they are silent now except for the endless screech and whir of a million bats that swarm in the black recesses of this desolate building.

As I walked from tier to tier, from stone picture to stone picture, these repulsive creatures, disturbed by the hollow sound of footsteps, tumbled in swarms about the evil-smelling vaults, execrating me and my intrusion. For seven hundred years, Angkor Vat, has been the private property of the lizards and the monkeys. Who was I to disturb their peace?

For an hour I had seen no human being. All about me was the most gorgeous architecture ever reared, and yet it was a corpse—a corpse that had maintained its complete physical being though unutterably dead. This depressing silence, this ghostly emptiness, this grim ruthless jungle that was waiting at the gates to spring again upon these god-hewn stones and devour them, all made me shiver and want to cry out against the doom that clanked beside me no matter where I turned.

What was that yellow streak—I started—that flitted like an enormous butterfly across a patch of distant sunlight? I hurried to investigate and found a Buddhist priest in his daffodil gown, wandering, even as I, along the endless corridors. He was one of an order that used this prodigious corpse for its monastery. Angkor was built as a temple to Brahma, but local followers of Buddha, like mice in a deserted dwelling, have taken several corners of the pile, and established shrines by setting up battered statues of Buddha and a few miserable candles.

These imperturbable statues, so calm and mysterious, sitting and smiling in the gloom, are startling when one comes upon them unexpectedly. In one courtyard there is a Buddha morgue, where several hundred images have been stored pell-mell. They are discarded and decayed, and yet one of the few gaunt priests that are always prowling about the temple almost obliterated me when I picked up a piece of a broken Buddha from the pile, and used it as a stepladder to reach the roof where I wanted to take photographs.

These ecclesiastics, but for their bright yellow robes, would be lost in the vastness of Angkor. Nevertheless, let the trespasser beware. There is a persistent rumor current among the natives that fabulous treasures are buried in the sealed crypts beneath the central tower, and these obstructed passages are guarded with special zeal by the priests. But if there is any great wealth buried here it is little used by its guardians, for more bedraggled disciples of Buddha I have never seen.

Angkor Vat, after all, is only the greatest and best preserved of a vast array of magnificent sandstone structures once enclosed in the city of Angkor Thom, which in the days of its glory had several million people and was the luxurious capital of a mighty empire. The number and dimensions of the city's ruins are staggering—and, oh, how melancholy, how indescribably desolate! How was it possible for such a race as the Khymers to disappear so absolutely? Did it happen in a day? Was this heavenly city, with its vast population, its armies, its palaces, its might and glory, surprised by its enemies and destroyed over night by the sword? What diabolical wrath was spent upon it! No sooner had the roar of tumbling battlements died away than that insatiable fiend, the jungle, rushed upon the prostrate magnificence and suffocated all but a few of the most indomitable giants.

Of the remaining buildings the Temple of Bayan is in a class of interest by itself. Mutilated, overthrown, the lodgment for a forest of trees and vines, it is still the most original and fantastic temple in the world. Formerly it contained fifty-one towers, each faced near the top of all four sides, with a great carved countenance of Brahma eight feet high. Although many of the faces are lost, a number remain, and the sight of them, looking calmly out to the four quarters of heaven as passive as Sphinxes, is weird and wonderful. The cracks and yawns in the joints of the stones upon which they are carved give each of them a different and contorted expression, some wry, some smiling, some evil. Lianas have crept across the eye of one; lichens and moss have blinded another. They peered at me from the treetops; they pursued me with their scrutiny like a bad conscience, no matter where I tried to escape. Stamped with the wisdom of a thousand years, they seemed to read my puny soul and mock the awe of them that rested there.

Slowly and wonderingly I climbed about these fabulous ruins. The sun set beyond the western jungle-tops, and before I realized that day had gone twilight enveloped me. Every bird became hushed; the faintest breeze seemed to hold its breath. Not even a cricket broke the pall of silence that sank upon this mighty corpse. From the shadows, death and oblivion crept forth to seize the city from the retreating sunshine; ghosts drifted beside me as I moved and dreamed through the gathering darkness. Loneliness—loneliness—in all this stupendous graveyard of man and monument, I stood—the only living human being.

## ～ XXIX. ～

# Dolce-Far-Niente

*a* LAZY haze floated over the ocean, blotting out the horizon and dulling the intensity of the equatorial sunshine. For an hour I had been lying on deck (since the deck as usual was my stateroom) absorbed in an enormous gray cloud that loomed mysteriously out of the fog and seemed to reach a hundred miles into the sky.

"Looks just like a gigantic mountain, doesn't it?" I remarked to the mate, pointing to the curious mass.

"*Looks* like a mountain?" he laughed, "—it *is* a mountain. It's the Peak of Bali."

Bali! A thrill ran through me. At last I was on the threshold of this amazing island, this little paradise in the Dutch East Indies that I had come so far to visit. At Saigon (where I had emerged from the Angkor jungles after a two-day voyage down the Mekong River) I had first heard about its lure—its beautiful people—its brilliant coloring—its unspoiled naturalness. Drifting about the docks, looking for a ship that would take me away—anywhere—I ran across an old tropical tramp who had combed the beaches of New Guinea and Sumatra, and knew every isle and city on which the sun of the equator blazed. *He* had been to Bali, and when he spoke of it, he might have been Adam telling Cain about the Garden of Eden. To him it was the most idyllic spot in the Pacific, chiefly because it was almost the only one not blighted by European culture and American tin cans. He assured me it was a siren isle, enslaving by its beauty and romance every one who looked upon it.

Long before he had completed his Bali panegyrics I had decided to go there—and right away. It occurred to me just before departing that I had not the slightest idea where it was, so I extracted my map of Asia and had the beachcomber show me the tiny emerald all but touching the eastern tip of Java—two thousand miles south and east of Saigon.

By good fortune there was an American freighter about to sail for Surabaya, the Javanese port from which one embarks for Bali, and the consul placed me on it as a deck passenger. The captain, like the dipsomaniac chief engineer of the *Adamson*, was a kind-hearted old piece of salt, and shared with me his meals and his canvas cots so that not for five minutes during the eight days across the equator was it necessary to descend to the deck occupied by the vulgar crew.

By one day only I missed connection for Bali and with nearly two weeks to wait for the next boat decided to get acquainted with Java. From the very outset this "Queen of the Indies" proved a disappointment. Though I managed to see almost every city and temple and volcano of major interest on the island, there was never a romance, never an adventure, because Java with all its gorgeous scenery, bizarre arts and picturesque swarms of natives has not a spark of personality. After Rajputana and the Punjab, the Javanese seemed like so many brown peas with about as much magnetism; after Angkor, the world-famous temple of the Borobudur in the center of the island, that makes all travel writers and archeologists jump up and down, was about as exciting as a red brick Baptist church on a corner lot in Kansas. Java is the most beautiful dumb-bell in the world. Her conventional Dutch overlords have put their own dull and ugly stamp upon a tame and passive race, and the result is painful. There is an atrocious harmlessness about the people, an utter negativity, that makes one want to stick pins into them or start a revolution. Had the boat to Bali not sailed when it did I should certainly have done one or the other.

All expectation, I landed at Boeleleng, the seacoast village on the north side of my island. The Saigon beachcomber was right. Here indeed was a little paradise, a south sea Eden, and the Eves whose beauty he had praised so highly. Erect as Dianas they moved about the streets, no more aware of their half nude bronze bodies than the fat yellow babies that trotted at their heels.

In Bali it is considered brazen and shameless to cover the breasts, and no respectable woman would think of doing so. Considerable trouble was caused recently by a native official, who having been molded by Dutch ethics, felt it immodest for his daughter to dress in the native fashion. In order to clothe her in the conventional Dutch manner and yet protect her from reproach, he commanded that *every* woman should wear a jacket, and all being thus debased no one could condemn his daughter. The new law met with indignant opposition, and except in Boeleleng, where the few foreigners live, has never been enforced.

Long before this island expedition I had learned that the pleasure of travel increases in direct proportion to the decrease of baggage. In consequence I left behind at the Surabaya consulate even my knapsack, bringing only my camera, a toothbrush, razor and soap. The small articles fitted snugly into the big breast pockets sewn on my one shirt and made from the sleeves which I had ripped at the shoulder from that same garment. I knew that to see and "learn" Bali I must walk, and to walk comfortably in such a torrid climate, one must not be burdened with non-essentials such as clothes and self-consciousness. If everybody else undressed properly for the equatorial weather, why shouldn't I? With twenty dollars (all that remained of the one hundred and twenty dollars I had left Calcutta with), a map, a staff, a minimum Malay vocabulary— the *lingua franca* of the Indies—and a light heart, I set forth to explore the island, to follow only my nose, planning to linger where fancy dictated and advance only when the spirit moved.

I knew that the centers of population and interest lay on the south side of the mountain wall, which, running east and west, rose abruptly from the north coast. After a leisurely inspection of care-free, lazy Boeleleng, I headed for the ridge, and had ascended half a mile above the sea when evening fell, and found me standing entranced before the magic of a tropi-cal sunset. The ball of fire was dropping straight through the crater of a sky-scraping volcano in the eastern tip of Java, inflaming the clouds above it and suffusing with amber the ocean, the jungles of palms along the coast, and the terraces of tiny rice-fields which climbed with astonishing agility up the steep slopes to where I stood. That night, for the first time since crossing the Malay Isthmus, I slept on the ground. There was no monsoon to plague me now, no cobras, no flood of water—only forest solitude amid the ferns, and soft caressing wind, and heavy odors of night-blossoms that carried mem-ory back to the garden of the Taj Mahal. I broke an armful of flowered boughs from the hibiscus trees, and, spreading them on the mountainside, slept peacefully upon this green and scarlet bed.

Awake with the sun, I bethought myself of breakfast. That

was easy to procure, as the trail was dotted with little hamlets, at each of which a dozen bananas could be bought for a penny. In place of a morning cup of coffee I secured a green coconut, and boring a hole drank its refreshing milk. This draught was so satisfying that for the month I wandered about the island I never tasted water—and who would have, with this vastly superior substitute always obtainable?

The farther away from the north coast one gets, the more unsophisticated the people become, and the more superfluous they consider clothes. Having descended the ridge, the equatorial palms again made their appearance in dense jungles, and under a great cathedral arch of them the pathway led. At each village my appearance caused more excitement than had been known in months. The vast population of pariah dogs clamorously heralded my approach, and all the villagers ran out to stare as I passed. Every community had its temples, old and crumbling now, yet with all their faded appearance there were traces of chisel virtuosity that indicated the high state of artistic civilization these people of Bali once enjoyed.

The third day I reached Den Pasar, the little metropolis near the southern coast, but finding it less interesting than the wilder aspects of the island, I turned to the east, tramping leisurely through terraces of rice and palm-hidden villages hedged with flaming hibiscus. For food I had coconuts, bananas and mangoes, and for a bed, the ground shaded by a grove of trees beside a stream of fresh cool water, or a spot on the shore beneath the fronded palms that stretched out hungrily toward the blue, blue ocean.

The east coast is entirely too rugged for roads, and is therefore the most aboriginal part of Bali. The beach extends unbroken for forty miles and is the only highway. Here, if anywhere, was Bali primeval—unknown, unsung, unspoiled. The coast is in the form of a semicircle, rotating about the base of the towering Peak of Bali which rises ten thousand feet from the sea and dominates every landscape on the island. With this great mountain always on my left and the indigo ocean always on my right, I spent three weeks idling along the palm-shadowed beach—the most care-free, most romantic weeks I had known since my quest began.

For a few days I lived with a hermit fisherman, sailing forth with him in his miniature outrigger canoe to set his nets. Ocean water was never so clear. One could look down into it for several fathoms and watch the roving schools of brilliant fish.

His living quarters could scarcely have been more Spartan—two poles covered with palm-leaves, braced against a boulder. For myself I matted a bed of fronds and slept on the sand. In Den Pasar I had bought paper and pencil, and when sunburn had put me out of the fishing business, I sprawled on the rocks of a near-by wooded promontory, and let the wind and the waves dictate to me a story for my American newspapers.

Becoming restless again, I moved on up the broad beachway. Fifteen miles brought me at sundown to a little cove where a family of salt collectors had built a very attractive hut of poles and matting in a dense grove of palms. They were bathing as I passed, father, mother, son and daughter, in a freshwater pool close to the house, and being half broiled myself and parched with thirst, I followed their excellent example. They did not know whether to be frightened or amused at my spirit of fraternity, but on hearing my desperate effort to converse in Malay, decided to take it smilingly. The mother rubbed coconut oil on my blistered arms; the half-grown son climbed a tree to secure for me a "fresh drink." Little by little their original timidity wore away, disappearing altogether when I offered the *père* a guilder and invited myself to dine on their frugal meal of rice and fish. The night brought forth as big and round a tropical moon as I ever saw, and a desire to cling to whatever human association I could find, if only to this simple-spirited family; so I remained all night, sleeping on my usual palm bed.

It was a novel sport assisting them next day in raking the salt deposits from the hollow logs they filled with water and left in the hot sun till the moisture evaporated. By the second evening I was quite captivated by this ingenuous household, and decided to pass the time until next boat-sailing on this idyllic spot with my hospitable friends.

I soon found out that surf-swimming was more pleasant than collecting salt, and spent hours each day in the ocean, hurrying for shelter from the sun the moment the protection of the water was lost. The two children, unlike the rest of the Balinese—who are not especially interested in aquatic sports—were marvelous swimmers and having been demoralized by my desertion of the salt business played truant themselves and answered their parents' scolding with shouts and splashing.

Most of all we enjoyed the twilight hour. Then the sea was still and the beach deserted. The boy and girl of our ménage had never before had so strange a companion as this curious white man, a white man who loved the water as they loved it. In consequence darkness always found the three of us still enjoying the cool calm sea. If hunger drove us back to the sand, Taja, the daughter, would fetch a supper from her mother's table. Then these brown children and I, speaking different languages, knowing different worlds, would sit on the beach under the rising moon eating our meal and laughing as merrily as if we were of one race and one mind. Communication of thought soon ceased to hamper us. A common tongue is not vital to understanding when there is congeniality of spirit.

In these romantic hours I forgot the difficulties that had beset me in the search for them. I forgot all previous existence, since in my shell of coconut milk these gentle Balinese had pressed a lotus bloom that dimmed all recollection of the past and deadened the call of the future. We obeyed the behest of Rupert Brooke; we heard "the calling of the moon, and the whispering scents that strayed about the idle warm lagoon." We hastened "down the dark, the flowered way." "Along the whiteness of the sand and in the water's soft caress," we washed our minds "of foolishness."

A week or so after my adoption by the salt collectors, groups of gaily dressed Balinese began to troop past our beach dwelling, all moving in the same direction. By means of gestures I asked Taja where they were going.

"Den Pasar," she replied, and with more gestures she added that her entire family was likewise going and wanted me to accompany them.

"But why?"

In answer Taja danced and sang and grew very excited… some sort of fête or celebration evidently…certainly I'd go.

The next day found the five of us tramping steadily toward Den Pasar. The road was lined with pilgrims like ourselves, all merry and eager over impending events. As we entered the outskirts of the town I heard the jargon of distant native orchestras, and realizing that the great volume of their sound indicated something beyond the ordinary, hurried in the direction, coming soon upon a magnificent procession before which I stood, with Taja beside me, gazing in wonder at the passing flashes of color. Long lines of women draped in vivid hues, marched in single file, on their heads bearing food for a banquet. Great towering floats of tinsel and gilt were carried along by a mob of struggling coolies. The community dancing girls, painted and crowned, acted as festival queens, and were borne aloft in gilded chairs surrounded by a body-guard of cavaliers. The *sine-qua-non* of the procession was the rout of savage monsters and ogres, made of paint and plaster, that roared and pranced through the crowded sidelines, scattering the shrieking spectators and being trailed by all the naked little urchins in Den Pasar. Every few feet a xylophone and cymbal band vigorously executed its three-note music, but they marched so close together nothing could be heard except a terrible din that was deafening. This glittering, hilarious, noisy spectacle wound its way through the village's palmy lanes and on to the temple, there to gorge itself to stupefaction.

Consumed with curiosity I hurried to find the English-speaking Dutch commissioner and to ask him if this Mardi Gras procession was just a circus parade—or what.

"It's a *funeral*," he replied.

Seeing my astonished expression he offered more information.

"I think the greatest spectacle in the Indies is one of these Balinese cremation ceremonies. The more prominent the dead person, of course the more elaborate the funeral. You are very fortunate to be here now—a rajah died a few days ago, and this is going to be the biggest cremation fête they've had for a generation."

And all this hilarity I learned was only the first day of mourning, the actual cremation not taking place till next day.

The beachcomber had been right in saying that the Balinese were a simple people; yet they have their own little vanities, one of the most peculiar of them being a love of mortuary display. When a person dies whose family is not rich enough to afford a triumphant cremation, he is embalmed and buried, and remains buried until a nobleman or plutocrat follows suit. Then amid the trumpeting and parades that distinguish the funeral of a lord, the bourgeois corpses are disinterred, and, attached to the end of the splendid procession, get full benefit of all the music and banqueting and ostentation, none of which their own small wealth could have commanded. Indeed, when a rajah shows signs of approaching death there are no cremations at all for a time as every one postpones the ceremony in the hopes that the rajah will die soon and allow the lesser dead to reap the great honor, and their families the greater glory, of participating in the funeral of a king. Then too, when the gates of Heaven open to receive the nobleman, who knows but that a few spirits of the common clay might not slip in?

In consequence of this custom, there were over a hundred other coffins in the second day's procession, each borne in floats of various sizes all the way from the rajah's ponderous masterpiece of glass and gilt down to the crude small box of coolie's bones.

The coffins presented one of the strangest of the many strange Balinese characteristics, for in place of the conventional oblong box, the corpse was encased in a gaily spotted hobby-bull made of wood and paper, and adorned with horns, glaring teeth and upraised tail. This vicious animal is carried on top the float, which in turn rests on the shoulders of the pall-bearers, and after being placed upon the pyre is burned to ashes along with the enclosed body. I could learn neither the origin nor significance of this custom. It had always been observed—that was all they knew.

The crowds of the second day's cremation festival were even more hilarious than on the first. A circus could not have caused as much excitement as this event. When the towering hearse came into view I saw that it was borne along by a mob of almost naked men, those in front pulling forward, those behind holding back—a conflict that subjected the unwieldy bull to dangerous tilting and inconstant support.

This struggle represented the reluctance of the soul to leave the body. Half the pall-bearers represented the "friends of Heaven," half the "friends of Earth." The "soul" dragged the corpse to the exterminating pyre; the "body" fought against the inevitable, and strained for prolonged earthly residence. The two forces were battling over the coffin as it labored slowly and haltingly toward the flames.

The most astonishing spectacle was yet to follow. When, after a great struggle, the coffin finally reached its goal, the saddle of the rajah's bull was displaced and the corpse itself, tightly encased in bamboo, was lifted out. Then began the climax of the ceremony. Suddenly the "friends of Earth," marshaling their strength for one supreme effort, seized the mummy and with shouting began to carry it away from the very gates of eternity. The "friends of Heaven," taken by surprise, were at first over-powered, but they did not abandon the field, and soon succeeded in halting the escape. The struggle was long in doubt. Scores of fresh recruits rushed to both sides and plunged into the crushing mass of fighting humanity. The corpse was lost in a sea of brown flesh. It was the final desperate rebellion against the torch, and both sides put forth hysterical efforts to assist their cause. The solid acre of sweating, yelling fanatical men were trampling on one another, clawing at the mummy, falling by the wayside, gasping for breath and devoid of the last shred of clothes. The yards of shrouding encasing the corpse became loosened and entangled a score of the fighters. The hundreds of spectators were as excited as the participators. They cheered on the side they favored, or unable to restrain their zeal, rushed to join in. Simultaneously, in a great circle at the edge of the glade, the hundred lesser dead were being consumed by the flames which sent forth great columns of smoke that hung ominously overhead, and mingling together made a solid wall about the mad battle within. The final dramatic touch for this incredible picture was the musical accompaniment, for twenty native orchestras outside the wall, frenzied by the general spirit of abandon, pounded wildly on their xylophones until their rolling notes could be heard even above the crackling of the hundred pyres and the shouts of the multitude. Not until both sides were utterly exhausted was the ill-used corpse dragged back to the pyre.

With Taja I stood wide-eyed on a near-by knoll and looked upon this extraordinary scene. Where on earth could it be equaled—this ruthless combat over the corpse, this swarm of garish colors, this pall of human smoke, this barbaric music, all melting together into one great savage spectacle? A wave of revulsion rushed over me. I saw instead of gentle peaceful children of Holland's island empire, mad savages stripped of their thin veneer of Dutch culture, reveling in brute instincts inherited from cannibal ancestors. To me it was desecration of the dead, the orgy of a pack of ghouls; but I realized that I had seen what so few have seen—Bali the real, the undisguised.

With the music gone, the food consumed, the pyres in ashes, it was amazing how quickly the crowds dispersed. Having five more days to wait before the Java boat sailed, I tramped back with my hospitable friends to our east coast home.

Not until the hour of departure did I fully realize how attached I was to them. Taja insisted on guiding me up the faint and precipitous trail which climbing five thousand feet abruptly from the sea led over the crest of Bateor Mountain and on to Boeleleng. Though it was a trying and dangerous route I knew that the reward of choosing this hardest way was worth the effort, for the beachcomber and the Den Pasar commissioner had both waxed enthusiastic about the astonishing picture one beheld from the summit of this mountain.

Indeed the picture was worth ten times the climb. As the

girl and I neared the top a great blue void opened on the island side and out of the void appeared two steaming volcanoes. We hurried to the summit and there stopped abruptly for below us a sheer drop of fifteen hundred feet yawned, and before us one of the most bewildering landscapes on earth met our eyes.

On one side of the brink where I stood, the ocean a mile below glittered in the sunlight. On the other side a thousand and five hundred feet below, the blue lake of Batoer half filled the enormous crater, the abrupt wall of which is twenty-five miles in circumference and eight miles across. From its center two perfect cones of lava and sulphur emerge, pouring forth smoke, and all too frequently streams of molten rock.

I stood dumbfounded by the sight; it was so unexpected and so awesome. I could discern tiny fishing boats on the blue mirror before me, and a sail out at sea behind. Squeezed between the precipice and the crater-lake a village appeared directly beneath, made of toy houses, while across at the foot of the volcanoes and on a part of the crater floor not covered by water there was another village, all but overwhelmed by a recent eruption.

Taja and I, to rest from our climb, sat on this wild wind-swept crater crest, looking out over the stupendous panorama. Neither of us spoke; words would have been futile. We had reached the brink at mid-morning, but it was well into the afternoon before this child of Bali and I said good-by. I have known happier moments.

Dejected and alone I descended the inside cliff by a zigzag trail, and climbed again to the rim on the far side. Just as twilight came I reached this goal and turned to look back over the gigantic picture. The lake, the dual cones, the granite walls, were symphonies in smoky blue. The great abyss was in heavy darkening shadows, even though the sun yet gilded the distant crest of the majestic Peak of Bali.

I sat in thoughtful mood on the edge of this mighty spectacle. To-morrow I would seek my ship and depart from these hospitable, entertaining shores. I felt deeply grateful to the island for the refreshing weeks of rare happiness it had afforded me. I had found what I had been seeking these many months. I had justified what I wished to believe. I could henceforth challenge the idea that there is no novelty left on earth, and I derived great satisfaction from the thought that if my spirit of romanticism were ever endangered by the materialism and artificiality of the Western world, I could always seek refuge and rejuvenation in this far-off land of the lotus, this Eden, this idyllic little isle, this Bali.

# ☙ XXX. ❧

# The Stowaway

ERE'S a stowaway, Captain. What shall we do with him?"

The skipper, looking at me sternly, heard my case stated by the officers who had found me in hiding. Knowing that he would not turn back the thirty miles to Surabaya for one stowaway, and that even though I were jailed on reaching Singapore, that would be better than being out of jail in Java, I could not repress a smile of triumph as I stood before him.

This smug attitude on my part was disastrous.

"*Drop him with the pilot!*" was the captain's only remark.

Pilot! Holy smoke! I'd forgotten all about that. Hadn't we been sailing three hours?

It had seemed three years. With only thirteen dollars left on my return to Surabaya from Bali, and with a consuming desire to get away from Java and on to China, I had reluctantly taken the only course open to me—stowaway.

A British passenger ship came along just at the right time,

and, in broad daylight, as conspicuously as possible, I went aboard, having first laundered and polished myself in the hope that I would be mistaken for the captain. It worked perfectly. Still pretending I owned the entire navigation company I tried all the first-class stateroom doors, and coming upon one unlocked, walked in to find myself in the quarters of some absent officer.

Before long the ship began to move, and the engines to throb music in my ears. One hour, two hours, three hours, passed; night came, before the door opened and a rather surprised head-steward asked me in suspicious tones please to explain my presence in his room and on the ship.

My explanation was not at all satisfactory, and I was dragged before the merciless captain with the above mentioned results.

Presently, in mid-ocean it seemed, we stopped; a skiff emerged out of the blackness; a rope ladder was dropped overboard, and I was roughly ordered to climb down it behind the pilot. Seated in the gyrating row boat I watched my ship sail on and disappear, followed by all the vociferous vituperations in my vocabulary.

The pilot ship was only a few hundred feet away, and on it I was as welcome as the black plague. I slept in a vacant bunk that night, far out at sea, mad enough and humiliated enough to die; and next morning went aboard an inbound Dutch steamer, returning to that hell-hole, Surabaya.

Next day the steamship *Minerva* (not her name), an American freighter, put into port sailing for Hongkong via Singapore, and before the captain, a grand old man with a magnificent sense of humor, could get ashore, I called on him and brazenly asked for a free ride.

He was so astonished he gave it to me, with qualifications, since such a gift was absolutely *défendu* with the United States

Shipping Board. He said if I could come aboard at midnight he would have the chief officer hide me in the vacant hospital, where I must stay hidden for at least twenty-four hours.

I obeyed his instructions to the letter, and for the twenty-four hours was secretly fed and cared for. Then the chief officer who had been my keeper, "caught" me and in a perfectly feigned rage marched me gulping with "fright" before the blessed old skipper, who, with twinkling eyes, played the rôle of indignation until the entire crew fully expected to see me hung from a yardarm.

When he was sure everybody had overheard this terrible tongue-lashing he took me into his cabin, gave me a cigar and ordered me to smoke it. This was my first offense with cigars, and when I began to turn a bit pale, the old skipper roared with amusement and thrust half a dozen more upon me with the suggestion that I smoke them all and learn how. The moment I got on deck the half-dozen Havanas were fed to the sharks, which no doubt died of apoplexy in short order.

Instead of being given to the cook as a galley-slave, as happens in most stowaway stories, the captain put me to work repairing his broken phonograph, and when I "repaired" it so that the records played backward as well as forward he was so delighted he released me from all work henceforth, except to finish reading *Vanity Fair* for him which he had started and found too dull to complete himself.

The *Minerva* had to tarry forty-eight hours in Singapore, where the captain of course permitted me to slip ashore unnoticed. Straight to the American consulate I went and with little difficulty arranged for a deck passage to Hongkong. The consul asked:

"What ship do you want to go on?"

"The *Minerva*." I replied unblushingly.

This matter being settled I hurried to present a letter of

introduction (sent me in Calcutta and fortunately clung to) from the President of an American rubber company to Mr. X., the local English manager in this rubber metropolis. As at Bangkok I was received along with my khaki shorts and knapsack, into the British-American colony, and for thirty-six hours "had a whirl."

The second evening, having dined at Mr. X's home, I donned one of his dinner coats, etc., and went with a party of his friends to dance at Raffles Hotel. For me it was a very merry party—until in the midst of it I saw the captain of the *Minerva* seated at a side table. He was staring in amazement, unable to believe that the destitute vagabond, the stowaway, whom he had charitably protected and the man in the dinner coat dancing with one of the prettiest women in Singapore, *could* be the same person. For fear he would think me a fraud falsifying my position, I thought it best to show him no recognition. All evening I met his quizzical glances with stony stares.

The ship sailed at two A.M. With not a moment to spare, I hurried to my host's house and changed my clothes for the old rough attire.

The captain, awake to superintend the departure, was on hand when I climbed aboard with proper papers from the consulate.

He snorted with mock indignation at seeing me on his hands again, and greeted me with a torrent of profanity.

"Oh, Captain, Captain," I exclaimed, "that's no way to welcome a legitimate passenger. Your Singapore agent has just sold me a deck ticket on your ship to Hongkong, and here's a letter from the consul authorizing it and requesting your good will."

"Deck passenger!" he roared. "Baaah! What's your game anyway? One minute I see you dressed like a dude gallivantin' around a ballroom floor—and the next minute you come on my ship wearing those confounded Boy-Scout pants and asking for a deck passage."

"Why, Captain," I replied, looking as abused as possible, "I've been eating peanuts in the park all evening."

"Hum! Are you quite sure you didn't eat some of the peanuts at Raffles Hotel?"

"Who, me?—at Raffles? Swell chance!"

"Well, if you weren't there, then I'm damned."

He was considerably more damned than satisfied with the situation. All during the five days' voyage to Hongkong the dear old captain was continually asking me questions in regard to my history and interests—without avail, as I was always very noncommittal. He was never quite sure I *was* the person he had seen at Raffles, yet neither was he sure that I *wasn't* Not until we parted company at our destination did I confess to the dual rôle.

"You're a disgrace to your family," he said savagely, but there was a twinkle in his sharp eyes. "If you'll admit it, I'll give you a box of cigars."

I admitted it, and then went ashore, vainly trying to subdue another one of the gruff old skipper's poisonous Havanas.

# Pirates!

IVE hundred dollars! That was what awaited me in
magazine and newspaper honorariums on reaching
the American Express Company where mail had
been accumulating since I left Calcutta. Five hundred dollars!
Now at last I could travel decently, buy a new outfit and cross
the Pacific in comfort. The very thought of it—the thought of
putting all the strain and destitution behind me and going
home in peace—made me purr with contentment.

"Quitter!" The still small voice at the height of my rejoicing
whispered its contempt into my ears. "Quitter! For seventeen
months you have been a vagabond, and now, just because
you've made a little money, you'd throw over your original
determination and spoil everything at this late hour for a private bath and a derby. The Royal Road to Romance!—all right
so far—but if you start paving it with money, this, Hongkong,
will be the end."

I realized the voice was right and appropriating four hundred dollars to spend on Canton jade and Macao gambling dens, reserved only one hundred dollars for my future travels.

Unless one has fought for a frugal existence during seventeen months, plotting and maneuvering to save a dollar, one can not comprehend the exquisite delights of suddenly having money to fling away as recklessly and whimsically as fancy dictates—and in China too where one has an urge to buy half the things one sees.

Nowhere is this so true as in Canton, especially if one is a jade-lover as I am. For two days I idled and shopped up and down Jade Street, returning to Hongkong proudly bearing two delicately carved bracelets, two pairs of pendant ear-rings and a necklace of fair green spheres that dazzled me every time I looked at them.

But I still had fifteen dollars left out of my surplus funds that must be expended, so I decided to gamble it away at fantan in the Portuguese colony of Macao, thirty-five miles distant on the mainland. Though Macao is only a small unimportant place, the boat service from Hongkong has paid its company well, for the Portuguese not only allow, but encourage, gambling establishments, which each week attract thousands of Chinese players and not a small number of Europeans. Sunday is always the great day at Macao. All the business houses in Hongkong are closed, allowing the employees, with their week's wages in hand, to take advantage of excursion rates and travel in crowds over to the fantan houses.

Choosing a Sunday for my visit I boarded the British steamer, *Sui An*, which, following her unvarying daily schedule, left her berth at Hongkong carrying seventy Europeans and some three hundred Chinese. It was the usual crowd, many of the voyagers being tourists going to Macao more out of curiosity than anything else. At luncheon time we were all very merry, talking of the "systems" by which we planned to make our fortunes. It was well that everybody ate rather heartily just before landing, for it was the last food we were to have for twenty-four hours.

As far back as 1550 the Macao area was the happy hunting-ground for Chinese pirates. (It still is.) In that year, as a reward for temporarily expelling the marauders, the city was ceded by a grateful emperor to the Portuguese who have held possession ever since, waxing rich on the revenues received from the gambling and opium houses. It is a quaint little port—medieval Portuguese in architecture, and Asiatic in population.

This was the place then where our three hundred and seventy passengers disembarked from the *Sui An* and scattered to the various fan-tan casinos with the understanding that we must be on board at five if we wished to return with the ship to Hongkong.

While fan-tan is a simple game, it is at the same time absorbing. One wins as often as one loses, almost, so that it is very fair and very popular. The house might not be able to meet demands were it not for the ten per cent commission it takes out of every dollar won. In place of a wheel spun to determine the winning number, as in roulette, a small pile of copper rings is dumped on the table, and drawn away, four rings at a time, until only four or less are left. This number remaining decides one's fate. The Chinese players stand about the table on the ground floor; the Europeans sit on a balcony above and send their stakes below in a basket. The house is always rich enough to pass around tea and candy gratis, enabling you to get a free meal even if you lose all your money.

Entering a reasonably respectable-looking establishment, I soon got to understand the method of play, and placing my coins at reckless random, won oftener than I lost with beginner's usual good luck. Very soon I began to realize what a valuable two hours had been wasted in wandering among the streets and churches, for these hours would have been worth fully twenty dollars each if more intelligently utilized. As five o'clock approached I was forty-five dollars ahead, and beginning to have visions of going back to America in my private yacht. The all-aboard warning came from the *Sui An.* Just one more play, then I'd rush out and jump on. I placed five dollars on the fourth number—and lost. Had I won that time I would have become a fan-tan fiend and not gone back to Hongkong till next day. But I lost, and suspecting that my streak of good luck had changed, rushed out of the casino, clutching my forty dollars, and on to the *Sui An,* the last passenger aboard. By what slender threads our destiny sometimes hangs! One small brass ring—a little thing—and yet how fateful.

Through the gathering twilight the little ship steamed onward toward Hongkong, her passengers boasting about the sums they had won, or grumbling at what they had lost. Nothing was further from our minds than piracy, yet at the very moment the resurrected spirit of skull and crossbones was ambushed in our track waiting to pounce with glee upon its fat-pursed, helpless victims.

Some ten miles out from Macao, the purser approached two Chinese passengers to ask for their tickets. To his amazement, he received instead a poke in the ribs with a revolver and an order to throw up his hands. The frightened man turned and fled down the passage, followed by wild shots from the high-seamen. This was the signal for a carefully planned assault. Simultaneously, in every part of the boat from saloon to steerage, the passengers found themselves confronted by masked men and leveled guns.

I was seated on the first-class deck trying to console a young English bank clerk who had lost his entire week's wages.

Along with every one else we jumped to our feet at the sound of the uncomfortably close revolver shots. Pandemonium had broken loose. Pirates, pirates, armies of them seemed to have swooped upon the deck from thin air. For an hour after leaving Macao the *Sui An* had been the peace ship itself, then presto!—she swarmed with yelling bandits, and the air sang with bullets. There was nothing magical, however, about the attack, except for the astonishing efficiency with which it was executed. There were sixty brigands in all. A number of them, to assist in deceiving the ship's officers, had boarded Sunday morning at Hongkong, bought round-trip tickets and to all appearances were nothing more than model Chinese gamblers. The remainder of the gang came aboard at Macao and stationed themselves in their allotted places, some first-class, some second-class, some steerage.

With the first shots two of the four Indian armed guards rushed to the scene. From three sides bullets were poured into their bodies before they had a chance to strike a blow in defense of the ship. The two remaining guards were beset by the wolves, and bleeding and unconscious, left for dead on the deck.

From the tangle of rushing, terrified people, a young Chinese girl, obviously the leader of the band, detached herself and ran up the ladder toward the captain's cabin just as the captain himself appeared on deck. She fired point-blank at him, and as he collapsed an accomplice beat in his skull. The girl, losing no time over her first victim, dashed to the cabin of the Chinese purser, who, she knew, kept the keys to the ship's safe. She found him, but not before he had time to secure his own pistol. The girl fired away at her second victim, and missed. He returned the fire, and did not miss. She fell into the arms of her confederates, shot through the shoulder, and while not killed was disabled the rest of the evening.

In ten minutes the *Sui An* was completely at the mercy of

the attackers, the captain was all but dead, the two murdered guards had been pushed overboard, the other two were unconscious, the engineers had been dragged on deck, and the passengers were huddled in corners, driven into cabins or stretched on the floor where they had prostrated themselves to escape the flying bullets.

The initial assault had been directed against the second-class passengers, who, being all Chinese, could be counted on to stampede the ship and make no resistance. But the pirates allotted to the saloon had not been idle. Speechless with astonishment every one of us stood, helpless and humiliated, with our hands as near heaven as we could get them. Personally I was not so frightened but that I could congratulate myself on being present to participate in this little pirate party—even though the price was fifty dollars and my hat and coat and belt and what was left of my pride. Neither could I help being tremendously impressed by the contrast of the ominous, tense quiet prevailing among the Europeans, and the chaos and howls and hysterics coming from the Chinese. The very composure of our group, its moral resistance to this outrageous treatment, began to disconcert our handful of assassins. They made no move to rob us; their eyes betrayed the fact that they were really the more uncomfortable of the two sides. I am inclined to believe an audacious blow, or an act of resistance, from one of us would have routed them completely, and perhaps saved the ship. However, whatever heroics were in our minds were never expressed, for the second-class Chinese, wild-eyed and squealing, began to pour into the saloon and along with them another dozen bandits came to the aid of the wavering first-class pirate contingent. Any resistance now was hopeless, and being ten miles at sea on a boat without wireless, there was no escape.

The systematic, orderly plundering of the *Sui An* now

began. We were crowded pell-mell into a narrow passage leading to the saloon, and as we squeezed through the entrance, one at a time, were thoroughly searched and relieved of whatever valuables we were guilty of possessing.

I would have tried to hide my gambling gains (fortunately the one-hundred-dollar reserve was still safe at Hongkong) in my shoe but the bandits didn't give me a chance to lower my arms. When my turn came they reached into my pocket and drew out the wallet and then seized my wrist-watch that had given such faithful service through all the vicissitudes of this story. They were welcome to the fan-tan money, but the watch they could *not* have. Not stopping to think that I might get a bullet in my ribs for my impetuosity, I suddenly dropped my arms and snatched the beloved old watch from the pirate's hands. I don't know why he didn't resist such impudence. Perhaps it was because the watch was small and battered and rusty, with my name and navy record engraved on the back. Anyway he let me keep it.

The wallet and money were not all I lost. My cap was so becoming to one of the gang he decided to wear it, and taking a liking to my coat and vest bought not three days before in Hongkong, he appropriated these also. The coat removed, my broad leather belt with an intriguing silver buckle, caught his eye, and off that came. I fully expected the trousers to go next—but nothing so immodest happened. In my coat pocket an unopened package of "Camels" was discovered, and my captors had the good grace to offer me the first cigarette and a light before pushing me along to make way for the next victim.

The man following me had only one dollar and twenty cents; they gave it back to him with a shrug. Another pleaded that his elk's tooth watch-fob had tremendous sentimental value; he was allowed to keep it. The plum of the white passengers was an unfortunate American tourist who was carrying around a roll of two hundred dollars. He insisted it was all the money he had in the world, and if it were taken from him he would be destitute—would starve to death in fact. The bandits were so touched by his recital that they gave him twenty dollars of his own money.

Our captors were nothing if not thorough. Suspecting some of us might be hiding or withholding valuables, we were all ordered to our staterooms, there to await a second and more sociable holdup.

From cabin to cabin the pirates went, threatening the passengers with smoking pistols and demanding in bloodthirsty tones the watch or wallet that was known to have escaped the initial search. Nine times out of ten nothing of the sort was known. It was only a ruse, but a very successful one, for those who *had* secreted valuables felt sure their treachery had been discovered, and in terror of their lives handed over their last cent.

Our bandits had a particular liking for European hats and shoes. Having seized all jewels and money, they added insult to injury by ordering their prey to hand over most of their clothes, so that later we stocking-footed and bare-headed passengers saw several pirates disembark tottering under a great tower of hats worn one on top the other, or perspiring under the weight of six overcoats.

Meanwhile the *Sui An* part of the time in utter darkness, was not standing still. In keeping with their faultless plan the brigands stood guard over the engine-room, and removing the rightful quartermasters, forced a passenger to take the wheel and steer to a rendezvous on the mainland. Again they showed sportsmanship, for on disembarking they offered the enslaved passenger one hundred dollars for his services.

Guided by a bright fire on a promontory, we sailed close in to shore, and there were met at once by a number of allied junks, which pulled alongside to receive the forty thousand dollars' worth of loot stripped from the unfortunate ship. When the stacks of hats, bundles of overcoats, silverware, rugs, furniture, dishes, supplies—every removable thing in fact—had been transferred to the junks, the sixty pirates, bearing their wounded queen, followed suit and had the audacity to send long cheers after us as the *Sui An* limped away, boiling with rage and humiliation, toward Hongkong.

It was nearly noon Monday before she crept in to the harbor, to the enormous relief of her owners, for when this ferryboat of long-tested reliability, in calm weather, failed to come home all night from a three-hour voyage, the wildest rumors as to her fate began to fly thick over the city.

As our little ship moved painfully toward her dock I was standing on deck in my shirt-sleeves beside the unfortunate American tourist who had lost most of his two hundred dollars.

"Lord, I'm hungry!" he growled to me.

"Oh, everybody's hungry," I replied unsympathetically. "But it's worth it having such a jolly adventure."

"*Jolly adventure!*" he gasped.

"Why, of course. I've never *had* such a good time."

"Idiot!" he burst out.

"Fossil!" I retorted.

## ∾ XXXII. ⌣

# The Bride of Heaven

RINCETON Court, at Peking, gave me a royal welcome. The first night after my arrival, the six Princeton men—some of them my classmates—who lived in this beautiful old Chinese house and taught in the local Y. M. C. A., gathered around the open fireplace in the living-room to hear my stories of adventure and to examine the trinkets and photographs I had on hand.

"What's this?" one of them asked, picking up a big yellow tusk I had placed on the table.

"That's a tiger's tooth. It's my good-luck talisman. A native in India pulled it out and gave it to me after a hunt I took part in, and insisted that if I'd carry it I'd always meet with good fortune. Ever since I accepted the tooth my fortune's been so *very* good I'm getting a little superstitious. For example, look at the once-in-a-lifetime inaugural I saw in Ladakh, and the just-as-infrequent cremation ceremony in Bali—and the escape from the cobra in Malay—and the *Sui An* pirates, and a dozen other things. Almost every break was in my favor up to

Hongkong, and from Hongkong here—well, it's been just one continual streak of luck. I wasn't disturbed once during my stolen ride to Shanghai with the seamen in the fo'castle of the *President Cleveland.* And on the Yangtze river-boat a family of Danish missionaries annexed me to their party so that I traveled up to Hankow almost free of charge. Then at Hankow one of the Red Cross Relief commissioners persuaded the conductor of the Peking express to let me ride in his first-class compartment the entire thirty-six hours on my third-class ticket."

"—And the very day of your arrival," broke in one of the six, "the Boy Emperor accommodates you with the first imperial wedding Peking has had in a generation. Your luck's disgusting."

This was an exceedingly pleasant surprise. I hadn't even known there *was* an emperor, much less a boy emperor. I supposed China had been a republic since 1912. In answer to somewhat eager questioning my friends told me the history of the young prince and the details of the impending wedding.

Up to 1912 the Forbidden City (the walled and moated district in the heart of Peking) housed what was perhaps the most glittering and extravagant court in the world. But in that year the Chinese, the most passive and indifferent of races, reached the point where they could no longer endure the corruption and decadence of the Manchu régime, and turned upon it with bloodthirsty revenge. Living previously in awe of the very walls of the Forbidden City, the rebels, encouraged by mob strength, broke into the most sacred recesses of the place in search of the baby prince whom the famous empress dowager had appointed to be the successor of the late emperor. Fortunately, the nurse had changed the boy's rich clothes for coarser ones, and smeared his face with dirt, by this ruse saving his life. The republic was established shortly after and the president allowed the child to live on as a state prisoner in one small corner of the palace.

The years passed, and the little boy, supported lavishly by the government, reached his seventeenth birthday. On this occasion the guardians of his imperial highness chose for him a wife, as is the custom, and, after affiancing the pair, informed them of the good news. Personal choice in such a matter is considered nonsense. Before I left Peking I saw a Y.M.C.A. debate advertised: "Should Free Love Become a Chinese Institution?" By "free love" the debaters meant the right to choose a wife personally instead of by deputy.

This wedding between the young emperor and his fifteen-year-old princess fiancée had at last come to pass. Even as my friends at Princeton Court told me about it, a great nuptial procession was forming before the bride's house.

At *four in the morning* this gorgeous spectacle moved through the moonlit streets of Peking, en route to the prison-palace. The entire city was awake, and people thronged the line of march. The usual public display of wedding gifts was missing. This had taken place in the afternoon when bearers, under guard, transferred the priceless collection ceremoniously through the streets from the bride's house to the palace. But there were more than enough added features to make up for this lack. Richly dressed Mandarins in embroidered robes and feather trimmed hats, led the cortège. A forest of pennants blazed and fluttered past...gold dragons on black silk, blue dragons on gold silk; and swaying lanterns, and gilded kiosques containing the bride's ceremonial robes, and princes on horseback surrounded by their colorful retinues. There was more than enough music. Last of all came the bride's sedan hung with yellow brocade, roofed with a great gold dragon, and borne along by sixteen noblemen.

I followed close behind the shrouded chair, and wondered about the state of mind of the little girl inside. Headed straight for prison, she was on the point of surrendering forever the freedom she had hitherto enjoyed. Educated and refined above this barbaric procession, she must have cringed from its savagery. Fifteen years old! Married to a boy she had never seen, distrusted and disliked by the republic, she would live always in danger from its suspicious partisans. This was the veil for her, a farewell to the world.

The procession wound its way to the "Gate of Propitious Destiny," one of the entrances to the palace, and halted before it. Torches flared. There was subdued confusion and whispers. Mandarins and court officials hurried back and forth. Slowly, darkly, the great gates swung open—I could look inside the courtyard and see the blazing avenue of lamps down which the procession would move up to the throne room where the emperor waited. Into the glitter and glamour of this "Great Within" the trembling little girl, hidden in her flowered box, was carried. Then as I watched, the gates boomed shut and the princess became an empress.

Before I left Peking, the young couple, half-suffocated by their retainers and servants, had settled down to married life in the imperial prison. The groom continued with his schooling under the personal direction of a well-known English scholar, who acts not only as a tutor, but as guardian, adviser and companion. Realizing that his pupil was sadly in need of exercise, the tutor prevailed upon the authorities about the time of the wedding to procure a saddle horse for him. Instead of getting an energetic animal as was desired, the Chinese officials scoured the country for the fattest, whitest, gentlest, sleekest pony that could be found. Into the diminutive courtyard of the boy's prison the meek-spirited little horse was brought, and having been lifted into a cushioned saddle on the pony's broad back, the youthful rider was led, with two gigantic groomsmen clinging to the white silk bridle, solemnly round and round the court. This was the imperial exercise.

Not to be outdone by the emperor with his tutor, the little queen had a tutoress, the daughter of an American missionary, who taught her the speech, modes and manners of the West. One day, when secluded in her own apartment the empress and the American girl exchanged costumes, each finding naive pleasure in looking as much like the other as possible. The empress was satisfied with everything about her new appearance except her finger-nails. They were not pink and glossy as were her friend's. So next day the tutoress brought along scissors and files and gave the Bride of Heaven a manicure—a simple caprice that transformed for a day the poor little Manchu prisoner into the happiest child in China.

I would have given much to have had the privilege of meeting this story-book princess, but the opportunity never came. There was so much that was romantic in her situation, and so much that was pathetic. Her isolation, her imprisonment, preyed upon my mind until my visit in Peking was almost ruined. In fact she appealed so to my sympathy I half-way fell in love with her. Without confessing to my Princeton Court friends that I entertained such impious sentiments for the emperor's wife, I spent one entire day composing a sonnet to this celestial child, and when the poem had been carefully copied on lavender paper I wrapped it about my magical tiger's tooth, and, with a prayer that it would reach the little lady, mailed the packet to "The Empress of China, Imperial Palace, Peking."

The talisman has not served her, I fear, as it served me. Not long after my departure from the capital, evil days descended upon the court. Revolution and anarchy swept over China. Once more rebels profaned the Forbidden City, and the white-faced little girl, along with her unhappy young consort, were driven out even from their prison. Their art treasures, their embroideries, their silks and jewels, were left behind to be stolen and scattered and destroyed. Homeless, friendless, throneless, the last of the Manchus have sought protection, it is reported, in a foreign land.

Naturally, because of these misfortunes, I feel certain that the tiger's tooth really never reached the empress, for if it had I firmly believe she would be empress still, leaning out the window of her silk-hung apartment, and waving a magnificently manicured hand at her imperial husband riding on his milk-fed pony below her in the courtyard.

## ∽ XXXIII. ∾

# Veni Vidi Bolsheviki

TWENTY days of respectability slipped by at Princeton Court—twenty happy, full, care-free, December days. I would *never* have left Peking had I not solemnly promised my family on departure from America in July that if they would sanction my descent into hobohemia I would be back home for the second Christmas. While indiscretions and blind wanderlust had wrecked these good intentions, I still felt duty-bound to return as soon after Christmas as possible, and so at the height of the Peking visit I extracted my threadbare map of Asia and studied it for hours.

Whither now? Japan, certainly, was too close and too potentially romantic to be slighted. It would be nothing sort of disgraceful to reach the Far East and not become acquainted with Fujiyama. This mountain was as important as the Matterhorn or the Taj Mahal. No, the question was not where, but how.

The least commonplace of the routes, in fact, the forbidden, abandoned route for tourists, was through northern

Manchuria to Harbin, thence to Vladivostok by the Trans-Siberian and across the Japanese Sea. With my tiger's tooth no longer protecting me, with an arctic winter at hand, with a Chinese bandit army in control of one-half the railroad and the officious Bolsheviks the other, only a determined seeker after novelty would have cared to travel this route. Its disadvantages were so numerous, the possibility of being delayed and harassed so great, my enthusiasm was only half-hearted when I began to make practical investigation. However, when the American and Bolshevik authorities refused point-blank to give me a passport, my ardor for Siberia—heretofore a very negligible quantity—burst forth in a holy flame, and with a determination fired by hatred of this injustice I vowed that now I *would* go, and defied all the officials in Asia to stop me. Thus for once my congenital perverseness stood me in good stead.

There was an even better reason than this for me to visit Vladivostok. On reaching Peking from the tropics it was my good fortune to be known to a Mr. S——, a permanent director in the Peking Y. M. C. A. Totally unequipped for severely cold weather, I was suffering from the north-China winter, when this accommodating friend—taking pity on my pirate-depleted wardrobe, came to the rescue and offered to provide me with one of his superfluous fur-lined overcoats if I really intended going to Vladivostok. That was the last straw. Passport or no passport, I *had* to go now or freeze to death.

From Peking to Mukden, one goes northeast for twenty-four hours. At the time of my journey Chang Tso-lin's bandit army had control of the railroad, and his cutthroat soldiers swarmed along the tracks all the way. On my train, however, nothing happened more exciting than having a hundred of these military brigands commandeer the dining-car, in which, having bought a third-class ticket, I was forced to take refuge myself during the entire journey.

From Mukden it is twenty hours straight north to Harbin. I was quite unprepared on leaving the train to find big blond people in shaggy fur hats, high boots, horsehide coats and fierce enveloping beards that dripped with icicles. Had I been a child I should have exclaimed aloud, "Oh, Russians!" It was like an unexpected meeting with bears.

Most of these Russians were anti-Bolshevik refugees who had settled in this miniature Moscow after the revolution. Though they were nearly all of the aristocracy and "intelligentsia," and though they had been residents in Manchuria several years, most of them were still having a bitterly hard struggle to live and were willing to accept any form of work. My hostess in Harbin was being instructed in Russian by a princess; our water was brought to the house by an ex-general in the czar's army; the janitor at the Y. M. C. A. had once been the lord of a ten thousand-acre estate. Hounded, despoiled, in rags, though they were, these unfortunate aristocrats were still gentlefolk, still holding high their heads, despising their base-born persecutors and their miserable betrayers.

The Bolsheviks did at least one good thing. They modernized the calendar, and by advancing it ten days made it coincide with that of other Western countries. Consequently in non-Bolshevik Harbin, the church Christmas comes three days after our New Year's instead of seven days before. Just the same there were special services on the evening of December twenty-fourth, in the typical bulgy-domed Russian church, with an Arctic blizzard outside sweeping and whistling about its spires.

What a contrast to the Christmas Eve of the previous year! Then I had been in sunny Spain under the shadow of the Alhambra, attending services in the ancient Granada cathedral with swarthy sun-loving Andalusians making up the congregation. It was balmy and radiant, with a languid breeze from the Mediterranean softening the atmosphere. People without top-coats promenaded gaily along the boulevards en route to church. Twenty thousand miles from there to Harbin, from languor to exhilaration, from orange blossoms to frigidity, from Spain to Siberia! After a year's peregrination I again go to church on Christmas Eve. Here the swirl from the tundras pierced to the marrow, as, wrapped in my fur coat, I fought my way toward the jangling chimes.

It was a tremendous relief to be inside, safe from the ravages of the howling blizzard. The building was faintly lighted, and decorated with images and pictures symbolic of the Greek Orthodox faith.

With a rush of icy wind and a flurry of snow, newcomers entered stamping the white flakes from their great boots, beating the circulation back into their frost-nipped faces, knocking away the icicles that hung in clusters from their ferocious beards and matted hair. With few exceptions, each person made a regular circuit of the icons, touching his lips to the feet of one saint's portrait, crossing himself and muttering some rigmarole before another, kneeling before a third and touching his forehead to the ground. Ugly and raw though the church was, it had something the mightiest cathedral might envy—a Russian choir.

To me there is sheer magic in Russian music. With all its volume and vigor it has the depth of sympathy and the height of sincerity. When the thirty voices began to sing Russian hymns without accompaniment to the bell-like sopranos and the full melodious bassos, the standing worshipers seemed transported into another world where there were no bitter cold, no hunger and no Bolsheviks. Outside the blizzard kept up its accompanying chant—whirr—whirr—whirr! The candles flicked perilously as the draughts crept in beneath window and door. But the song soared on above everything, if strange in word, undoubtedly a doxology in spirit:

> Praise God from whom all blessings flow,
> Praise Him all creatures here below—

Whee—whee—swirl—swirl—the windstorm was singing its own Te Deum—

> Praise Him above, ye heavenly host
> Praise Father, Son and Holy Ghost—

Whirr—whirr—a rattling of windows—a trembling of walls as the blast from the frozen north lashed at the little church, only to be met defiantly by a woman's voice, singing as clear and high as the wind, and by a bass who in dropping to his deepest tone found the sympathetic vibration of the building itself, and with powerful resonance shook it back at the blizzard.

While in Harbin, I was frequently a guest at the home of the family of a refugee Russian nobleman who, having been a director of the old czarist railroad system, had no difficulty in finding a lucrative position with the Chinese Eastern Railroad running south toward Mukden. Though he then had the most palatial home in town, it was nothing compared to the pictures of the regal estate his family once possessed in European Russia. "It's been a terrific drop from that to this," said the mother of the household in perfect English, "but we were fortunate to escape with our lives and enough valuables to enable us to get away. Those dreadful Bolsheviks seized everything we left behind, and burned what they could not remove."

That was the signal for a general denunciation from everybody of the Soviet. They were bandits, murderers, traitors and worse. The czar's régime, almost forgotten about by most people, was praised as blindly as the Bolsheviks were damned, which made me a bit suspicious that their arguments were more personal than logical. Demitri, the twenty-year-old son, chafed more than any one at their fall. His eyes would sparkle with hatred of their despoilers when he talked of them, and his vows never to relax this hatred were terrible to hear.

Demitri's experiences in Russia had made him absolutely callous to the blood and brutality he saw daily here in Manchuria. With the utmost nonchalance he told me about the decapitation of six Chinese bandits, locally called Hung Hutzers which he had witnessed some weeks before my arrival:

"Head choppings in Harbin are a form of public entertainment. Everybody goes. There must have been five hundred people watching those six Chinks get their heads cut off. Two trumpeters marched through the streets announcing the performance, and behind them was driven a cart to which the poor devils were chained. This procession trumpeted and clanked its way out to an old wall beyond the city limits where the six Hung Hutzers, half-frozen from cold, were made to kneel, about six feet apart, with their hands tied behind them and their necks close to the ground. You should have seen the executioner! He was the worst-looking villain of all. He motioned to us to stand back, but we didn't; we were too curious. We paid for it though, because when the first blow came, and the head dropped on the ground, the front line got splashed by the spurting blood. You should have seen me jump then. I had to go to a tea-party afterward, and didn't want to get my clothes soiled. We didn't push so close after that. The executioner might have been cutting weeds for all the emotion *he* showed. He just wiped off his sword and walked over to the second fellow. Swish—crunch—thud!" Demitri gave a graphic demonstration with his arms how it was all done.

"The fourth bandit certainly had nerve. He turned around

and watched the third man lose his head. That seemed to fluster the executioner—anyway he missed his blow, and had to strike three or four times—and with the fourth man seeing it all. Those Hung Hutzers are a funny lot. This one no doubt had murdered twenty people. He didn't mind dying—but to be hacked by an ill-aimed sword—that made even him cringe. It certainly was a bloody business."

"Demitri!" I exclaimed. "And you stood there watching all this, and it didn't make you sick?" I was a bit pale merely from listening to his realistic description.

"Oh, it did a little the first time. I saw so many, though, I got bored after a while. They got only what they deserve. There were six less Hung Hutzers after that big party. That left only fifty millions."

Meanwhile I had struck an immovable wall in the Bolshevik passport bureau. The authorities did not know whether or not it was according to rules to let visé-less Americans pass. At least, they thought, here is an opportunity to harass an American into persuading his recalcitrant government to recognize them; or, at worst, by being obdurate, they may get an official request from the consul, and that in itself is some recognition. So they informed me they could do nothing without his sanction and appeal. This the consul refused to give. Neither side would budge, and I was in as much of a dilemma as I was in Peking.

In this crisis, my guardian angel came promptly to my aid, in the disguise of a young English resident of Harbin. This man was on friendly terms with the Bolsheviks, and on hearing of my predicament assured me he could disentangle it. Following his instructions I bought a fresh package of cigarettes, and in his company, we braved the bureau once more, calling upon the chief official himself. My companion slapped the Bolshevik on the back, thrust a cigarette upon him, shoved my application blank under his nose, pointed to the dotted line and said "Sign here!" The trick was done in ten seconds. Grasping my passport I walked out of the building in a daze, hurried to the station, boarded a Trans-Siberian train, and rolled away across the frozen plains toward Vladivostok.

As usual I bought only a third-class ticket, and, not knowing a single word of Russian, being in a suspicious and inhospitable country, and having been absolutely excommunicated by the American consuls in Peking and Harbin (whose parting shot had been that they jolly well hoped I *would* land in prison as a warning to other reckless Americans), I felt it the better part of valor to remain—for the first time of the many times I had bought third-class tickets—in my third-class compartment without trying to bribe the conductor, or ride in the dining-car, or the engine, or Trotsky's private Pullman. This virtuous behavior was especially difficult since all the de luxe sleeping-cars were empty.

At the border line between Manchuria and Siberia, the passport officials were suspicious of my visé, and fired innumerable questions at me in Russian, none of which I understood. Likewise I resolutely refused to understand French, German or Chinese, and as the English-speaking inspector was not present they threw up their hands in despair and let me pass.

My first taste of real Bolshevism came the moment we reached the Vladivostok station, for on the next track stood a long line of ramshackle box cars packed with miserable-looking men and women. This was a train of political enemies being sent back into European Russia across seven thousand miles of bitterly cold tundras. Such a trip would take four weeks and result in the death of some of the passengers, but death!—what's that to the Bolsheviks?

The American "Y" director, on learning of my presence in town, invited me to reside with him and his wife, a proposal I gladly accepted. Before I had been with them twelve hours, we were awakened at two o'clock in the morning by the sound of soldiers marching into our court. More than apprehensive, I rushed with my host to the dining-room window and looked from our second story window down upon eight soldiers and two officials. I felt sure they had come for me and began to recall the American consuls' renunciation at Peking and Harbin. I could not appeal to them to liberate me from a Siberian dungeon. Perhaps I'd be deported to Moscow on one of those terrible trains. Perhaps I'd be shot without a trial, or merely disappear. Well, anyway, it would be an interesting adventure.

The two officials stamped noisily up-stairs, and halted before our apartment. In the suspense the "Y" director and I ceased to breathe. They knocked at the door, and as my host went to meet the ogres I turned tragically to the window and looked out for one last time upon the moon-flooded city and the glittering frozen harbor and the arctic stars. All this I must leave, the freedom of the sea and the winds, the law which for months I had been unto myself. They evidently thought I was a spy. I would be cross-examined and commanded to acknowledge the Red flag. A thousand deaths first! Never would I bow to anarchy! Never!

Meanwhile the Bolsheviks had been received. I heard conversation in Russian, and expecting them to arrest me at once began to register my most martyr-like expression.

But the blow never fell. The officials had the wrong apartment. The soldiers went on up-stairs, and in a few minutes came down with a Russian my American friends scarcely knew. In the frosty radiance of the moon we watched him led away in the direction of the infamous police bureau. He was never heard of again.

And then I went back to bed, disappointed and disgusted with the Bolsheviks.

Vladivostok, her trade obliterated, her streets thronged with refugees, her social order still in chaos, was half starved, and, in late December, with no fuel, half frozen. The only source of income for most of the gentry in town was the pawning of their personal property at absurd prices to shop-keepers in the market. This great bartering place was the one animated part of the city, for there all day long the buyers and sellers thronged to and fro, as picturesque a sight as one could find in a white community. Everybody, though poor and ragged, was wrapped in shaggy furs and topped with enormous Cossack hats. Russian peasants from the plains, hungry Russian students, Russian beachcombers, soldiers, exiles, criminals, riffraff of every color and description. One morning while I was wandering about the market a typical tatterdemalion vender greeted me in perfect American. Familiar speech coming from one of these human bears surprised and interested me. He proved to be a deserter from the American expeditionary forces in Siberia, who, not daring to return home, was earning a meager living selling Red Cross supplies he had stolen from that organization.

New Year's Day was approaching, and with it the grand patriotic mass-meeting of the more ardent Bolsheviks. The town was hung with red flags and plastered with red posters advertising the event.

On the night of December thirty-first, I had an early supper in order to get a seat at the mass-meeting, and pushed out into a blizzard that had been brewing all day. It seemed as if the entire city was moving in the same direction. I found the auditorium seething with laboring people, dock workers, mechanics, their wives and children. Crimson blazed about the walls and stage; crimson flags draped themselves over balcony and chandelier.

At ten the program began—Bolshevik songs and music,

Bolshevik moving-pictures showing the Red soldiers entering Vladivostok. As the time passed, so did the vodka, and as the temperature inside the building rose with excitement, outside it was dropping with incredible rapidity far below the zero mark. About eleven, the popular Bolshevik leaders began to harangue the already feverish audience. At a quarter to twelve the trump card was played. The commanding general of the local armies, a young, dominant, dignified figure, mounted the platform from his seat among the "people," and with a fire and power such as I have rarely seen on any platform hurled defiance at their enemies and courage and glory at their cause. At one minute of twelve he reached his sensational climax, and stretching his arms out to the fifty-piece brass band stationed in the balcony at the stroke of midnight shouted, *Internationale*.

There was a crash of music and the strains of this stirring song leaped to the rafters. The people were overwhelmed with emotion by the dramatic effect of the perfectly timed trumpets. Some cheered, some wept, the rest of the two thousand stood on their chairs and waving diminutive red flags joined in the music:

> Arise, ye members of starvation!
>> Arise, ye wretched of the earth!
> For justice thunders condemnation,
>> A better world's in birth.
> No more tradition's chains shall bind us,
>> Arise, ye slaves, no more in thrall!
> The earth shall rise on new foundations,
>> We have been naught, we shall be all!

I left the building in a daze, as emphatically anti-Bolshevik in sentiment as ever, but deeply impressed by the faith of the party's constituents in the righteousness and justice of their cause.

## ∾ XXXIV. ᵕ

# Welcome to Japan

THE New Year's Day blizzard played havoc with local
shipping. The one boat from Japan, on her weekly
journey to Vladivostok, had become so heavily encased
in ice half-way across the Japanese Sea, her captain had been
forced to turn back, and in consequence of her failure to
appear after five days the rumor spread that she had sunk. Just
as I was resigning myself to retracing the long desolate journey
back to Harbin and Mukden as the only other way of reaching
Japan, the diminutive steamer, battered and broken, limped
into port behind an ice-breaker, resembling an iceberg rather
than a ship.

Fortunately, I had begun to negotiate with the Bolshevik
and Japanese authorities for my release from Vladivostok on
the very first day of my arrival there. Yet after two weeks my
passport was not in order—and sailing-time was at hand. In
this unhappy situation the American and British consuls came
to the rescue with an inspired idea—they would make me an

official courier, and thus at one swoop circumvent the passport nuisance all transients had to endure.

As I had dined at both consulates and had come to know both consuls in a very friendly way, they had concluded that despite my temporary vagabond career I was a perfectly safe person with whom to entrust official mail destined for Yokohama. Each of them gave me special passports, and a fifty-pound sealed mail-pouch. I was impressed with the fact that I must not let the sacks out of my sight day or night, since they contained diplomatic correspondence of the utmost value.

Both consuls had presupposed, naturally, that I would book first-class passage, there being only first and steerage; nor did I disillusion them. But I had only twenty-five dollars, and while the American mail at Yokohama might contain new capital—again it might not. It was injudicious to expend my entire fortune on a two-day voyage across the Japanese Sea, so I stood on the first-class deck until my friends were out of sight, and then, dragging the mail-pouches behind me, descended into the depths of the ship.

At first it was so dark I could see nothing—only smell the proximity of innumerable Japanese. Gradually the hold became clearer, and I saw row after row, tier after tier, of Japs all lying side by side on hard uncompartmented bunks, all smoking, all expectorating, all eating. Instantly, for the first and only time in my life, I became seasick.

The moment we reached open water the sea, still tossing furiously from the recent storms, began its onslaught. We rolled and dived and stood on end. All the three hundred other steerage passengers followed my bad example and became sick en masse. There were half a dozen crated dogs among us and they suffered from *mal de mer* more than the other animals, groaning and whining pitifully, and shrinking as far as possible from the plate of bones the steward thoughtfully placed under their noses. In a few hours our hold became so foul, asphyxiation would have overcome me had I not resolved to risk a breath of air on deck.

Still dragging my ton of mail, I climbed the gyrating ladder and emerged through the trap-door of the hatchway. Everything was buried under ice. Spray and screaming wind struck me in the face, Boom—hiss! The ship dived and an enormous flood of water roaring over the gunwales half drowned and completely drenched me. Roused from steerage-stupor by the ice-water bath, I clambered up the steep ice-caked steps to the promenade deck, and, accompanied by vicious gusts of wind, plunged into the first-class saloon. Not a single person was to be seen. There was only one first-class passenger, a Norwegian sea-captain, and even he had sought refuge in his cabin. Having known him in Vladivostok I did not hesitate to seek him out and ask for dry clothes, as my entire wardrobe was soaked when the waves struck me on deck. His heart being as big as his girth (he weighed all of two hundred and fifty pounds), he promptly had me use his cabin as a dressing-room in which to change to an outfit of his, which, while ample enough for two of me, was most acceptable nevertheless. All afternoon I remained in his cabin, and being very willing to abstain from supper in the steerage cesspool, continued to stay all night, using a hard, lumpy mail sack for a pillow.

Next morning the struggle with the Japanese purser began. With smiles and smirks he courteously but firmly demanded that I either pay for first-class transportation or vacate. Just as courteously, just as firmly, and with just as many smiles and smirks, I refused to do either. He intimated that unless I met his commands I would have to face the consequences with the immigration authorities at Tsuruga, where we landed. I still refused to move, feeling that no matter how bad the punishment might be in Japan it couldn't be nearly so bad as enduring another twenty-four hours with three hundred poisonous Japs in the hold. The kindly Norwegian kept me supplied with fruit and cookies from his own table, and that was all I wanted anyway with the ship doing handsprings every five minutes.

At dawn on the second morning we entered the mountain-bound bay of Tsuruga. Hill and dale were deep in fresh snow; the storm had fled, leaving the sky and sea brilliant with morning sunshine. One long devouring look at such beauty— one deep intoxicating draught of such air—and I was ready to face any music that might await me.

The music was loud and long. Every passenger and all the freight on the ship were discharged while the immigration and custom officials and I waged war. My indignant resentment at the idea of traveling steerage with *Japanese* so antagonized them they would have sent me straight back to Vladivostok on the return trip, had I not waved aloft my official letters, with eagles and seals spread all over them and threatened the entire Japanese Empire with the combined wrath of the American and British governments if they continued to delay a government courier.

Tsuruga is such an unimportant little port that the authorities were not greatly experienced in problems such as I presented. They didn't understand half my excited English and couldn't read the letters—but the mail-pouches were eloquent pleaders for my release. Thanks to them I was at last permitted to land, and once ashore I jumped on the first outgoing train before the officials could change their minds.

By no means, however, did my departure end the matter. A government detective joined me and was my very shadow for an entire week. It was impossible to move without his surveillance. I was annoyed at first, but came to see the funny side of it and rather enjoyed making his pursuit as hectic and exhausting as possible. To Ama-No-Hashidate (a long, narrow, pine-covered peninsula jutting across the mouth of a naval harbor, and considered one of the three "Great Sights" of Japan), he followed me, and to Kobe, and Kyoto, and Nara. But at Nagoya he became so utterly weary from the rapid pace I set him he didn't care whether I spiked all the fortification guns or not, and without further effort abandoned the chase leaving me to travel on northward feeling neglected and incomplete without a spy at my heels.

## ᴄ XXXV. ᴐ

# The Challenge of Fujiyama

*P*OETRY. Japan is filled with poems. There is one, the great national epic, that dominates all others, made not of rhyme and meter, but of rock and snow and forests and gracefully, tenderly beautiful lines—the poem Fujiyama.

Whenever Japan is mentioned the first picture that comes to the minds of most people who have never visited that country is one of this famous snowcapped volcano. To most foreigners this incomparable mountain is the symbol of Japan itself. They may never have heard of the shrines at Nikko and Nara; or of Miyajima and Matsushima, bywords for scenic beauty in Japan. But who is there so far removed from civilization that he has not the graceful sweep of Fuji's skirts impressed upon his brain by the thousand images he has seen drawn and painted and photographed on almost every object of art and industry that is Japanese? The entire nation is obsessed with "Fujimania." The people are so enamoured of the mountain's soaring slopes and diadem of snow, that they believe it to be an embodied goddess and make pilgrimages from the ends of the empire to ascend and worship her. No house is complete without a colored print of Fuji hung on the wall; in contemplation before it the greatest poetry of Japan has been inspired. Many a foreigner who has had the good fortune to look upon this fairy peak agrees with the Japanese that it is not merely the most beautiful natural object of this island empire, but of this earth.

The ascent of this beguiling Queen of Mountains had been my chief purpose in visiting Nippon and though it was now well into January, and though everything was buried under snow and ice, my enthusiasm was so deep-seated I was not in the least discouraged. Neither was I impressed when every one I questioned in Kyoto assured me, between peals of derisive laughter, that neither I nor any other human being could reach the twelve thousand, four hundred-foot summit of Fuji at the present season, when it was a solid uncompromising iceberg lashed with savage blizzards.

As my train sped at night from Kyoto on to Yokohama, I realized that our route lay around the base of the mountain, and I scarcely dared go to sleep for fear I should remain asleep through the dawn and miss the long-awaited glimpse of my pet peak. At last, at sunrise, I saw it! Glittering from base to summit with ice and snow, it struck me as the most inspiring picture I had ever seen, and I felt that my adoration had not been wasted on an unworthy object. I was ready to leap from the train then and there in response to the siren's call, and would have, had we not been traveling about forty miles an hour.

What a relief it was to reach the American and British consulates at Yokohama and deliver the mail pouches! While these had become a real burden, considerably hampering my movements, I was not forgetful of the fact that without them I would never have been allowed to land in Japan at all. Then, too, they brought about a most agreeable association with the Yokohama consuls, who in turn introduced me into the local foreign colony and helped to make my fortnight's residence in their city a memorably happy one.

Like Marseilles, Calcutta and Hongkong, Yokohama found me penniless. I borrowed sufficient money to cable the Memphis *Commercial Appeal* which had by now published over thirty of my contributions, and ask for fifty dollars "advance royalties" on the story of my "Fujiyama Ascent." Immediately the money came back. Now I *had* to climb.

I began to look around for sources of information about winter mountaineering in Japan. Very little progress had been made, when, by good fortune, I learned with a mixture of astonishment and delight that Fuji had been conquered the previous February—for the first time in winter, by a Colonel Lees and a companion, both Englishmen.

I lost no time in locating Colonel Lees, and learned to my increasing satisfaction the details of the mountain combat which the Britishers had pushed to a spectacular victory the winter before, gaining for themselves the honor of being the first to ascend Fuji after her annual burial in ice.

I now became unreasonably optimistic. Here was a supremely romantic, supremely original idea that inspired exultation in the very thought. If others had climbed it I could try. Colonel Lees was not so confident as I was. His successful fight with Fuji had not been made without a great deal of preparation, organization, hard work and preliminary recon-naissance of the mountain itself, and even then only on the third attempt. The sound arguments against my attempt greatly overbalanced those in favor. First of all I would have to go alone, for every one I approached on the subject had the usual misconception of the expedition and thought it in the same class with going over Niagara Falls in a barrel. In the second place, the date of my expedition would be in the dark of the moon, while Colonel Lees' trips had been made in full illuminating moonlight, "without which," he said, "I am sure the ascent can not be made, as the short winter daylight is not sufficient."

In the third place, being a vagabond, I carried only a knapsack for my worldly possessions, and among many things it did not contain were the necessary snowshoes, ice-axes, rubber boots, blankets, helmets and fur coats.

And so, after long discussion, Colonel Lees argued me out of the idea. It seemed too barren of all hope, too fraught with madness. As a substitute, I reluctantly turned my steps with a herd of tourists to stereotyped temples at Nikko. But as the train left, in the early morning, I happened to glance south, and there, like the ghost of Banquo, rose the haunting siren, pale, proud, majestic. I turned my head away; raised the shade to shut her from view; all in vain. She taunted me even through the curtain.

I hated Nikko. I paced the platform with impatience waiting for the train to take me away, and, once more back in Yokohama, hurried out to Colonel Lees' residence to announce that, winter or no winter, I meant to climb Fujiyama. Seeing I was not to be dissuaded he began to face realities with me.

Opposed to my many liabilities, my assets seemed few indeed. Stubbornness, a tough constitution and a camera were all I had.

The first obstacle, lack of a companion, was not removed. It was simply ignored. Having no one to catch me if I started sliding, I solved the problem by wearing three pairs of pants. The second obstacle, moonlight—that too, was ignored. I'd pray for stars. As for equipment, Colonel Lees very generously made me the loan of his fur coat to sleep in the night before the final dash, his ice-ax and snowshoes. I collected woolen contributions from all my friends, and bought, in fact, only one article, sharpened iron ice-creepers, the forging of which I superintended myself. These crampons are magic wings to the winter climber. With them lashed to heavy boots I was prepared to challenge the old mountain, to trample up and down her ice-armed sides and to throw rocks into the big hole in her skull. Without them, any attempt would be first-degree suicide, though I doubt if one could get far enough up even for that.

And so, alone, I left for the battle-field, not knowing one word of Japanese or whither I was going except to a place called Gotemba, where began the trail that led, sooner or later—if one did not freeze or slip—to the pinnacle of scenic Japan.

Colonel Lees had kindly prepared for me a list of food items that would be needed. I immediately lost the list, and at Gotemba, accompanied by a highly amused coolie, went from shop to shop buying what scanty provisions the little village afforded. My larder finally consisted of unappetizing sandwiches made from sweet bread and sour ham, and two pints of brandy.

For twenty-four hours I tried, without success, to get a guide to climb with me. While there were scores of guides, willing enough in summer, not one of them had ever made a winter ascent—nor ever intended to, though he were offered all the money in Japan. I stormed and threatened; I cajoled and pleaded, dangling handfuls of yen before their eyes. I might as well have tried to get a guide to purgatory. Finally, losing all patience, I told the entire village to go to that very place, and vowed that I would climb the volcano alone, if for no other reason than to show these miserable Gotembans what jellyfish they were.

It was with great difficulty that I obtained a coolie to carry my baggage to the base of the mountain, where I was to spend the night before the final dash, and even then I had to pay part of his wages in advance. He felt sure I'd meet my finish on the icy slopes and default. Realizing that he was no doubt right, I agreed. This matter having been settled, Katsu and I, amid pitying stares from the villagers, at noon on this bitterly cold January day, set out upon the long, steep, ice-covered trail that led to the base station of Tarobo, from which point the actual climb begins.

Tramping through deeper and deeper snow, we reached the four-thousand-foot shelter about dark, and having built a fire tried to counteract the frigidity of the draughty hut. But with night the merciless cold descended, and a dozen fires could not have kept us warm. Sleep was fitful. The hours dragged shiveringly past. At four in the morning I decided it would be as pleasant to glissade to my death as to freeze. Disentangling myself from Colonel Lees' bearskin coat, I routed the last vestige of irresolution and anxiety with a heroic drink from the brandy bottle, lashed on the magic spikes beneath Japanese straw snowshoes (for the snow from this point up, while deep, was frozen hard, making the Canadian shoes useless) and bade farewell to Katsu. Our parting was touching indeed; the coolie never expected to see me again, and I owed him six yen.

If Fuji had lured me on, then she played false to the conventional code of her sister sirens, since a more auspicious reception I could not have desired. My prayer for stars had been answered—there were twice as many as usual, and while it was zero weather at this four-thousand-foot elevation, it was the still windless type that makes cold endurable. In the dim light the ghostly peak before me, barren of all vegetation, glimmered like a colossal cone of white sugar. Cold thrills ran through me. This was the climax of adventure, the glorious finale of months of sensational living. I had defied everybody, risked everything, on this one throw. It was to be the acid test, the iron trial of endurance. This was my twenty-third birthday, and here was a chance to celebrate it by dashing to pieces the age-old tradition that Fuji could never be climbed in winter single-handed. I glared at my enemy. It glared back at me. "Fool!" it seemed to say, "you presume to do alone that which has been fatal to whole parties of climbers! Go reach for the moon—you'll get it as easily as my summit." The danger of my adventure suddenly appalled me. I quaked with apprehension, but Danton's clarion call to his hard-pressed French again came to me:

"*L' audace, encore l' audace, toujours, toujours l' audace!*" To hell with discretion! I would not turn back!

# ☙ XXXVI. ☙

# To the Peak!

EFORE I had gone half a mile, from out of the Pacific that beat at Fuji's fringe, the sun burst forth and gilded the icy peak above me with gleaming fire. It was soon broad day, a superb snow and crystal and sapphire day that made one rejoice to be alive.

If the climb was not quite so bad as the reports concerning it, it was only because nothing could be as bad as that. I had anticipated a long desperate struggle—and found it. I had been warned of steep ice-banks, sloughs of snow, screaming blizzards. In abundance I found them all. I had resigned myself to freezing about half-way. Here I was disappointed, for while a thermometer would have registered at least twenty degrees below zero, the vigorous exertion underneath three layers of woolen clothing kept me sufficiently thawed. Such a climb as this demanded no great physical power or special skill in mountain-craft. Guides would have been superfluous, for the trail was buried under ten feet of snow and ice. The only essential articles were the thin needle-like spikes and the ice-ax, both of which bit into the surface with all the trustworthiness I had hoped for. It would have been impossible to move a single yard without them. One would have launched forth on a toboggan-slide of five miles and a drop of seven thousand feet which, while it would have broken all records of the sport and been highly exhilarating, might have become too hot from friction to be comfortable. With them the climb was physically possible. Stamp, stamp, stamp, with the spikes; higher and higher up the increasingly precipitous slope; chop, chop, chop, with the ice-ax. This weapon was attached to my wrist by a six-foot rope, to prevent its escape in case I dropped it. Had that happened my indispensable ally, unleashed, would have skated home to Tarobo in less time than it takes to tell it, and I would have been left in a position that would have been extremely embarrassing. When I slipped or stumbled, as I did time and again, a quick drive with the iron pick would steady me and give me a chance to reestablish my crampons in the ice.

Though it was a breathless morning when I left Tarobo, by the time I had reached eleven thousand feet I had mounted into the realm of hurricanes, and began to suffer in consequence. The wind beating into my face would have frozen nose and chin, had I not kept the blood circulating with friction. The last few hundred yards was a desperate battle against the final, frantic, resistance of Fuji's blizzard guardians. More than once I was on the point of retreating from the blast before I was completely annihilated but some devil inside urged me higher and higher into more perilous territory. "To the peak! To the peak!" So I wound my muffler tighter and crawled on.

Each step brought me nearer, till at last the rim was reached. In a rage the icy blasts gathered their forces for a counter-attack, and sweeping unobstructed from the wide cold heavens struck with such terrible force that I had to lie flat upon the ice and fight to keep from being blown off the top of the mountain. Though the sky was clear and though the sun shone with unusual ardor for January, the views I had from the summit were merely blurs of flying snow-clouds lashed into fury from the rocks and driven hither and thither by the screaming blast.

The cold was tormenting, and could not long be endured once climbing had ceased. The necessary pictures must be taken at once or not at all. Working as quickly as circumstances permitted, I unleashed my hitherto infallible camera, only to find that the aperture, closed at Nikko to a pin-point opening for a time exposure, had broken or frozen and now would not expand. I cursed the wind and snow for this diabolical trick. Freeze me all it would, but spare my camera. Pictures I *must* have to prove that I had made the climb! Pictures I *would* have! Crouched down behind one of the half-buried summit huts, I drew off my outer gloves, and, racing against frostbite, unscrewed the lens. I tried to pry open the thin steel leaves; the snow froze in my eyes and I could not see clearly enough for so delicate an operation. Unable to effect my purpose by gentle methods, I tried force and gouged out the leaves bodily with my knife. Drawing a visiting card from my wallet I cut a pasteboard disk, punctured it with a hole of the proper size, and thrust it against the shutter.

Meanwhile I could tell by the feeling that my ears were frozen. My nose was white as snow; fingers refused to bend; but the camera was saved. With considerable pain I restored circulation in the afflicted extremities, and crawled over to the edge of the seven-hundred-foot deep crater with my machine open. Although the swirl that met me almost dashed it out of my hands I managed to make three half-sighted exposures of the great hole, and fled. One of them recorded. It was the first photograph ever taken on Fuji's crown during the ice season.

In descending, the wind was behind me and Taboro before.

It was early, scarcely three o'clock, so I decided to slacken the relentless pace I had set on the ascent. I had not known how much time the climb would take, so to be on the safe side had driven myself ruthlessly all morning. Now that the climax was past, I decided that a well-earned rest would be appropriate. So, creeping down below the blizzard belt, I drove my ax deep into the ice, and propping my cumbersomely-shod feet against this support, lay back on the forty-degree slope. How comfortable it was to relax, and what a view!

For five thousand feet straight below me, Fuji's dazzling skirts swept downward and outward, gently decreasing their gradient from forty degrees to four with such uniformity of curve and grace of line I decided the Japanese were right in believing that the peak *was* a goddess which rose by magic from the fields in a single night, two hundred and eighty-six years before Christ.

I could think of no other mountain so superbly situated. Even the mighty Matterhorn, glowering over half of Switzerland, is overlooked by the yet loftier Rosa. Fuji stands solitary, isolated, unobstructed by even the smallest foot-hills. It rises twelve thousand and four hundred feet straight from the Pacific's isle-studded sea. Few beacons in the world are so far-reaching as the hoary head I perched on. While in summer the lesser peaks of Japan reluctantly doff their arctic caps, this sky-scraping mountain clings tenaciously to hers throughout the year, and on clear days, to ships one hundred miles at sea, flashes her message: "Here am I, Fujiyama!"

What a magnificent shoot-the-chutes lay beneath me, not so much as a pebble to obstruct a coaster until the forest was encountered four miles below. I could not resist a childish urge to send something dashing and skating down the slope, just to see how fast it would go. My balky camera deserved such a fate, but I was merciful and launched instead an empty brandy-flask. Like a streak of lightning it leaped and slithered down, down, down, until in a few seconds it became a melting speck and disappeared into the vast hem of Fuji's skirt.

While I lay on my icy bed the sun beamed down over the expansive panorama, and as I looked the low-lying blanket of clouds which for the moment had screened everything from view and made Fuji an island of ice in an infinite ocean, was driven by the wind away from the lakes and woods and sparkling sea that snuggled at my feet. How heartily I agreed with the first half of the Japanese proverb: "You are a fool if you do not climb Fuji,"—yet not less heartily did I agree with the last half: "—but you are a worse fool if you climb it twice!"

Every season there are twenty thousand people removed from the former category of fools, for though the climbing season lasts only six weeks in midsummer, the faithful gather in droves from far and near and swarm up the sacred lava-strewn slopes like ants in never-ending streams. Fuji is the most frequently-climbed mountain in the world.

Six routes to the top have been established, each served by ten huts, at which, during the season, a climber can find food and lodging for the night. The pilgrims, usually clad in white garments, sing out lustily as they trudge upward the Shinto formula: "*Rokkon sojo O yama keisei,*" meaning, "May our six senses be pure and the weather on the honorable mountain fair."

The volcano is by no means extinct.[1] From 286 B.C. to 1707 it periodically disgorged all the elements of hell, and then after a final outburst, it subsided, but wisps of steam still curl upward from the crevices in the lava rock, indicating that while Fuji "may have a clear, cold head, she also has that rare

---

[1]Fuji remained quiescent during the terrible earthquakes of September, 1923.

accompanying characteristic, a warm heart." Nature is so cruel and untrustworthy in Japan it would not be surprising if the steam-wisps some day develop into an obliterating whirlwind, and once more strew death and disaster over Nippon's fair fields.

All this and more that I had learned drifted through my mind as I sat enthroned on my gigantic icicle, and looked through half dreaming (and half frozen) eyes out upon the glittering Pacific. If I quite forgot how insecurely I was stuck on the slope, I was reminded of it with terrible and sudden violence; for in absent-mindedly shifting my position my clumsy shoes slipped off the ax support, and instantly, with my crampon brakes turned skyward, I began to glissade Taroboward with all the speed and self-control of the brandy flask. But the fates had reserved my finish for another day. Before I fully comprehended what a suicidal plunge I was launching upon, the tape connecting my wrist with the ax became taut, and I was stopped dead. Dear old ice-ax! I had roped it to my arm so that in case it should slip from my grasp it would not slide back to Tarobo, but it was I that had slipped and the ax that had held.

Only then did I realize how prodigal of time I had been. The sun had disappeared behind a spur, and the early short-lived dusk of a January day was near at hand. Rallying from the fright of a moment before, I drove my crampons once more into the surface and began again a steady downward stamp, stamp, stamp. By six o'clock a faint glimmer from the stars was the only light. And now another serious danger faced me. In the darkness I would not be able to find Tarobo or the trail leading through the impenetrable forests that lay in a wide belt about Fuji's base. But again fortune favored me. Just as the last trace of day departed, a speck of light suddenly appeared in the abyss far below, and I shouted with joy, for I knew it was a signal bonfire the faithful but uneasy Katsu had lit to guide me home. Straight to the lighthouse and to safety I steered my course, and an hour before midnight the harbor was reached. Katsu's face beamed with delight on seeing me still alive with his six yen—and so did mine, especially the frozen, swollen nose and chin part of it.

Fatigued almost to unconsciousness, I painfully turned back for one last glimpse of my defeated mountain. I expected her to curse me for having humiliated her in single combat, for having trod disdainfully upon her forbidden summit. I expected her to hurl down avalanches of snow and ice in vengeance, but when I met her star-illumined gaze—it was serene. I think—'twas passing strange—I think I saw her smile at me and whisper: "Young man, I do not care; I called to you. You came. Few others have. My homage and my benediction." But it may have been the ravings of a brain that by this time was delirious, or the rustle of the night wind murmuring through the pines.

## ↶ XXXVII. ↷

# The Last Battle

ATSU had baggage other than overcoats and snow-shoes to carry back to Gotemba;—he had me to carry as well. My feet, the circulation stopped by the crampon thongs, were frost-bitten, and walking, over the rough and slippery trail through the forest, painful beyond endurance. Although I could not tell the coolie all this, not speaking one word of Japanese, my behavior must have been eloquent enough, for while I was wondering how we'd ever get to the hotel, he strapped our baggage high on his enormous shoulders and then, to my astonishment, picked me up and strapped me on top the pack, seemingly ignoring the fact that I weighed fifty pounds more than he did and was a foot taller.

As I had requested my hotel proprietor to be prepared for our return by night, he was still up when we staggered in about 4 A.M., after the most distressing and difficult eight miles of the forty thousand or so described in this narrative. Too groggy myself to assist them, I watched Katsu and the proprietor carefully unbind my frozen feet, and with friction bring them back to life. An enormous wooden family bath-tank, six feet square, filled to the brim with hot steaming water, awaited me, and into it my attendants precipitated their half-conscious charge. Oh, joy! Oh, bliss! Such ecstasy was worth climbing Fuji to experience. For two hours I was allowed to parboil, with Katsu on hand to see that I didn't go to sleep and drown.

At dawn on a Wednesday I crawled into the great pile of soft comforters; Katsu "tucked me in," slid the paper walls tight about me, and then, perhaps for the first time—knowing his "responsibility" was safe and sleeping—gave a thought to himself.

A sound of children playing in the courtyard awakened me. The sun was flooding my mat-strewn room. It was Thursday morning.

As quickly as stiff and aching muscles permitted I rushed back to Tokyo—four hours north—and burst into a reliable photography shop with my precious films. In the dark-room, holding my breath with apprehension, I watched the negative of Fuji's crater take shape. It was not a very good picture, but it was unmistakably what I claimed for it. Exuberant beyond description, I seized a wet print and rushed over to the editorial office of the *Japan Advertiser*, the biggest English publication in Japan, to ask if they would buy my story.

"Got one about your swim across the Pacific?" the editor asked scoffingly. He believed my statements were all inventions.

"But the crater picture!" I cried in despair. "What better proof do you want?"

He called in the editorial staff for its opinion, and they all agreed that the photograph was undeniably Fuji's crater, and from the snow it contained, obviously taken in winter. My story was vindicated and I was made to tell it to the entire staff.

The following Sunday the article was conspicuously published in full with a half-dozen pictures—the one of the crater, incidentally, being upside-down.

Immediately I spent the *Advertiser's* fifty-dollar check on fine raiment, and prepared to enjoy the hospitalities which the published accounts of my climb and my previous travels had stimulated. All was ready for a week's whirl when the steamship *President Madison* put into port en route to Seattle, short one seaman. The American consul, in appreciation of the mail-pouches I had brought from Vladivostok, had kept a sharp lookout for vacancies on American-bound ships where he could place me, and here, with unexpected suddenness, an opportunity to work my way home presented itself. He rushed a messenger to my quarters to deliver the glad tidings. I must act at once; the ship was to be in port only a few hours.

The messenger found me carefully dressing for a dinner-party. My dinner clothes, borrowed from an obliging friend, lay freshly pressed on the bed; a snowy new dress shirt with a new pair of pearl cufflinks, a new pearl-and-silver evening watch-chain, a new hat and shoes and cane, a glorious new Japanese silk scarf, awaited the meticulous parting of freshly-trimmed hair.

I was stunned by the news. *Seaman*—fo'castle—dungarees—paint—wops and Swedes and *work*—Oh, *lord*!

"What's the matter? Don't you want to go?" the messenger asked in surprise, seeing the way I was glaring at him.

Of all the things on earth I wanted little, at the time I wanted this thing least; yet such an opportunity might not come again for weeks—and my funds after paying for the chain and scarf were already trembling on the edge of nothing. There was no escape. I must go. Sick at heart, I wrote a hurried note of apology to my hostess, saying that I had just received news demanding my "immediate return" to America, and that I was "sailing" at once on the *President Madison*. With my new dress shirt as a tip, I gave the note to the messenger for delivery.

Out came the dilapidated old knapsack; into it was chucked the silk scarf and the pearl chain and the new derby. On went the corduroys and the Fujiyama boots. Oh, baleful world!

Ready to die from disappointment, I stamped vindictively down-stairs and over to the consul's office, where he gleefully gave me a letter to the captain of that cursed ship.

Early next morning we sailed. The sun was beating on distant Fuji's graceful glittering slopes. Never have I known such a poem—never have I beheld such a queen. Soaring up and up into the morning sunlight she flashed farewell to me. Enchanted as usual by her snowy majesty I stood motionless on the deck and feasted my eyes for one last time on that divinely beautiful and perfect mountain-goddess.

"Hey, you, by the rail—lay off that star-gazin'—this ain't tea-time—get a broom and sweep this deck 'fore I break yer neck!" Thus the bo's'n dragged me back to earth—or rather, back to sea.

For ten days we remained at sea, and each day I loathed the ship more. It was my first experience as seaman on a passenger-boat—and it will certainly be the last. On a freighter a man's life is his own; the ship belongs to him, its decks, its bridge, its hold. He brooks no repression other than the bo's'n's. But how different are passenger boats. Here the crew members are menials, being roused at 5 A. M. to manicure and "holystone" the promenade deck in order that the passengers may not soil their dainty feet during their early morning constitutional. On the *President Madison* we twenty-four seamen were bunked in tiers in one crowded compartment in the depths of the hold, where the odors of fetid food, drifting in from the galley alongside, were always with us. Fortunately, we were so dead tired by night, we did not know or care whether we were breathing air or laughing-gas.

After a week out I became so bored sweeping snow off the decks all day (a perpetual motion, as it seemed never to cease snowing) I threw down the detested broom, and picked up a midiron which a careless passenger had left lying beside the indoor golf set supplied by the ship. It was the first time I had held a club since I left Kashmir, and in my enthusiasm for it I quite forgot my contest with the snow. I teed the leashed ball and tried to drive it all the way back to Yokohama. This was *so* much more fun than deck-sweeping. What a pleasure it would be to get back to the links in America! Swing—swing—yes, indeed—golf was a great game.

Just in front of me was a fellow-seaman painting winches. He glanced up suddenly, and looked over my shoulder with such a horrified expression that I dropped the club and glanced around prepared to dodge a falling mast.

What I saw was worse than that. There behind me, arms akimbo, speechless with wrath, stood the *captain* of the *President Madison*, one of the most notoriously hard-boiled skippers on the Pacific, surrounded by a number of officers with whom he was making a *tour of inspection*. He nearly exploded. A lower-than-worms seaman deserting his broom and playing golf with the clubs consecrated to the first-class passengers!!! This was no place for me. He was purple. I made a wild leap for the broom and dived headlong down the nearest ladder out of sight. I fully expected to pass the rest of the voyage in the brig, but as my companion seaman turned over his pot of paint on the hardwood deck in the excitement, the captain forgot me in venting his wrath on this new criminal.

The last night I stayed up until morning, to watch for the first light-ship, and in Puget Sound forgot to work looking at the snow-clad giants that stand guard there.

Seattle was by no means home. My despairing parents were awaiting me in Memphis, Tennessee, and thither I was bound—nor would I spoil the consistency of my Royal Road by whining for help just because I was on the American continent. The *President Madison* paid me fifteen dollars; on this I got to Portland with fifteen cents left for breakfast. The father of one of my Lawrenceville roommates was there to greet me, and to see to it that the Portland *Oregon Journal* not only accepted and printed my Fujiyama story, but also paid me thirty-five dollars for it.

By foregoing a Pullman half-way, I got to Denver. Here I was the guest of Governor and Mrs. S——, with whose son I had roomed at Princeton. Introduction from my host to the *Rocky Mountain Times* was all that was necessary to persuade its worthy editor to buy my Fujiyama story. However, fifteen dollars was all he would offer. The ticket to Kansas City cost sixteen dollars—so I borrowed a dollar from the governor and reached this new destination.

The Kansas City *Star* was more generous, asking if I would accept forty dollars for my Fujiyama story. I would! Better far than this good fortune was finding my original comrade of this story, the man with whom I'd left America, bicycled across Germany, climbed the Matterhorn, and the Trocadéro—Irvine Hockaday—at home. He had preceded me around the world, and reached Kansas City, where he lived, nine months before. For three days and nights we never stopped talking, for his adventures had been as dramatic as mine, and each was impatient to hear how the other had fared.

Forty dollars!—and only twelve hours to Memphis. I had long since lost my hat—the fur-lined overcoat given me in Peking was in rags; Irvine's mother put me to bed while she sewed together my corduroy suit; my shoes, which had climbed Fuji, were disgracefully battered—*but* I had forty dollars and only three hundred miles to go.

On the evening of my departure, a red-cap, carrying my two-pound knapsack, escorted me into the most expensive compartment the special extra-fare Florida Limited de luxe could possibly provide. In this glittering blaze of glory I returned to my paternal hearth on the first day of March, six hundred days after my departure from New York, fully and finally aware that be it ever so luxurious, after all there is no place like home.

THE END

Richard Halliburton was a writer, lecturer, and world traveler. He published numerous books in his short lifetime, including *The Royal Road to Romance*, *Glorious Adventure*, and *The Complete Book of Marvels*. Halliburton is known for having paid the lowest toll to cross the Panama Canal, which he swam in 1928, paying 36 cents. Born in Tennessee in 1900, Halliburton died in 1939 as he and his crew attempted to sail a Chinese junk, the *Sea Dragon*, from Hong Kong to San Francisco as a publicity stunt. The vessel was unseaworthy and went down in a storm, apparently shortly after Halliburton sent out his last signal: "Southerly gales, squalls, lee rail under water, wet bunks, hard tack, bully beef, wish you were here—instead of me!"